FALLEN ANGEL

Sandipan Deb is an IIT-IIM graduate who, after three years in the corporate world, shifted to journalism. He has been the managing editor of *Outlook*, the editor of *The Financial Express* and was the founder-editor of *Open*. He is also the author of *The IITians: The Story of an Extraordinary Indian Institution and How Its Alumni Are Reshaping the World*, which has been translated into Chinese and Korean. He lives in Delhi and is currently working on a novel, *The Last War*. A collection of his writings over the years can be accessed at: sandipanonline.com

GW00400097

FALLEN ANGEL

The Making and Unmaking of Rajat Gupta

SANDIPAN DEB

RUPA

Published by
Rupa Publications India Pvt. Ltd 2013
7/16, Ansari Road, Daryaganj
New Delhi 110002

Sales centres:
Allahabad Bengaluru Chennai
Hyderabad Jaipur Kathmandu
Kolkata Mumbai

Copyright © Sandipan Deb 2013

By arrangement with Aardvark Media

The views and opinions expressed in this book are the author's own and
the facts are as reported by him/her which have been verified to the
extent possible, and the publishers are not in any way liable for the same.

ISBN: 978-81-291-2111-0

10 9 8 7 6 5 4 3 2 1

The moral right of the author has been asserted.

Typeset in Minion Pro 10.5/13.3

Printed by Replika Press Pvt. Ltd, Haryana

Contents

Prologue

'SO WHY DID MR GUPTA DO IT?' JUDGE JED S. RAKOFF ASKED, as he prepared to deliver his sentence on Rajat Gupta.

It was a question that many thousands of people had been asking in the twelve months since Rajat Gupta had been indicted for insider trading. To almost everyone who had ever known Gupta, or even just heard of his accomplishments, it was—and would remain—an epic enigma. And many of those would never believe that Gupta was guilty.

For nearly two decades, he had quite simply been one of the most respected and admired men in global corporate and humanitarian circles.

Rajat Gupta was among the seventy-two people the US government had charged with being part of the largest insider trading ring ever busted in Wall Street history. At the centre of this unholy web had been Raj Rajaratnam, the Sri Lankan-born hedge fund trader, who was already serving a sentence of eleven years in a Massachusetts prison. Of the seventy-two indicted, sixty-nine had either pleaded guilty or been convicted. Gupta, however, had insisted that he was innocent. In fact, the evidence against him, unlike that against the other defendants, had been entirely circumstantial. The government had also been unable to establish—if Gupta really had passed on tips to Rajaratnam—that he had ever made any financial gains from this.

But the sheer mass of the circumstantial evidence had been damning. On 15 June 2012, Gupta had been pronounced guilty. Yet some members of the jury had been seen weeping after they had passed the verdict.

The prosecution had asked for a prison term of ninety-seven

to 121 months. The defence had done their own calculations and pleaded that Gupta's crimes deserved six to twelve months. In fact, the defence had argued for a probationary sentence, with the stipulation that Gupta would have to perform rigorous community work for a specified period. Two ideas had been proposed, the more innovative of which was that Gupta be sentenced to work in faraway Rwanda, living a hard life, atoning for his sins, and helping that war- and poverty-ravaged nation get back on its feet. The Rwandan government had offered wholehearted support. The defence had argued that given Gupta's brilliant management track record and his extraordinary commitment to bettering the lives of people across the planet, it would be the perfect punishment: he would suffer, yet the world would benefit from his talents and expertise.

More than four hundred people, including Bill Gates, former UN Secretary General Kofi Annan, industrialist Mukesh Ambani, and New Age guru Deepak Chopra had written to Judge Rakoff, requesting leniency. Many of the letter-writers said that Gupta was the finest human being they had ever met.

On 24 October, Indians around the world were celebrating Dussehra, the festival of good triumphing over evil. In cities, towns and villages all across India, effigies of Ravana, the king of Lanka who had kidnapped another man's wife, were being burnt in a shower of flames and fireworks. But for the many Indians inside the courthouse at 500 Pearl Street in New York City, the mood could not have been more sombre, the suspense more chilling. It was sentencing time.

Assistant US Attorney Robert Tarlowe, who had led the prosecution during the trial, reiterated what the government had been emphasizing: that Gupta's crimes warranted a long prison term precisely because he had been so eminent a person. He said that the sentence must not give the impression that there was 'a two-tier system of justice'.

Gupta's lawyer Gary P. Naftalis said that he 'was an iconic

figure, someone who had been a role model for people around the globe for his work'. His fall from grace was of 'Greek tragedy proportions', he 'is a man who has suffered punishment enough'.

Then Gupta, in a dark blue suit and light blue tie, stood up and spoke. This was the first time he had spoken to the court, because he had been called as a witness in the trial. According to a *The New York Times* report, he 'appeared more haggard and strained than he did during his month-long trial'.

'The last eighteen months have been the most challenging period of my life, since I lost my parents as a teenager', Gupta said. 'I have lost my reputation that I have built over a lifetime. The verdict was devastating to my family, my friends and me. Its implications to all aspects of my life—personal, professional and financial—are profound. Much of the first year seemed surreal to me; however, since the trial, I have come to accept the reality of my life going forward.' He said he regretted 'terribly the impact of this matter on my family, my friends and the institutions that are dear to me'. He hoped that his fate would not negatively affect the institutions he had been associated with—and in some cases built. Every time he looked at his wife, his daughters, and members of his extended family, he was 'overcome with a deep sense of letting them down'.

'Your Honour, as I come before you to be sentenced, the overwhelming feelings in my heart are of acceptance of what has happened, of gratitude to my family and friends, and of seeking forgiveness from them all', he said. 'It is with these feelings that I hope to move forward and dedicate myself to the service of others.'

It was then over to Judge Rakoff, widely acknowledged as one of the most brilliant and fair judges in the United States of America. As he read out his fifteen-page sentencing order, he also made impromptu comments.

'The court can say without exaggeration that it has never encountered a defendant whose prior history suggests such an extraordinary devotion, not only to humanity writ large, but also to individual human beings in their times of need,' said Rakoff. 'I think the record [...] is that he's a good man, but the history of this country and the history of the world are filled with good men who do bad things.

'When one looks at the nature and circumstances of the offence, the picture darkens considerably. In the court's view, the evidence established, to a virtual certainty, that Mr Gupta, well knowing his fiduciary duties, brazenly disclosed material nonpublic information to Mr Rajaratnam at the very time, September and October 2008, when our financial institutions were in immense distress.'

Yes, the evidence was wholly circumstantial, but, said Rakoff, it 'was not only overwhelming, it was disgusting in its implications. A terrible breach of trust'.

As for the Rwanda community service proposal, Rakoff called it 'very innovative', and then turned Naftalis's logic back on him. 'I think if everything you told me about Mr Gupta's character is correct, and I think it is, he would be doing this regardless of a court order or not. So looking at it in a cynical kind of way, it is not punishment.' A prison term was necessary. 'Others similarly situated to the defendant must [...] be made to understand that when you get caught, you will go to jail.'

The sentence was then handed down. Two years in prison, plus one year of supervised release (which is somewhat similar to being out on parole), and a $5 million fine. Judge Rakoff denied a request from Naftalis to allow him to remain free during his appeal. He was ordered to report for prison by 2 p.m. on 8 January 2013. However, the judge agreed to recommend that Gupta should be sent to the minimum security prison in Otisville, New York, though the final decision on this would be taken by the Federal Prisons Bureau.

According to media reports, Gupta showed no visible reaction when the judge announced the sentence. 'Just behind him,' reported *The New York Times*, 'his wife, Anita, pinched her fingers tightly into her eyes, which were hidden behind dark sunglasses. His four grown daughters, who attended their father's trial nearly every day, were teary-eyed throughout.'

Preet Bharara, the Indian-born US Attorney for the Southern District of New York, who had led the relentless hunt-down, said in a statement: 'With today's sentence, Rajat Gupta now must face the grave consequences of his crime—a term of imprisonment. His conduct has forever tarnished a once-sterling reputation that took years to cultivate. We hope that others who might consider breaking the securities laws will take heed from this sad occasion.'

As Gupta left the court with his family, Naftalis told the gathered journalists: 'Mr Gupta maintains his innocence and will vigorously pursue an appeal. We continue to believe that the facts of this case demonstrate that Mr Gupta is innocent of all of these charges, and that he has always acted with honesty and integrity.'

Case No. 11-cr-00907

THE UNITED STATES DISTRICT COURT FOR THE SOUTHERN District of New York, with jurisdiction over the counties of New York, Bronx, Westchester, Rockland, Putnam, Orange, Dutchess and Sullivan, is affectionately referred to by the New York legal fraternity as the 'Mother Court'. After all, it was the first district court to hold a session under the sovereignty of the United States, on 24 September 1789. In December 2000, the new courthouse building on 500 Pearl Street was dedicated and named after Daniel Patrick Moynihan, legendary US senator, and former ambassador to the United Nations and to India.

On the morning of 21 May 2012, a crowd of journalists waited in front of the courthouse to intercept the man whose trial was about to begin. A man whose life had been the sort of near-magical immigrant success story that lay at the heart of the American dream. A man who had spent the last two decades of his life moving among the richest businessmen, the biggest philanthropists, the most powerful statesmen in the world. Former (and the first non-American-born) head of McKinsey & Co, the elite and secretive management consultancy firm; special advisor to former United Nations Secretary General Kofi Annan; confidant and consultant to heads of state; former chairman of the board for The Global Fund to Fight AIDS, Tuberculosis and Malaria; former member of the boards of iconic American firms like Goldman Sachs and Procter & Gamble. Sixty-three-year-old Rajat Gupta was a corporate legend with a career that could only be described as awe-inspiring.

He was also the biggest name in corporate America ever to have been accused of insider trading. His criminal trial was about to begin.

As Gupta arrived, wearing a navy blue suit and a red and yellow polka-dotted tie, accompanied by his wife Anita, his four daughters—Geetanjali, Megha, Aditi and Deepali, and his lawyer Gary P. Naftalis, the journalists surged forward, thrusting cameras and microphones before them. But Gupta had nothing to say, and his handsome patrician face retained its customary calm.

Gupta's indictment and trial were the slipstream of the biggest insider trading trial (and conviction) in the history of Wall Street. A year and ten days ago, Sri Lankan-born billionaire Raj Rajaratnam, head of the Galleon Group, which ran a clutch of hedge funds, had been found guilty on fourteen counts of security fraud and conspiracy. He had been sentenced to eleven years in prison. In December 2011, pending appeal at a higher court, Rajaratnam had begun serving his term, the longest ever awarded for insider trading, at a federal prison in Massachusetts.

Gupta had been close to Rajaratnam. He was among the five people in the list Rajaratnam had dictated to his executive assistant in 2008, who were to be given access to the Galleon boss immediately, no matter how busy he was. The US government was now charging Gupta with having passed on confidential information to Rajaratnam, who had made a killing on the stock market based on this.

Why would a man of Gupta's stature and accomplishments have done so—if at all, that is, he had? Even the US government seemed unsure. Gupta's indictment was rather vague on this count, stating merely that he 'benefited and hoped to benefit from his friendship and business relationships with Rajaratnam in various ways, some of which were financial'.

It seemed obvious that the investigators had not been able to put their finger on any concrete quid pro quo agreement that Gupta may have had with his friend. Quite simply, there was no evidence that, if indeed Gupta had been leaking insider information to Rajaratnam, he had made any money out of it. And Rajaratnam could offer Gupta nothing other than money, since Gupta had everything else in much greater measure than the hedge fund manager: status, respect, impeccable reputation. In fact, he hardly lacked money either; his personal financial advisor pegged his net worth at $130 million.

The evidence on which the government had based its case against Gupta came down finally to three phone conversations that Rajaratnam had had in 2008 and one in 2009. One of them had been tapped by the Federal Bureau of Investigation (FBI), who had been on Rajaratnam's trail for quite some time, but the other two calls had not been. But phone records showed that they were calls made by Gupta to Rajaratnam, and the timing of the calls appeared highly significant.

All these phone conversations took place while the financial markets were facing their worst crisis in eight decades, the result of widespread and incredibly reckless trading in extremely high-risk mortgage-based securities. On 24 January 2008, the National Association of Realtors announced that 2007 had seen the largest drop in existing home sales in the US in twenty-five years, and 'the first price decline in many, many years and possibly going back to the Great Depression'. On 10 March, the Dow Jones Industrial Average hit its lowest level since October 2006, down more than 20 per cent from its peak just five months earlier. Six days later, investment bank Bear Stearns was acquired for $2 a share by JPMorgan Chase in a fire sale, with the Federal Reserve providing up to $30 billion to cover possible Bear Stearns losses.

In July, IndyMac Bank went into receivership, the fourth largest bank failure in US history. In the same month, major banks and financial institutions that had invested heavily in mortgage-backed securities reported losses of approximately $435 billion. On 7 September, the government took over Fannie Mae and Freddie Mac, which, at that point of time, owned or guaranteed about half of the US's $12 trillion mortgage market. On 14 September, investment bank Merrill Lynch was saved from collapse by being bought over by Bank of America. The next day, Lehman Brothers filed for bankruptcy protection. On 17 September, the US Federal Reserve lent $85 billion to insurance giant American International Group (AIG) to help it avoid insolvency. The next day, a Wednesday, US Treasury Secretary Henry Paulson and Federal Reserve Chairman Ben Bernanke met with key legislators to propose a $700 billion emergency bailout through the purchase of toxic assets. Bernanke told them: 'If we don't do this, we may not have an economy on Monday.'

On the afternoon of 23 September 2008, Gupta joined members of the Goldman Sachs board on a conference call. The board wanted to discuss some extraordinarily good news. While the country was petrified about how far the contagion would spread, and how many more hallowed Wall Street institutions would go belly-up, America's most prudent investor, Warren Buffett, 'the Sage of Omaha', had just agreed to invest $5 billion in Goldman Sachs.

The conference call ended at 3.54 p.m. Sixteen seconds later, Gupta called Rajaratnam's office. It took a minute to locate Rajaratnam—he was not at his desk—so he could take the call. The conversation lasted fifty-six seconds. Immediately afterwards, at 3.58 p.m., just two minutes before the markets closed, Rajaratnam bought $27 million worth of Goldman stock. Almost exactly two hours later, Goldman announced the Buffett investment. The bank's shares spiked in after-hours trading. The next morning, when the markets opened, Rajaratnam sold, and walked away with a cool profit of nearly a million dollars.

The US Attorney for the Southern District of New York, Preet Bharara—like Gupta, an Indian-born American citizen, and the man who had spearheaded the investigations—believed that Gupta had called Rajaratnam to tell him about Buffett's offer. If this was true, it was a classic case of insider trading, when the market player gets hold of information that is not available to the public at large and acts on it to make a quick buck.

On 3 October, ten days after Gupta's phone call, in a desperate measure, President George W. Bush signed the Emergency Economic Stabilization Act, creating a $700 billion Troubled Assets Relief Programme (TARP) to purchase failing bank assets. Accounting rules were eased to prevent the collapse of more companies and financial institutions. But the next week was the worst week for US stock markets in seventy-five years. The Dow Jones lost 22.1 per cent, and Standard & Poor's 500 index dipped 18.2 per cent. Paper losses on US stocks now totalled $8.4 trillion as against the market highs of the previous year. A frantic US Federal Reserve announced that it would provide $900 billion in short-term cash loans to banks, and around $1.3 trillion directly to companies outside the financial sector. On 11 October, central bankers and finance ministers from the Group of Seven leading economies met in Washington and agreed to urgent and exceptional coordinated action to prevent the credit crisis from plunging the world into a depression.

On 24 October, during a wiretapped conversation, Rajaratnam told a colleague: 'I heard yesterday from somebody who's on the board of Goldman Sachs that they are going to lose $2 per share. The Street has them making $2.50.' A minute later, he says, 'I'm gonna whack it, you know', and laughs with unrestrained glee.

He had just sold Galleon's entire position in Goldman, and avoided, according to the prosecutors, a loss of more than $3.6 million. The day before, Gupta had been told during a Goldman board meeting that the company had lost almost $2 a share, worse than Wall Street's expectations. And phone records showed that just twenty-three seconds after the board meeting ended, Gupta had called Rajaratnam and spoken to him for thirteen minutes.

On 29 January 2009, a day before Procter & Gamble announced its quarterly earnings, Gupta, who was attending the World Economic Forum at Davos in Switzerland, participated in a P&G board meeting via conference call. Earnings were discussed. A few hours later, the government alleged afterwards, Gupta called Rajaratnam and spoke to him for eight minutes. Later that day,

Rajaratnam's Galleon funds short-sold about 180,000 P&G shares, and ended up making a profit of more than $570,000.

Gupta had angrily denied accusations that he had been supplying insider information to Rajaratnam. In fact, when in March 2011 the Securities & Exchange Commission (SEC), the market watchdog, filed an administrative action against Gupta for the same alleged misdeeds, he had sued the SEC right back. The maximum that the SEC could have done to Gupta was give him a rap on the knuckles and perhaps impose a fine and restrictions on trading in stocks, and the matter would have ended there. But Gupta sued, asking to move the matter to federal court. He did not want the slightest blot on his reputation and he was willing to fight it out.

His court filing read, 'Mr Gupta denies all allegations of wrongdoing and stands ready to mount a defence against each and every one of the Commission's charges. Yet under current Commission rules, Mr Gupta would be deprived of a jury trial, the right to use the discovery procedures of the federal court to shape his defence and the protections of the federal rules of evidence, which were crafted to bar unreliable evidence.' It went on to say that the SEC action '"unfairly and unconstitutionally" singles him out', as he was to date the only person not employed by a broker-dealer ever charged by the SEC in administrative proceedings.

But Wall Street sentiment was already turning against him. Right after the SEC allegations came to light, investment banker Michael Farr said on 2 March 2011 on CNBC: 'If the allegations are true, this guy's a jerk, you know, a major jerk. On Wall Street, there is no more precious currency than trust… There have to be real hard consequences for people who commit these sorts of transgressions.' Other Wall Street traders appearing on US TV echoed his views.

However, it could be argued that this sort of talk smacked more than a little of sanctimoniousness. The CNBC show host pointed out to Farr that people believed that what Rajat Gupta had been accused of was 'endemic' on Wall Street. And one could further argue that the US investment community—shaken by the market collapse and public perceptions that ran a narrow spectrum from rage to revulsion—was trying extra hard to appear as a bastion of fair play and financial ethics. It would be perfectly happy to throw to the wolves a man like Gupta, who was not a member of the community, and certainly not a key player in any way in the suicidal stampede of greed that had led to a global economic crisis.

In August 2011, Gupta and the SEC agreed to drop their respective actions against each other. But on 26 October, the United States Attorney's Office filed charges against Gupta on five counts of securities fraud and one count of conspiracy to commit securities fraud. He surrendered to the FBI and pleaded not guilty. He was released on the same day on $10 million bail secured by his Westport, Connecticut house, once owned by retail chain magnate J. C. Penney. The white eighteen-room mansion, which Gupta purchased in 1999, sits on 2.28 acres and has more than 12,000 square feet of living space.

Gupta was also asked to surrender his passport and barred from leaving continental USA till further notice.

He had just become the fifty-sixth person charged in the biggest insider trading probe ever in US history. Of the fifty-five people charged before Gupta, fifty had either pleaded guilty or been convicted at trial.

By suing the SEC, Gupta had started off a chain of events, the full consequences of which he might not have worked out at that time. Much later, on 19 June 2012, after the verdict had been passed in the Gupta criminal trial, K. P. Nayar, US correspondent for *The Telegraph*, the Kolkata daily, wrote: 'A prominent New York lawyer colourfully compared Gupta's lawsuit against the SEC's administrative action to a road accident in which a drunken driver fatally hits a pedestrian and the police charge him with driving a car with an expired registration. But the driver, in turn, files a case against the police challenging the citation ticket and as a result, the police comes back after the driver accusing him of driving while intoxicated and also slaps a murder charge caused by reckless driving.'

Gupta had chosen his lawyer well. Gary Naftalis, a tall, white-haired, big-nosed sixty-nine year old, was a superstar among defence lawyers specializing in white-collar crime. In a forty-year career, he had successfully defended clients like investment bank Salomon Brothers, brokerage firm Kidder, Peabody & Co., former Walt Disney Company CEO Michael Eisner, and even the New York Stock Exchange. This is how a *The New York Times* (27 October 2011) profile piece described him: 'Over the years, Mr Naftalis has developed a reputation…[for] his unassuming style and low-key intelligence. He rarely raises his voice, peppers his questions with humour and doesn't bother with the hand-tailored suits favoured by some high-flying defence lawyers.'

The day Gupta was arrested and charged, Naftalis had issued a statement categorically declaring his client's innocence. 'The government's allegations are totally baseless,' he said. 'The facts in this case demonstrate that Mr Gupta is innocent of any of these charges and that he has always acted with honesty and integrity… He did not trade in any securities, did not tip Mr Rajaratnam so he could trade, and did not share in any profits as part of any quid pro quo.'

Coincidentally, Naftalis was also a close friend of Jed S. Rakoff, the federal judge in whose court Gupta would be tried. In fact, Rakoff had presided over the 2009 wedding of one of Naftalis's sons, who was also a clerk for the federal judge.

In the courtroom, Gupta sat with Naftalis and his team, and his family sat in the audience right behind him.

The moment that Gupta's entire life seemed to have led up to had arrived. Under US law, this man, who had been orphaned as a teenager in India, and then fought his way up to reach the very pinnacle of the US corporate world, was facing as long as twenty years in prison if convicted on each of the securities fraud charges and as long as five years if convicted of conspiracy. He could also be fined as much as $5 million.

The trial for Case No. 11-cr-00907, US v Gupta, US District Court, Southern District of New York (Manhattan), was beginning.

The Karmayogi

RAJAT GUPTA'S LIFE IS AN ASTONISHING SAGA OF OVERCOMING towering odds through a near-superhuman combination of intelligence, hard work, discipline, equanimity and humility. His friends and associates repeatedly use the Sanskrit word 'karmayogi' to describe him. He himself, in several interviews, has referred to the teachings of the Hindu sacred text the Bhagavad Gita as central to the way he approached his life and career. 'I owe my success to the basic, underlying philosophy of India,' he told the Indian magazine *Business Today* (22 April 1994), soon after McKinsey had announced that Gupta would be its next chief. 'It goes back to the fundamental philosophy of the Gita, which is that you worship work and do it for its own sake and don't judge it by what results you achieve. Concentrate on doing your best in what you do.'

His quiet humility is legendary. Journalist Nicholas Lemann, in his long article on McKinsey in *The New Yorker* magazine dated 18 October 1999, was alarmed enough to write: 'Rajat Gupta, the head of McKinsey, [is] a man whose air of intense calm, quiet and unobtrusiveness, is almost unsettling because it counterposes so dramatically with what a big shot he is.' As far as his school friends and college mates are concerned, he never changed— success and wealth did not affect his values or behaviour in any way. His designation, power or status made little difference to Rajat Gupta the person. 'Even after he rose so high, he was always very responsive to emails and messages,' said a friend from his IIT days. Gupta and his wife were ever-willing to host their families and friends at their Westport, Connecticut home. 'I've always wondered how he managed to pack so much into his schedule,' said the friend. 'He had an extremely demanding job, yet he would always be able to make time for you when you were in town. It was quite amazing.'

The amount of love and admiration Gupta has received throughout his life for his humanitarian work is, quite simply, awesome.

In fact, he almost seems to be a perfect man.

In a 2001 interview with the *Academy of Management Executive Journal* (Vol. 15. No. 2), certainly one of the most exhaustive he has ever given, Gupta was asked what he thought his core values were. 'Overall, I would say that one obviously aspires, but to what level you achieve it is for someone else to judge, but I very much believe in the philosophical concept of karmayogi,' Gupta replied. 'You just do what you think is the right thing, don't really get attached to the fruits thereof, or don't worry about the results. Do it with the right intentions, do the best you can, and the results will be whatever they will be. It's a fundamentally, deeply held philosophical thought. So my colleagues often ask me, if something doesn't go right: "Aren't you unhappy about it?" I say: "Well, I did everything in my power to do, I did the best I could, I always had the right intentions, and the outcome was not what it was. Well, so be it! Try it another day." It happens all the time; I serve clients the best way I can. Great client projects, but nothing happens afterwards, no relationship, no follow-on work. Well, I did everything I could, but it didn't happen. I think if we judge ourselves by results too much, we're always out of balance. Either we are far happier than we should be, or far sadder. Sometimes the results are not because of what you did, but because of circumstances. Sometimes the results are in spite of the best you did.'

The website friendsofrajat.com was set up within days of Gupta's indictment. It hosts an open letter signed by some of India's top business leaders, from Mukesh Ambani, chairman, Reliance Industries, and Adi Godrej, chairman, Godrej Group, to Yogi Deveshwar, chairman, ITC, and K. P. Singh, chairman, DLF; globally renowned executives like Rana Talwar, former CEO of Standard Chartered Bank; and others like spiritual guru Deepak Chopra and former world badminton champion Prakash Padukone.

Reads the letter: 'The Signatories are extremely concerned that the portrayal of Rajat Gupta in the press and blogosphere have promoted impressions of him that are entirely inconsistent with the Rajat we know. Rajat has built several world-class humanitarian and educational institutions, a legacy that will outlive all of us and greatly benefit future generations. The REAL Rajat known to us over several decades is completely at odds with the public narrative. To our collective knowledge, which spans a lifetime and covers hundreds of friends, Rajat has always upheld the highest of ethical standards; been judged, without a chance to tell his side of the story; and been mis-characterized by people who have little or no knowledge of him... We fully stand by him in his rights to presumption of innocence; in his efforts to clear his name and in his cause to win back his well-deserved reputation for integrity in all aspects of his life and his dedication to humanitarian causes.'

The site also carries dozens of messages from people who have worked with Gupta or known him in a personal capacity, and also from people who have never met him, but been inspired by his life and works.

◆

Rajat Kumar Gupta was born in Kolkata on 2 December 1948 to Pran Kumari Gupta and Ashwini Kumar Gupta. His father worked as a journalist for the Ananda Bazar Patrika Group, which would go on to become the largest media company in eastern India. Rajat was the second of the Guptas' four children. A sister had been born a year earlier, another would appear two years later, and a brother when Rajat was ten.

Ashwini Kumar had been involved in India's freedom struggle against the British, and had been jailed several times. By the time India gained independence, in August 1947, Ashwini had become a favourite of Ashok Kumar Sarkar, the owner-editor of the company's flagship Bengali paper *Anandabazar Patrika*, which had played an important role in the country's freedom movement. In 1954, when Rajat was five, Ashwini Kumar was sent to Delhi to start a new edition of the company's English paper, the *Hindusthan Standard*. Rajat was enrolled in Modern School, one of the most prestigious schools in the capital city—its alumni include some of India's most famous industrialists, journalists, surgeons and civil servants.

But awful tragedy struck the Gupta family when Rajat was still in his teens. Ashwini Kumar passed away when Rajat was fifteen, and two years later he lost his mother. Suddenly, he was alone in the world, the eldest male member of the family, with three siblings.

The Gupta siblings refused to be separated from one another. 'We decided to live by ourselves,' Gupta said in his 1994 *Business Today* interview. 'It was pretty unusual in those days. Normally, we would have been sent off to live with various relatives. Instead, we asked a spinster aunt to come and live with us. All of us were good students, so we all had scholarships.' It also helped that his late father's employer let them keep the Delhi house.

Since then, Gupta's life and career has been an astonishing and inspiring story, for he seemed to achieve perfect success in everything he set his mind to. He ranked fifteenth all-India in the Indian Institute of Technology (IIT) entrance test, and chose to do his graduation in mechanical engineering at IIT Delhi. He excelled in his studies at IIT, was extremely active outside the classroom, and was by far the star of his batch. He appeared in or directed seventeen plays (in English and Hindi) in his five years there; was a brilliant debater; represented IIT Delhi in soccer; and was active in student government, being elected to the highest student post in the campus—General Secretary (Students Affairs Centre). At IIT, he also met his future wife, Anita Mattoo, who was two years junior to him.

He graduated in 1971, in the top 15 per cent of his class, with the Director's Gold Medal for the Best Graduating All-Rounder, and had several options to choose from: a highly prestigious job offer as management trainee from ITC, the tobacco giant (now a diversified conglomerate), a seat at the country's top business school, the Indian Institute of Management at Ahmedabad, and an MBA admission with financial aid at the Harvard Business School. Gupta decided to go to Harvard.

'I had got a wonderful job at ITC, [but] I told [them] that I wasn't going to join them,' he told *Business Today*. 'They wouldn't believe me because nobody had turned them down. So, they actually paid my airfare to come and meet them in Calcutta to explain why I wasn't joining them.' In ITC's legendary 37, Chowringhee headquarters in Calcutta, Gupta met a board consisting of the company's top executives, including chairman Ajit Haksar. He explained that he was going to Harvard; and they understood. It was the first time Gupta had sat in an aircraft, or indeed, seen one up close.

The success story continued at Harvard. Gupta graduated in 1973, as a Baker Scholar, the business school's top distinction, awarded to the top 5 per cent students in every batch. Yet McKinsey turned him down for a job in the campus interview, because he had no work experience. But Gupta had set his heart on McKinsey—it was the first time in his life he had met with any sort of failure—and convinced Walter Salmon, one of his professors, to speak to the firm. Salmon obliged, calling up his former classmate Ron Daniel, then in charge of McKinsey's New York office. Clearly, Salmon was a persuasive man. McKinsey did something extraordinary—it flew Gupta down to New York, and after a day-long interaction, decided to hire him after all.

In 1994, at the age of forty-five, after having worked in the

US and Scandinavia (where he grew McKinsey from a small operation to a large thriving entity), Gupta, then heading the Chicago office, was elected by McKinsey's 427 partners as their next managing director. Interestingly enough, it was Daniel who called Gupta to inform him. Daniel had also been managing director, and was now the chairman of the election committee. Gupta took over on 1 July 1994, for a three-year term.

Gupta was not only the first non-US-born managing director of McKinsey, but also the youngest ever.

He was elected twice more, and stepped down in 2003, abiding by the rule that he himself had introduced: a McKinsey managing director would be allowed a maximum of three terms. 'I was elected quite young and I could do five terms, if not more,' Gupta explained in the 2001 interview with the *Academy of Management Executive Journal*. 'So I decided that, in an institution like ours, it is important that there is always renewal and change. It is very difficult for an individual, himself, to voluntarily step down; at least I thought it would be if I got closer to it. So I said in my first term, let me put in a term limit of three terms, and make sure that there is an incentive or a requirement for me to step down. Whatever I could do in nine years would be sufficient. If I couldn't do it in nine years, I would never be able to do it, and there would always be great value in renewal and change in the leadership. And that is one philosophy that I have adopted in everything.'

After giving up his managing directorship, Gupta remained a senior partner at McKinsey, though he was increasingly involved in various global philanthropic projects. Some of these were to do with India, born out of his deep personal commitment to his country of birth.

In fact, Gupta's later life has been characterized by a strong desire to give something back to societies and institutions which he felt had made him what he was. He was in Davos attending the World Economic Forum in January 2001 when news broke about the devastating earthquake in Gujarat which claimed thousands of lives. Within hours, he had started raising funds for the victims, and had set up an informal organization that would, in time, become the influential American Indian Foundation, with former US President Bill Clinton as its Chief Patron. Gupta was one of the moving forces behind setting up the Global Pan-IIT Alumni Association, which brought together IITians from all over the world with a specific mandate to be an agent of change in India. He also sat on the Harvard board.

Gupta retired from McKinsey in 2007.

◆

Friends from Gupta's IIT days recall a young man who was brilliant but unassuming, a natural leader who, however, never imposed his will on anyone, extraordinarily disciplined yet keen to enjoy every aspect of campus life.

Ashok Syal, co-founder and managing director of information technology solutions firm Sumpraxis, based in Chantilly, Virginia, lived a few rooms away from Gupta's room for five years in Aravali hostel at IIT Delhi. 'I remember Rajat very, very fondly,' he says. 'He was a very very social person, so he had a lot of admirers, a lot of friends.'

More than four decades later, Syal still marvels at the way Gupta managed to balance academics and all his extra-curricular activities. 'He spent such a busy life!' he reminisces. 'I remember meeting him sometimes, rushing back from some drama rehearsal or something, and saying, "I only have four hours to prepare for today's exam." But even those four hours were enough for him. Because, as you know, he was a topper.'

All this must have required a great amount of discipline. 'Absolutely,' says Syal. 'He is the most disciplined guy I have ever met. No matter what time of the night he had gone to sleep, he would get up early in the morning. He was very particular about having his meals at the right time. He would take on a lot of responsibility and manage everything perfectly, and on time. And we never saw him shabbily dressed. Now, IIT students usually don't care about how they look and what they are wearing, but not Rajat. His clothes were always clean, and he was smartly turned out. I think he knew that having lost his parents, and with three siblings to take care of, he had to maintain discipline.'

Writing on friendsofrajat.com, IIT classmate Harbinder Gill recalls: 'For most of us [IIT] was the first time we lived away from our families. Our adolescent hormones and new-found freedom formed a dangerous mixture and we were all seventeen going on fourteen. As much as allowed by our busy academic schedule, we spent every waking moment on some inane prank or the other, which would today be considered sexist or even harassment. Except Rajat, who seemed to be seventeen going on thirty. He was a stabilizing force that provided us with a moral and ethical compass that kept us from doing something really stupid... His pensive nature, peppered with a razor-sharp wit and a self-denigrating sense of humour showed us that fun doesn't have to be at the expense of others. We were in the same hostel for five years, and being from the same neighbourhood in Delhi—Rajinder Nagar—we often travelled home together for the weekends. I am sure he didn't realize how educational our conversations were for me, as I compared his deep thinking to my shallow plans for the weekend and the near future... When the rest of us went gallivanting in Delhi University's richly co-ed campus, Rajat was busy volunteering his services around IIT, assisting with student affairs, hostel management, etc.'

For one day every year, Gupta would put on a dhoti and kurta, which, Syal guesses, had possibly belonged to his father. 'He would wear those in memory of his father, and he was not shy or defensive about it at all,' recalls Syal. 'He would go everywhere wearing his dhoti and kurta. And everyone respected him for that.'

It is clear that Gupta's father had been a very strong influence on him, and as a young man, he truly missed him. Late one night, Syal was returning to his room after music practice, when he saw the light on in Gupta's room. He knocked and entered. 'Rajat had a very big steel trunk. He had opened it and was in a very pensive mood. I asked him, "What's happened?" He said, "Today is my father's death anniversary." I think that trunk was full of his father's belongings, and he always carried it with him. That night, he spoke about what a great childhood he had had in Calcutta, about his father, and that now he had to look after his brother and two sisters. It was a very private moment, and it was very moving and touching.'

In the *Academy of Management Executive Journal* interview, Gupta acknowledged his father as his 'role model'. 'If I look at a role model and a value statement, though not in every aspect of life, I would certainly pick my parents,' he said. 'I'd pick my father, whom I observed, who died when I was fifteen. He was a freedom fighter, a real Gandhian. And he had a philosophy of life that was very much of a giving nature. So just observing what he did was probably the most important influence. He had very high standards of integrity and high thinking. And he believed in simple living. I don't think I would say I followed him in that regard. I'm far more materialistic a person than he ever was. He was a very simple person. But those things have shaped me.'

The Mother Teresa Factor

IN HIS FINAL YEAR AT IIT, GUPTA'S LEADERSHIP SKILLS FACED THEIR toughest test till then. Dr Subramaniam Swamy, who would go on to be a prominent national-level politician, had come down from Harvard University to teach Economics at IIT Delhi. As Ashok Syal recalls, soon after joining IIT, Dr Swamy, who had strong Hindu nationalist Rashtriya Swayamsevak Sangh (RSS) credentials, began spreading the message of Hindutva in the campus. Even during the most turbulent phases in independent India's political history, the IITs have traditionally been islands of apolitical calm. Student elections have always been fought on the basis of the abilities of candidates, and never on political or ideological lines. Dr Swamy garnered support from some students and a lot of Class IV staff at the institute. An RSS shakha (branch) was set up on the campus, where members would meet for early morning drill.

This spilled over into other aspects of student life. Students swayed by the Hindutva philosophy started warning Western music enthusiasts like Syal that they should play only Indian music. They threatened that if students played rock and roll in public fora, they would be booed and stoned. Some even started talking about a dress code, that jeans should not be allowed on campus. Dr Swamy's followers began digging up dirt on the institute's director, Dr Dogra, and holding demonstrations against him. 'The campus got divided,' says Syal. 'The situation became very bad.'

Then Gupta decided to do something about it. He firmly believed that religion and politics should not be allowed into the campus, and he was willing to fight for what he believed. A campaign was launched under his leadership. He began meeting students and convincing them to join him. 'It was a matter of principle for him,' remembers Syal. 'He said we cannot sit around and let the institute and its academic and social life be politicized. We used to meet in his room, make posters, strategize.' In the end, his campaign prevailed. The director was emboldened by the students' support to ban the formation of shakhas on the campus. 'Rajat was a brilliant manager and leader already, while he was still a student,' says Syal. 'If he didn't have those qualities, he could never have pulled off what he did against Dr Swamy.'

This campaign is perhaps what Anjan Chatterjee, who was Gupta's junior at IIT and then at McKinsey, is referring to when he writes on friendsofrajat.com: 'Rajat has a tremendous amount of courage—to follow through with his convictions no matter how unpopular, no matter how daunting. He sets high barriers and breaks through the walls in-between, he has done this time and time again...I have seen him stare down militant student protestors at IIT who threatened to harm the institute by telling them, "We are not afraid. If you burn down the buildings we will call in the fire engines and rebuild."'

When in 1994 *Business Today* contacted a former senior manager of ITC who had interviewed Gupta for the management trainee job twenty-three years earlier, he still remembered the bright young man. Apparently, when asked the attributes of a leader, Gupta had said: 'One who can motivate his colleagues and get things done without making his teammates feel that it was the leader who had actually got the work done.' Gupta's maturity and confidence had stuck in the interviewer's mind.

'When Rajat was applying for his graduate scholarship to Harvard, Professor Dogra gave him a recommendation that went something like: "Here is a student who saved our campus from a great disaster,"' says Syal. 'That was a very big thing to say.'

Strangely enough, today, Dr Swamy claims he remembers Gupta as a student, but cannot recall any such movement led by him. In fact, he says that he gave a glowing recommendation to Gupta when he was applying to Harvard, and, as a former

Harvard professor, his words should have carried considerable weight when Harvard was deciding whether to offer Gupta a graduate scholarship. At that time, a student from India getting financial aid at Harvard was a very rare event.

Even at the elite and highly competitive Harvard Business School, Gupta stood apart from the crowd, without even seeming to try. A May 2011 article by John Helyar, Carol Hymowitz and Mehul Srivastava in *Bloomberg Markets* magazine quotes John Carberry, a senior investment banker who lived in the same Boston dormitory and was Gupta's friend: 'Sometimes we'd still be doing cases at 2 a.m., but he'd be done by 11 p.m. and lying on his bed, watching Johnny Carson. But if you had problems with your schoolwork, he'd always help.' He recalled that at a time when students at Harvard Business School were overwhelmingly white, Gupta stood out culturally and intellectually. 'Gupta was unassuming and humble,' he said. 'When he spoke in class, though, everyone put their pencils down and listened. He was the smartest guy in my section, just brilliant.'

Gupta himself explained it thus in an interview: '[The Harvard experience] was sort of classic. You always feel you're going to flunk in the first month. They give you so much to do that you say this is impossible. But once I got over that initial scared feeling, it was relatively easy. Because the IITs give you a wonderful education, better than you get anywhere, actually.'

◆

In the nine years during which Gupta led McKinsey, the firm's revenues nearly tripled, from $1.2 billion to $3.4 billion. The number of partners more than doubled, from 427 to 891. McKinsey opened twenty-six new offices globally under Gupta, who pursued expansion in India, China and other emerging markets. But these years were also turbulent years for the firm. It enthusiastically rode the dotcom boom, only to see many of its clients go bust. Other big clients too went bust, the most notorious case being energy trading behemoth Enron, led by former McKinsey partner Jeffrey Skilling. Skilling was convicted of corporate fraud and sent to prison for twenty-four years.

Enron had been one of McKinsey's biggest clients, paying it as much as $10 million a year in fees, and it was McKinsey's advice that had been crucial in turning an old-economy gas distribution company into a (seemingly) stunningly successful new-economy energy derivatives trader. However, when Enron imploded, as its duplicitous and illegal accounting practices came to light, it took down its audit firm Arthur Andersen with it, but McKinsey emerged unscathed. Gupta ordered an internal inquiry, which concluded that McKinsey had had nothing to do with the financial structuring skullduggery. Yet a piece in the British weekly *The Observer* on 24 March 2002 referred to McKinsey in its headline as 'The Firm that Built the House of Enron'.

Even while he was head of McKinsey, Gupta had been becoming increasingly involved with initiatives that went far beyond the corporate world. After relinquishing his managing directorship in 2003, Gupta transferred his remarkable energy and intelligence to philanthropic and developmental projects. As can be expected, the number and scope of the missions he either spearheaded or was involved in is breathtaking.

While in McKinsey, he served as advisor to then-United Nations Secretary General Kofi Annan, and developed an extensive set of recommendations to reform the management of the organization. But Gupta's principal areas of interest have been health and education, especially in emerging nations.

In 2002 he became a founding board member (the only one from the private sector) of The Global Fund for AIDS, Malaria and Tuberculosis, and went on to become its chairman. The Global Fund describes itself as 'a unique public-private partnership and international financing institution dedicated to attracting and disbursing additional resources to prevent and treat HIV and AIDS, TB and malaria. This partnership between governments, civil society, the private sector and affected communities represents an innovative approach to international health financing.'

Today the Global Fund claims to be 'the main financier of programmes to fight AIDS, TB and malaria, with approved funding of $22.9 billion for more than a thousand programmes in 151 countries. To date, programmes supported by the Global Fund have provided AIDS treatment for 3.6 million people, anti-tuberculosis treatment for 9.3 million people and 270 million insecticide-treated nets for the prevention of malaria.' According to friendsofrajat.com: 'In partnership with the UN Secretary General's Special Envoy for Malaria, Ray Chambers, Mr Gupta devised a programme to distribute bed nets and artemisinin-combination therapies (ACTs) to fight malaria in at-risk populations. The programme helped to reduce deaths caused by malaria by 50 per cent.'

When in 2006 Indian Prime Minister Dr Manmohan Singh launched the Public Health Foundation of India (PHFI), it was to a large extent a Gupta initiative. PHFI is a first-of-its-kind public-private partnership in India, focused on research to inform public policy, creating schools of public health across the country, and establishment of health systems at the state level. Dr Singh appointed Gupta as the founding chairman of PHFI. In addition to developing and catalysing the idea, Gupta also raised $50 million to establish the foundation, including a $20 million grant from the Bill & Melinda Gates Foundation. Today, PHFI is India's largest health research hub, with Institutes of Public Health in six states.

Gupta worked closely with the Bill & Melinda Gates Foundation for over a decade as strategist and advisor. In 2001, he set up the American Indian Foundation (AIF), under the patronage of his friend, former US President Bill Clinton. Since then, the AIF has raised over $100 million, which it has deployed across India, developing partnerships with over 115 non-governmental organizations (NGOs) in India, according to the foundation's website. Gupta was also a founding board member of India's Emergency Management Research Institute and Health Management Research Institute, and had served on the boards of the Global Health Council, the Global Business Council and the Harvard School of Public Health. He was also on the board of the Rockefeller Foundation for more than three years, focusing in particular on global health issues.

Gupta had also been extremely active in the field of education. He had been involved with the Indian NGO Pratham right from the time it was set up in 1994 to provide education to slum children in Mumbai. Pratham is today India's largest NGO in the educational sector, and has served more than 3 million children in 47,000 villages across nineteen states in India.

However, if Gupta had had one dream project in education for his country of birth, one could say that it was the Indian School of Business (ISB). Completely his brain child, Gupta persuaded India's top business leaders to get involved in the project, which envisaged a business school to rank with the world's very best, both in terms of faculty and facilities. ISB's world-class 270-acre Hyderabad campus opened its doors to students in 2001, with Gupta using his network to forge partnerships with some of the world's top-ranked business schools, and get some of the best management professors from across the world to take visiting faculty positions at the institute. ISB is today one of the country's most respected (and, one must mention, also one of the most expensive) business schools, described by Dipak Jain, former dean of the Kellogg School of Management, as 'a world-class facility and faculty with western infrastructure, Indian heart and a global soul'.

Gupta also worked with top Russian investment banker Reuben Vardanian to set up the Skolkovo School of Management, Russia's first business school, modelled after ISB. In China, he served as a board member of Tsinghua University's School of Economics and Management, working with founding chairman (and former US Treasury Secretary) Henry Paulson to establish the school. He also served on the boards of Harvard Business

School (and as chairman for three years), Kellogg School, Wharton, and MIT Sloan, as well as a trustee of the University of Chicago and the Weill Cornell Medical College.

Rajendra Singh Pawar, founder-chairman of the NIIT Group, whose businesses include one of the world's largest talent development companies, was a year junior to Gupta at IIT Delhi, and succeeded him as general secretary (students affairs centre). He vividly remembers how the ISB idea germinated and how Gupta adroitly managed the whole project, from inception to completion.

In the mid-1990s, Pawar and some other IIT Delhi alumni met Gupta when he was visiting India. 'Initially, we were thinking of doing something for IIT Delhi,' he recalls. 'Rajat was very committed to the IIT cause. He said we must do something. We must make IITs more broad-based. At that time IITs were only focused on engineering, other than the humanities departments. He said: 'Why not create business schools within the IIT concept?' But we realized after a few rounds of discussions that it would not be possible to do something new and bold and radical within the IIT system. I remember his gentle yet firm passion to do something for the IITs. But the idea was not getting traction.'

But Gupta stayed with the idea of a world-class business school in India. The original plan was to set it up in the country's commercial capital, Mumbai. But these efforts seemed to be going nowhere, when the then chief minister of Andhra Pradesh, Chandrababu Naidu, stepped in dramatically. Naidu called Gupta in Mumbai and asked him to come and meet him at Hyderabad. The deal was done almost literally over one meeting. The Andhra government offered land and other support to the project, and Gupta's idea had found its feet.

While ISB was being planned, there were many contentious issues, but Pawar remembers Gupta dealing with them 'in a very humane way. His sensitivity to individuals always surfaced whenever there was a complicated situation. He was serene, patient, mindful, thoughtful, never flustered.'

Gupta's personal leadership style had not changed since the day of his ITC job interview when he had defined his concept of leadership. 'He was not a leader who made great pronouncements and excited people,' says Pawar. 'He would draw people out, get their ideas, coalesce them. If the discussion was drifting, he would intervene. He was not a visible solicitor of opinion. He would just look at Rahul Bajaj (industrialist), or look at me, and we would speak. If there was something contentious, he would put it aside and say, "Let's take that up in the next meeting." And between the two meetings, he would do a lot of background work—what was involved, the issues, the pros and cons, the sensitivities. He was the complete antithesis of the dominant visionary leader. He would never get up on a mountain and shout: "Follow me!" And he would never want to hear things like: "Oh, what a great leader you are!" He would be thoroughly embarrassed by that sort of thing. He drew people out and sought their help.'

In December 2008 India was hit by its own Enronesque scandal, when it came to light that leading information technology company Satyam Computer Services had been falsifying accounts for years and that the promoters had siphoned off billions of dollars. M. Rammohan Rao, the dean of the Indian School of Business, was a member of the Satyam board and had in fact chaired a board meeting on 16 December which approved some highly suspicious investments. The resultant hammering of Satyam stock on Indian bourses and Nasdaq forced Rao to reconvene the board meeting and hurriedly withdraw approval. But the cat was already out of the bag, and within days the full scale and gory details of the shocking corporate fraud emerged.

The scandal left ISB facing a massive public image crisis, and Pawar recounts the calm, clear-headed way Gupta resolved it. 'It was a tricky situation,' says Pawar. 'But Rajat was very clear and he dealt with the issue with great finesse. He said there was nothing that denied Rammohan Rao the right to remain a professor. We should retain him with all dignity. Yes, he cannot hold the dean's office, but his intellectual capability—and his quality as a teacher—has not been affected in any way. A teaching role and an administrative role are two different issues.'

Like the vast majority of people who have come in close contact with Gupta, Pawar is an unabashed admirer of the man. 'His selflessness was visible every minute that one spent with him,' he says. 'He was always gentle, determined, even tranquil. His ideas were always clean and simple. It was not like we have to do something so that we get something out of it, but this is something we have to do. There was no self-interest ever in his thinking. Take the whole ISB project. There was really nothing in it for him—there was no cause and effect equation that he was considering on a personal basis at all. It was just the basic goodness of the man.'

Indeed, feels Pawar, Gupta's 'goodness' may be his only imperfection. 'People have told me that if he had a weakness, it was that he was sympathetic to people who did not deserve his sympathy. It was all out of the great goodness of his heart. And he had this inability to say no. When he came to Delhi, everyone would invite him home—lunch, dinner, whatever. And we would wonder: how the hell does he find the time to meet all his commitments? But he always did.'

In January 2012, when the preliminaries leading to Gupta's trial had begun, I wrote a column on livemint.com, the website of the Indian financial daily *Mint*, on my personal encounters with Gupta. Here are some relevant quotations from that piece:

'In 2002, while researching a book I was writing, I met a galaxy of extremely successful [IITians]... Later, going through my notes and recalling my interactions with them, I realized that of all these people, Rajat Gupta, then worldwide head of McKinsey, was the man I had found most difficult to fathom. In fact, though I had spent several hours talking to him, in the US and in India, face-to-face and on the phone, I knew nothing about him as a person. Either he was the perfect guy—highly intelligent, unfailingly courteous, never a hair out of place—or he had built an impenetrable wall around himself; I could not get the slightest glimpse of what could lie behind it. If, that is, there was a wall at all.

'All the others I met let down their guard at some point of time—they joked, reminisced, told me anecdotes, digressed. Not Gupta. In his undergraduate days in IIT Delhi, he had excelled academically, and also been very active in sports, theatre and student government. He had even made time to woo and win [his future wife]. And this, when he had lost both his parents by the time he completed school, and had [three] siblings to take care of! It seemed incredible. "How on earth did you manage all this, and at such a young age?" I asked him.

'We were speaking over the phone, and there was an almost undetectable pause before he replied, utterly calmly: "I suppose it was all a matter of prioritization."

'"…I suppose it was all a matter of prioritization." I will never forget that answer: bland, logical, powerful, and neatly ending all discussion on the topic being discussed.

'Did Rajaratnam manage to breach Gupta's wall (if there was one), re-prioritize his worldview? We may never know for sure, whatever the final verdict.'

On 18 May 2012, during pre-trial hearings for Gupta's insider trading case, Judge Rakoff ruled that he would allow Gupta's lawyers only limited time to talk about his humanitarian activities. 'Forewarned of the hill I have to climb,' said Naftalis, urging Rakoff to reconsider his decision. 'You're talking about one of the renowned and active humanitarians in the world who has worked to eradicate AIDS, malaria, tuberculosis.' He said he should not be forced to play down Gupta's generosity when prosecutors will try to convince jurors he was motivated by money to commit insider trading.

Retorted Rakoff: 'If Mother Teresa were here and charged with bank robbery, the jury would still have to determine whether or not she committed the robbery.'

The Stockster

RAJ RAJARATNAM, A TAMIL FROM SRI LANKA, WAS BORN IN
Colombo on 15 June 1957. In 1971, the family migrated to
England, where he went to school at Dulwich College, whose
two most famous alumni occupy two opposite edges of literature:
P. G. Wodehouse with his British humour, and Raymond Chandler
with his American hard-boiled detective fiction. Rajaratnam has
claimed in interviews that he is a great Wodehouse fan.

After studying engineering at the University of Sussex,
Rajaratnam moved to the US and did his MBA from the Wharton
School of the University of Pennsylvania. Graduating in 1983, he
joined Chase Manhattan Bank as a lending officer focusing on
the technology industry. In 1985, he joined boutique investment
bank Needham & Co. as an analyst, and rose rapidly to become
president in 1991. In 1992, he started a hedge fund for his
company, the Needham Emerging Growth Partnership. Within
a few years, he had bought it, renamed it Galleon, and was on
his way to becoming one of the biggest hedge fund players in
the world. He was not yet forty.

In 2008, *Forbes* magazine listed him as the 262nd richest
American, worth $1.5 billion. The next year, even as the net was
closing in on him, he had improved his ranking to 236, with
$1.8 billion, and was the richest Sri Lankan-born individual in
the world.

By 2008, the Galleon Group was one of the ten largest hedge
funds in the world with over $7 billion in assets. Even though
technology had been one of its primary areas of focus right
from the beginning, Galleon had not only survived the internet
bust of 2000, but flourished. Between 1999 and 2002 its flagship

operation, the Galleon Diversified Fund, rose 43.7 per cent, while Standard & Poor's 500 (S&P) Index of the largest US companies collapsed, falling 37.6 per cent. In fact, the Galleon Diversified Fund claimed in 2009 that it had climbed 21.5 per cent a year on average since 1992, compared with 7.6 per cent for the S&P 500 Index.

The hallmark of the Galleon Group's operations was swift decision-making and quick entries and exits. Over a nine-month period in 2009, for example, it bought and sold shares of more than 600 companies—and apparently with great insight. In a statement released in September 2009, the fund announced that for the year till date, it had returned 22.3 per cent on a net annualized basis. This, while financial markets across the world were being devastated, and venerable entities like Fannie Mae, Freddie Mac, Lehman Brothers and Bear Stearns had crumpled.

Just a month after he had made public these triumphant numbers, Rajaratnam was arrested by the FBI.

As one can easily imagine, the creator and ruler of the Galleon empire was a man in a hurry. Rajaratnam was smart, he was networked, and he worked hard—any executive who was more than five minutes late for the 8.35 a.m. meeting that started every Galleon day was fined $25. He frequently described himself as a 'warrior' and his market chatter was liberally sprinkled with sports and military terms. But his tremendous ambition had led him to play fast and loose with the laws, right from the beginning. It was as early as 1998, only a year after he set up Galleon, that the authorities had started sniffing around.

That year, Roomy Khan, an Indian-origin employee of chip-maker Intel Corporation, was caught on a security camera in her office, faxing confidential documents to Galleon. Khan pleaded guilty and received three years' probation, but the case against Rajaratnam was too hard to make. Given the volume and speed at which a hedge fund like Galleon traded, it was more or less impossible to pinpoint the source of just one trade. The

Rajaratnam file was closed in 2002.

Then in 2004 the Internal Revenue Service found that Rajaratnam and Galleon executive Gary Rosenbach had participated in a sham tax shelter to hide $52 million in income in 1999. To settle the case, Rajaratnam agreed to pay $20 million in taxes, penalties and interest, and Rosenbach paid $13 million. They then sued the lawyers and promoters who had created the shelter, saying they had not understood that the shelter might be illegal and demanding that the promoters cover the penalties they paid. In 2008, a panel of arbitrators found in their favour and awarded Rajaratnam and Rosenbach more than $10 million in damages and interest from people involved in the shelter.

(In the early evening of 23 September 2008, after Rajat Gupta's alleged tip-off to Rajaratnam about Warren Buffett's $5 billion investment in Goldman Sachs, it would be Rosenbach whom the Galleon boss would call into his room and tell him to buy as much Goldman stock as he could before the stock market closed for trading.)

In 2005, the SEC had discovered that Galleon had repeatedly violated civil rules in share transactions. Galleon paid about $2 million in penalties, profits and interest to settle the case.

In October 2006 Andrew Michaelson, a young lawyer at the SEC, began investigating some stock trades involving a small hedge fund called Sedna Capital, run by Rajratnam's brother, Rengan Rajaratnam. He soon realized that there could be some insider trading going on, and the trail led to Galleon, which had duplicated most of Sedna's suspicious trades.

In March 2007 the SEC received an anonymous letter, alleging insider trading and other skullduggery by Galleon (the identity of the writer is still unknown). By then, an SEC team was already going through the company's electronic correspondence; after several months of meticulous work, they found enough suspicious fragments to issue Rajaratnam a subpoena. On 7 June Rajaratnam came in for an all-day session of giving testimony.

Apart from the usual questions which Rajaratnam would have surely been expecting, Michaelson wanted to ask him about a particular instant messaging (IM) exchange Rajratnam had had with someone using the handle roomy81. The two seemed to be discussing chip-maker Advanced Micro Devices (AMD), and something didn't seem right.

When Michaelson asked Rajaratnam about roomy81, careful to make the query sound entirely casual, the hedge fund manager said that that was Roomy Khan, a former Galleon employee (Khan had briefly worked for Galleon in 2000). When questioned further, Rajaratnam said he could not recall whether he had ever talked to Khan about AMD.

But five days after Rajaratnam's deposition, the investigators turned up an IM exchange dated 9 January 2006 between rajatgalleon and roomy81, where roomy81 had said: 'donot buy plcm till i het (sic) guidance.' PLCM was the ticker symbol for Polycom, a manufacturer of voice and video equipment. It appeared that Roomy Khan had an inside track on Polycom's financial information.

Investigators found that Rajaratnam and Khan had called each other frequently after that IM exchange, and had begun trading heavily in Polycom stock. At the end of January, when Polycom announced record quarterly earnings, Khan made $300,000, and Galleon more than twice that. One of Khan's phone contacts was a Polycom vice-president of Indian origin named Sunil Bhalla. The investigators guessed that he was Khan's source.

In July 2007, Michaelson noticed that there had been several large purchases of stock options in Hilton Hotels immediately preceding an announcement of the chain's takeover by the Blackstone Group. One of the perceptive traders was Rajaratnam; another was Khan. The SEC gave Khan's name to the FBI, and a background check revealed that Khan had a criminal history, and that it involved Rajaratnam.

On 28 November 2007, two FBI agents confronted Khan

at her home. After an hour of stonewalling, she broke down and agreed to cooperate. Apparently, in late 2005, faced with financial difficulties, she had approached Rajaratnam and asked for a job. Rajaratnam had responded by asking her whether she had any sources of inside information. Khan said she knew someone senior in Polycom who told her what was going on in the company. She agreed to pass on whatever she got to the Galleon boss, hoping that this would get her a position at Galleon, and also that Rajaratnam would pass on some inside tips to her.

On 2 July 2007, Khan came to know from Deep Shah, an Indian-origin executive at rating agency Moody's who happened to be a friend and roommate of Khan's cousin, that Blackstone was announcing its Hilton deal the next day, and the price it was paying for each Hilton share was in the mid-$40s, about $10 higher than what Hilton stock was then currently trading at. She informed Rajaratnam, and Galleon Tech Funds (whose stated mandate was to invest in the technology sector) bought 400,000 Hilton shares that day, which he sold a few days later at a cool profit of over $4 million. Khan made $630,000 and paid Shah $10,000 (Shah is currently absconding and is believed to be in India).

Within a week of the Hilton coup, Khan had another hot tip, this time from another Indian-origin friend working in Market Street Partners, a consulting firm that did investor relations work for companies. Google was to announce its quarterly results on 19 July, after close of trading, and its earnings per share (EPS) would be down 25 cents from the last quarter, while the market was expecting an improved EPS. Rajaratnam started short-selling Google, and after the company released its results, exited with a profit of more than $9 million. Khan made about $500,000.

Having revealed all this under FBI grilling, Khan knew she had no option but to go along with whatever the agency wanted—which was to record her calls with Rajaratnam. She quickly agreed to do so.

By March 2008, the government had enough 'dirty' call recordings to get court approval for a thirty-day wiretap on the trader's cell phone. The order was renewed through the rest of the year. The Rajaratnam recordings led to taps on other phones and identified other conspirators, harvesting a huge crop of direct evidence. By 16 October 2009, when Rajaratnam was arrested at his $18 million home on Manhattan's Sutton Place, the government had taped thousands of calls, the SEC had issued more than 230 subpoenas for phone numbers, and reviewed at least 8,000 call records. Over the course of the investigation, the agency gathered nearly ten million documents.

On the day of his arrest Rajaratnam was due to fly to London to launch a $200 million fund to invest in the Sri Lankan stock market. But at 6.30 a.m. he answered his bell to find six FBI agents at his doorstep. They informed him that he was being arrested for insider trading. According to Rajaratnam, as he was being led away, an agent called B. J. Kang told him, 'Take a good look at your son. You're not going to see him for a long time.' Then he said, 'Your wife doesn't seem so upset. Because she's going to spend all your money.' (The FBI has officially denied that Kang said any of this.)

Five other people were arrested and charged on that same day. They were Rajiv Goel, who worked at Intel Capital as a director in strategic investments; Anil Kumar, a director at McKinsey & Co.; IBM senior executive Robert Moffat; and Mark Kurland and Danielle Chiesi, CEO and senior executive, respectively, of the $1 billion hedge fund New Castle Partners.

At the hearing, the prosecution asked Judge Douglas Eaton to hold Rajaratnam in prison pending trial, saying that he had 'enormous incentive' to flee the country. Eaton, however, set Rajaratnam's bail at $100 million, to be secured by $20 million in assets and guaranteed by his wife and four others.

Among those who came forward to stand guarantee for Rajaratnam was Geoffrey Canada, chief executive of the Harlem

Children's Zone, a charity that runs after-school programmes and workshops for poor children and their families. If Rajaratnam did flee, Canada stood to lose everything he owned, including his house and his pension. But Canada was confident; he had known the hedge fund man for years as a philanthropist and supporter of Canada's charity. 'I have not had a moment's doubt, knowing Raj and his character,' he told the media persons gathered outside the courthouse. 'I'm not worried about it at all.'

Among the five other people arrested on that day, Robert Moffat was certainly the biggest name. Moffat, senior vice-president of IBM's systems and technology group, was perhaps the closest confidant of CEO Samuel Palmisano and widely considered a candidate to succeed him. Born in a working-class family, he had joined IBM as a junior programmer in 1978 and risen through the ranks to one rung away from the pinnacle. On the way, he had managed large divisions, turned around terminally floundering business units, and saved his company billions of dollars a year by creating a whole new supply chain management system. His loyalty to IBM and Palmisano was the stuff of legend in the company.

But in 2002 he had met Danielle Chiesi and that first brief encounter, engineered by Chiesi, would trigger off a relationship that would ultimately ruin Moffat's brilliant career and reputation.

Chiesi, a former teenage beauty queen—she had won the regional Southern Tier beauty contest at her home town of Binghamton, NY, when she was fifteen—joined Wall Street brokerage firm Mabon Nugent & Co. as an analyst in 1988. There she met Mark Kurland, who would be her mentor and off-and-on lover for two decades. She left the firm in 1991, worked for various companies, married, divorced, and in 1997, joined Bear Stearns's asset management business, where Kurland was CEO. Soon afterwards, Kurland set up an equity hedge fund within Bear Stearns called New Castle.

Chiesi, who covered technology companies at New Castle,

loved her work, and was fully aware of the arsenal she brought to the job. Information was power, and she was willing to use her considerable charms, enhanced by low-cut tops and short skirts, to get men to reveal information that would be useful to her. To her credit, she never made a secret of it. It was widely reported in the media that she would tell men: 'I love the three S's...sex, stocks and sports.' Trading business information, she would say, was 'like an orgasm'.

In 2002 she asked a senior IBM executive, who was a friend, to introduce her to someone in the company who was a star: someone, as she put it, with 'game'. Her friend introduced her to Moffat at a conference. The first meeting was short, but Chiesi knew he was her man—as head of IBM's global supply chain, he spoke regularly with the biggest technology companies in the world, both vendors and customers. And he was close to the CEO.

Chiesi made sure she kept in touch, and soon a business friendship developed. They would regularly swap ideas and discuss industry developments. Some time in 2003 they began sleeping together, and Moffat started revealing confidential information to Chiesi, who supplied it to Kurland.

It is unclear when Chiesi started giving information to Rajaratnam, but by March 2008, when the US government started tapping the Galleon boss's phone, they were in regular touch, and exchanging tips. In July 2008, Chiesi had a number of phone conversations with Rajaratnam on internet services company Akamai Technologies. Chiesi had a friend in Akamai who had told her that Akamai would announce disappointing quarterly results, and its share price would definitely fall.

On the phone, Chiesi was to tell Rajaratnam, barely able to suppress the jubilation of a hunter after a good kill: 'I just got a call from my guy at Akamai and I played him like a fine-tuned piano...Between the two of us, the way we should play it is, we should short [the Akamai stock] dead, we should short it dead... I don't know about you, baby, but I'm thrilled.'

Noting that Akamai is going to announce its results on Wednesday, Rajaratnam says that they have three trading days to capitalize on the advance information.

'We go slow,' says Chiesi, her voice now breathy in anticipation. 'We just keep shorting, every day. Nobody knows anything. Short, short, short. Nobody's going to know anything…and we have the chance to jab this thing down so huge…! That's the best thing I heard today. How about you?'

Rajaratnam agrees that for him too, it was the best thing he had heard that day.

New Castle made $2.3 million from shorting Akamai stock, and Galleon raked in $3 million.

Some inside information—what is technically termed 'material nonpublic information'—that Moffat provided to Chiesi, and of which the government had evidence from the wiretaps, concerned pioneering tech company Sun Microsystems, which IBM was considering acquiring in 2009. While IBM was conducting a due diligence on Sun, Moffat had access to the firm's complete financial information, including future guidances and quarterly earnings forecasts. He passed on the numbers to his lover, and New Castle made money. He also kept Chiesi in the know about his own company's quarterly results announcements in advance.

(IBM finally did not buy Sun. In January 2010 the company was acquired by Oracle Corporation for $7.4 billion; Sun was merged with Oracle USA Inc. to become Oracle America, Inc.)

Another top technology executive Chiesi cosied up to was Hector Ruiz, CEO of AMD (Ruiz has not been charged with any irregularities, and has consistently denied that he had an 'intimate relationship' with Chiesi). In June 2008 AMD was in talks to spin off its manufacturing business, Fabco, creating a joint venture that would be 50 per cent owned by an Abu Dhabi sovereign wealth fund, Mubadala Investments. IBM was involved in the discussions because it had been asked by AMD to provide a licence for the use of its technology as part of the reorganization. Moffat was

IBM's point man for the talks. With access to the two men in charge of the deal, Chiesi was soon getting detailed information that no other analyst had. Amazingly, she persuaded Ruiz to let her sit in on one of the confidential meetings between him and Moffat. As the deal progressed, Moffat kept her updated. She in turn regularly briefed Kurland about the developments. New Castle bought 199,400 shares.

On 22 August, Moffat told Chiesi, 'The Arabs are gonna pay $2.1 billion…for a 50 per cent stake in Fabco.' He would have been mortified if he had heard her discussing him with Rajaratnam just a few days earlier.

CHIESI: My parents have a lake house in Candlewood and so Moffat and his daughter are coming this weekend.

RAJARATNAM: Moffat has kids?

CHIESI: Yeah, he's married and has kids. Why are you surprised?

RAJARATNAM: I thought he was single. He looks like a single guy, you know, he's got a swagger.

CHIESI: No, he's more like the geeky type, not charming like how you are.

All told, according to the government, Galleon and New Castle made $20.8 million from insider information provided by Chiesi and other sources.

At six in the morning on 16 October 2009, five FBI agents arrived at Moffat's Connecticut house with a warrant to arrest him. But Moffat was not at home. The workaholic executive, as was his routine, had left home at 5.30 a.m. and was already in his office. His wife Amor called him and informed him about the visitors. 'What's going on?' she asked.

'I don't know,' said Moffat. He left for home immediately, sprinting down the parking lot to his Lexus. It was the last time anyone saw him at IBM.

That evening, he was released on $2 million bail. The next day, he resigned from the company to which he had devoted thirty-one years of his life.

After agonizing for months, Moffat agreed to plead guilty to one count of conspiracy and one count of securities fraud involving insider information that he had passed to Chiesi. 'I disclosed this information to Ms Chiesi intentionally, and I knew that what I was doing was wrong,' he told the court in March 2010. He described Chiesi as a 'friend'.

Mark Kurland was the first of the Galleon defendants to be sentenced. He admitted his crimes but attempted to minimize their significance, saying he was only a 'minor' player in the ring. Kurland argued he was significantly less culpable than Moffat, the tipper. He also tried to shift the blame to his former colleague and lover. Chiesi, Kurland's lawyer declared, 'is responsible for involving him in the unlawful inside-trading conspiracy'. Kurland was sentenced to twenty-seven months in prison and fined $900,000.

Chiesi was made of sterner stuff. She refused to plead guilty and, days before her trial began, she told a Reuters interviewer: 'There is not even a chance we will do one day in jail. We didn't do anything wrong.' While out on bail, she attended classes in French cuisine—her grandfather had owned a famous French restaurant in New York.

But as the trial progressed, her resolve crumbled. After more than twenty of the forty-seven people in overlapping networks charged with insider trading had pleaded guilty, Chiesi decided to do so too. By then, according to *The New York Post* (20 January 2011), she was on the anti-anxiety drug Cymbalta and seeing a psychiatrist. She sobbed and told the court, 'I ruined a twenty-year career in my field that I truly love and I have been extremely devoted to. I brought disrepute to what is an honourable profession.' She apologized to her family and to the judge. But, till the end, she refused to turn anyone else in.

In an interview with *Fortune* magazine published in July 2010, Moffat showed little self-pity, but 'rebuffed the notion that he hadn't paid a price for his crimes, noting that by leaving IBM he was giving up an estimated $65 million in lost stock options and pension that he would have collected when he retired at sixty'. He told his interviewer: 'The biggest thing I've lost is my reputation.' Moffat's lawyer had advised him not to talk about the case or his relationship with Chiesi, but when told that *Fortune* intended to write about the affair anyway, he said: 'Everyone wants to make this about sex. Danielle had an extensive network of business people. And she added clarity about what was going on in the business world…I know in my heart what this relationship was about: clarity in the business environment.'

On 14 September, Moffat was sentenced to six months in prison, beginning in April 2011. He immediately appealed that he would like to begin serving his term earlier, so he could be out of prison in time to attend his son's college graduation in May. The request was granted.

On 20 July 2011, Chiesi was sentenced by Federal Judge Richard Holwell to thirty months in prison, two years of supervised release, and 250 hours of community service. The sentence surprised many, since her boss Kurland had got twenty-seven months. 'I anticipate to survive,' Chiesi said in response to what she expected from her prison experience.

On 18 October she started serving her term in the Federal Prison Camp in Alderson, West Virginia. There would be no more designer outfits for her for some time. Prison rules at Alderson required inmates to wear a standard-issue khaki uniform with a belt, work boots, and shirt tucked in. However, electric hair-dryers, hot combs and curling irons were available on request for prisoners.

Rajaratnam remained steadfast with his 'not guilty' plea. He was a 'warrior' and had once compared himself with the great boxer Muhammad Ali. When the jury brought in a guilty verdict, the prosecution asked for a sentence of nineteen-and-a-half to twenty-four-and-a-half years. 'Raj Rajaratnam's criminal conduct was brazen, arrogant, harmful, and pervasive,' it said in its court filing. 'He corrupted subordinates. He corrupted entire markets. Day after day, month after month, year after year, Rajaratnam operated as a billion-dollar force of deception and corruption on Wall Street.' The prosecution argued that the sentence needed to 'reflect the seriousness of Rajaratnam's criminal activity and to deter others—particularly in the hedge fund and money management world—from engaging in a crime that is far too rampant'.

In response, Rajaratnam's lawyers filed that the sort of prison term the prosecution was asking for was an outrage. 'The government asks the Court to ignore Raj Rajaratnam the human being and to sentence a caricature instead,' said the filing. 'The real Raj Rajaratnam—the man who emerges from the full record including the hundreds of letters the Court has received—is a kind, generous and hardworking person, a dutiful son caring for his elderly parents, a loving husband and father, a loyal friend, and an exceptionally generous philanthropist. Although the jury found that Mr Rajaratnam crossed the line by engaging in insider trading while managing investment portfolios at Galleon, the record also shows that the trades in question accounted for less than 1 per cent of his trading activity, and that Mr Rajaratnam leveraged his personal success to help thousands of people in need, including family, friends, employees, acquaintances and perfect strangers. The government ignores all this, and instead of providing a fair and objective description of the defendant's conduct, resorts to unfounded ad hominem attacks, sketching a one-dimensional caricature driven by "greed, arrogance, hubris and egomaniacal desire" to commit crimes of "historic" proportions, comparable only to the vilest financial frauds—Enron, WorldCom, and the Madoff Ponzi scheme—each of which ruined the lives and livelihoods of scores of victims.

'The government relies on this distortion because it requests a distorted sentence—nineteen-and-a-half to twenty-four-and-a-half years of imprisonment. At the high end, the requested sentence is more than four times longer than the longest sentence imposed in these cases to date and would guarantee Mr Rajaratnam's death in prison. The requested sentence is so disproportionate to the sentences imposed in other insider trading cases that the government cannot cite a single insider trading case as precedent, lest it reveal that no comparable sentence has ever been imposed.

'The government's request that Mr Rajaratnam be imprisoned for an unprecedented nineteen-and-a-half to twenty-four-and-a-half years must be put in context. The average sentence imposed for manslaughter in 2010 was seventy-three months; for kidnapping and hostage-taking, one hundred and sixty-three months; for sexual abuse, one hundred and nine months; for robbery, seventy-seven months; for arson, seventy-nine months; and for child pornography, one hundred and eighteen months. The maximum sentence that the government is seeking in this case exceeds the average sentences imposed in all of these categories by more than ten years. Indeed, of all the offences for which the Sentencing Commission keeps statistics, the only category where the average sentence even approaches the sentence the government seeks here is murder, at two hundred and seventy-seven months—still sixteen months shy of the upper end of the government's request. This Court's statutory mandate is to impose a sentence that is "not greater than necessary", a bedrock principle of sentencing law that the government ignores completely. That mandate cannot be fulfilled by a sentence longer than the average sentences for murder or the other violent offences listed above.'

Judge Holwell finally decided that eleven years—one hundred and thirty two months—was the right prison term for Rajaratnam.

Of the six people arrested on the morning of 16 October 2009, only two men would not go to prison. Both had pleaded guilty, had testified against Rajaratnam at his trial, and were Indian-origin classmates of his from Wharton.

Rajiv Goel of Intel Capital had been supplying insider

information to the hedge fund boss for years. In January 2007, a week before Intel Corporation announced its quarterly results, Rajaratnam contacted Goel. Over the next two trading days, Galleon bought a million-and-a-half shares of Intel. But on 16 January, the day Intel was going to go public with its results, Goel called Rajaratnam. Galleon abruptly quit its bull position on Intel, and sold all the shares it had acquired just days before, at a profit of about a million dollars. A few hours later, after the markets closed, Intel announced its numbers, which were below expectations, and the stock price fell by 5 per cent. By selling in the nick of time, Galleon had avoided losses of about $1.4 million. This arrangement continued quarter after quarter. Goel would let Rajaratnam know what Intel would announce, and the hedge fund would take appropriate action.

On 7 May 2008, wireless service providers Clearwire Corporation and Sprint Nextel Corporation announced a joint venture combining their broadband networks. Intel Capital, which was Clearwire's largest shareholder, put $1 billion into the venture, its biggest investment ever. For three months leading up to the announcement, Goel and Rajaratnam had been in close touch. On 19 March, on a call that the FBI was tapping, Goel said: 'I was supposed to meet Sriram'—Intel vice-president Sriram Viswanathan—'today. I didn't. I got tired today, so I came home a little early... But we should be meeting tomorrow. I'll tell you, the Sprint thing is not happening in the short term. OK?'

Rajaratnam grunted in response.

'Uh—there—there's a meeting—there's a board meeting,' Goel said. 'Intel has a board meeting, in fact, today. Yeah, today. Uh, and, it's not happening to—today at the board meeting. That much I—I can tell you.'

But the next day, Goel had news. 'Yesterday our board approved this deal,' he told Rajaratnam. Four days later, Rajaratnam purchased 125,800 Clearwire shares.

Galleon did two more big trades in Clearwire stocks in the

next one-and-a-half months, each time a few days before some news broke in the media about the Clearwire-Sprint deal, which caused share prices either to rise or to fall. On each occasion, Galleon made money—a total of close to a million dollars.

Goel received his payoff by giving Rajaratnam access to his personal trading account. The Galleon boss bought and sold stocks on Goel's behalf and made money for him. For example, he had made Goel $78,000 by trading in Hilton Hotels stock after the tip-off from Roomy Khan. There's a fairly hilarious conversation between Rajaratnam and Goel, which the FBI recorded on 7 October 2008. The Galleon boss had just bought for Goel some shares of outsourcing company PeopleSupport, in which Galleon had a 25 per cent stake. But after he'd bought the shares through Goel's trading account at online brokerage firm Charles Schwab, he noticed that Schwab was billing Goel at a price 50 cents higher than what PeopleSupport was then trading at.

RAJARATNAM: Yeah, so at 1.10, [when] I went in and put it to buy the stock, [it] was at 931.

GOEL: Yeah.

RAJARATNAM: Or 932. But 1.12 is the time, right?

GOEL: Yeah.

RAJARATNAM: Now I'm also on Wall Street and I see the time and sales. I always monitor it here, right?

GOEL: Yeah.

RAJARATNAM: You know what the fuckers did? They took the […], they printed for you at 965 and 970, which is ridiculous. It's like 50 cents above where the stock was trading, right?

GOEL: Yeah, yeah, yeah.

RAJARATNAM: And I can see on the […] I have Level 3 machine I can see where it trades, OK?

GOEL: OK.

RAJARATNAM: And it was selling at 931, 932, 933... They don't know that I know that, right?

GOEL: Ah, OK.

RAJARATNAM: Right.

GOEL: (Unintelligible)

RAJARATNAM: So I call the guy at Charles Schwab, right?

GOEL: Yeah.

RAJARATNAM: The guy says what's your mother's maiden (Unintelligible)? I just fucking bullshitted, right? I said Alka. (Voice overlap) Right, he said, no, different name. What's your email? I said intel.com, right?

GOEL: Yeah, yeah.

RAJARATNAM: But he said no. But then he said what's your home number? I gave him the home number. You know I pretended to be you, right?

GOEL: Mmmm.

RAJARATNAM: But, when he calls up, so, this is what I, there's a guy...you have a pen and pencil?

GOEL: Huh?

RAJARATNAM: (Unintelligible) pencil, with you?

GOEL: I'm sorry.

RAJARATNAM: A pen.

GOEL: You're breaking up. I can't call you.

RAJARATNAM: Pen.

GOEL: You can call...

RAJARATNAM: Call me on my...(Voice overlap)

GOEL: No I can't get through.

RAJARATNAM: Call me on my landline.

GOEL: I can't get through on your landline.

RAJARATNAM: Call me on my landline.

GOEL: All phones are busy. I can't. Can you call me on my cell from your land?

RAJARATNAM: What?

GOEL: Can you call me on my cell phone from your landline?

This is all quite funny, except that what is actually happening is that Rajaratnam has inside information on PeopleSupport, since Galleon, because of its 25 per cent shareholding, has its own man on the company's board, and Rajaratnam is using that information to trade for Goel and make him some quick bucks.

Goel and Rajaratnam had been friends and the families had holidayed together in France in 2007. But once he was arrested and charged, and wiretaps of his phone conversations with his friend were played to him, Goel quickly agreed to cooperate with the prosecution and spilled the beans. As a result, he got away with a fine of only $10,000. He was also sentenced to two years' probation and ordered to forfeit $266,000 he had made from illegal trades. While delivering the sentence, US District Judge Barbara Jones said that Goel 'showed good sense in deciding to cooperate' with the government.

The other man who pleaded guilty and provided damning evidence against Rajaratnam was Anil Kumar, director at McKinsey and close associate of his former boss, Rajat Gupta, in more ways than one.

It was Kumar who had introduced Rajaratnam to Gupta while he and Gupta were raising funds for Gupta's dream project, the Indian School of Business, in 1999.

The Firm

IF ONE DOES A GOOGLE SEARCH FOR THE PHRASE 'MCKINSEY mystique', 4,300 results pop up. That's just one indicator of the aura the firm (or as loyalists call it, the Firm) has enjoyed over the decades. The Firm is elitist (it's packed with Ivy League MBAs), secretive (its approach to public relations has been compared to that of Greta Garbo), prefers to deal with top levels of management in client firms, and works almost exclusively in the area of high corporate strategy with far-reaching long-term impact. It has routinely topped 'most prestigious consulting firm' surveys ever since such surveys began.

And it's not even the largest consulting firm in the world. In terms of revenue, it comes in at seventh place. However, it is certainly the most expensive. And that's the way McKinsey has always wanted to be: not the biggest, but certainly the most exclusive. (Or that is what it has always been, except, say, detractors, during the years Rajat Gupta was at the helm.)

Judged in terms of McKinsey alumni who went on to head global corporations, the Firm could easily be called the most influential company in the world. Its alumni have been CEOs of enterprises as diverse as IBM, American Express, Westinghouse, Levi-Strauss, Vodafone, Morgan Stanley, HSBC, Boeing, BMW and Sotheby's. The McKinsey website claims that 'more than 230 [former McKinsey executives] are CEOs of companies with more than $1 billion in annual revenue.'

Naturally, it's hard to be a McKinseyite. Only about one out of a hundred young MBAs who send in their resumes to the Firm every year makes it through the gruelling interview and selection process, and is offered the job of an 'associate'. Only one in five associates becomes a principal, or junior partner, in six years' time. Most of the others are gently shown the door. Only half of the principals go on to become directors. And throughout his career, the McKinseyite goes through intense training sessions (starting with an indoctrination in the Firm's core belief systems), constant global exposure (it is routine for a partner based in Berlin to join a team in Shanghai for a specific six-month project), and working hours that only the toughest or the truly initiated can or are willing to survive.

In many ways, McKinseyites are a cult. They dress similarly (conservative dark suits, a fedora hat was also mandatory till the early 1960s), think similarly (the McKinsey strategy models), are understated to the point of almost obsessively shunning the public limelight, consider themselves to be—in some manner—'chosen', and have access to an intensely loyal old boys' network. When the Firm's image seemed threatened by the Kumar-Gupta insider trading scandal, the British business daily the *Financial Times* reported on 25 November 2011 that 'its senior people have gone delving back through history—the Firm's own and that of other institutions, including those with which it is most frequently compared'. In an interview to the paper in June 2012 Managing Director Dominic Barton said he had been 'thinking what happened with the suppression of the Jesuits in the 1700s. This may seem strange, but [it was] an organization that was thriving and doing well and all of a sudden was severely challenged.'

Though the Firm was set up in 1926 by James O. McKinsey, whose name it still bears, the man who built the McKinsey system and transformed it into a unique entity was a Harvard law graduate called Marvin Bower who headed the Firm from 1950 to 1967, and who is even today revered as the Firm's patron saint. Bower laid down five guiding principles for every McKinseyite:

- To put client interests ahead of Firm interests
- To serve the client competently, i.e. better than the

situation calls for and better than client managers typically expect

- To adhere to high ethical standards in everything McKinsey executives do
- To preserve the confidence of clients and client personnel
- To maintain an independent position, being ready to differ with client managers and telling them the truth as we see it even though it may adversely affect Firm income or endanger continuance of the relationship

Bower, in his own career, followed these tenets to the T. Says the McKinsey website page on Bower: '...He could be blunt. Jack Crowley, a retired director, recalls the time that Bower, in a client meeting with a CEO, bellowed out, "The problem with this company, Mr Little, is you." And there was a deathly silence. It happened to be totally accurate. That was the end of our work with that client, but it didn't bother Marvin.' Individuals in the firm who worked with Bower told stories about how he turned down opportunities to counsel prominent business leaders such as Howard Hughes, and when he refused to help the US government devise a bailout plan for American Motors. If he felt it was not in a company's interest for McKinsey to serve it or that top management was not committed to change, Bower wouldn't accept the company as a client.

Bower's heart and soul were entirely dedicated to the institution he had created. When he retired in 1968, he sold his McKinsey stock to the other partners at book value, rather than at its real market value, which would have been at a premium so large that it might have forced the company into debt. The McKinsey website adds that he also required older partners to sell their stock to younger partners well before they retired. 'Young people have got to get some shares,' he said. 'They have to gain a sense of ownership.' Bower passed away in 2003 at the age of ninety.

A few things Bower said in an interview he gave to *Fortune* magazine (on 1 November 1993) will surely startle anyone today. Asked by the interviewer which period in the firm's history had worried him most, he replied: 'Now... Have we grown too fast? Have we begun to think too much about money because we've got so much coming in...? People who make a lot of money get to thinking about having four homes to keep up, or maybe they want to buy a yacht. If an individual consultant has to make a professional decision on the spot and he has too many obligations, I worry that he is likely to make a decision to attract a client who shouldn't be attracted.'

This is precisely the sentiment that lies at the core of the criticism of the way Rajat Gupta ran McKinsey in his nine years at the top.

If one considers McKinsey's growth—in terms of revenue, global spread and people—the Gupta years were unmatched in the Firm's history. Revenues nearly tripled, the number of partners more than doubled, and McKinsey became a truly global corporation. If it had been any other company, Gupta's tenure would have been seen as a great triumph. But this is not any other company. McKinseyites today look back at the Gupta years with mixed feelings.

For whatever story the Firm's balance sheets and the bank balances of its senior partners may tell, the Gupta years were also turbulent years, both externally and internally. Rapid growth also coincided with some high-profile debacles, and Bowerites, who today once more have tight control over the Firm, are not above blaming Gupta's focus on growth as one of the reasons for the debacles.

However, it must be argued in Gupta's defence that the managing director of McKinsey is hardly in a position to thrust a strategic direction down the throats of senior partners. Gupta has himself explained the scope of his role as the Firm's helmsman. 'The nature of the task is being first among equals: you're not anybody's boss,' he said in the *Academy of Management Executive Journal* interview referred to earlier, soon after he was elected to a third term. 'If you tried to do that, you would not succeed. I personally feel very much that I'm there to serve; it's a servant leader kind of style. I've been elected at the pleasure of my fellow partners. I'm there to make them successful. It implies genuinely convincing them that I care about their success.'

Also, anyone who has worked with Gupta—and NIIT Chairman Rajendra Singh Pawar, quoted in Chapter Three, is just one example—describes his leadership style as remarkably muted, with great emphasis on building consensus around any decision to be taken. In fact, in the same interview, Gupta mentioned this as something others may perceive as one of his weaknesses, but implied that it was actually one of his strengths and was based on some deeply held personal beliefs. 'I think one of the things they would probably say is…about listening, about taking other people's point of view. Another thing that I do, I am not a very exact, confronting person at many times. So it's more to do with drawing people out and making them come to their own decision and realizing why a particular decision is good for them and for the firm. Oftentimes, that means that I am not as direct as I probably should be, and sometimes my colleagues, of course, find that a very frustrating process, and they think, "Why don't you say what you exactly mean?" Well, I'm trying for you to realize what is the right thing… No one says I'm not decisive, because I can be decisive, but I let the decision sort of evolve and percolate, rather than lead from the front, saying, "Here's the way we're going."'

So, if McKinsey deviated from Bower's sacred tenets under Gupta, it certainly did so with the assent of at least a majority of the senior partners.

One must also remember that Gupta came to head McKinsey at a time when the dotcom boom was beginning to rip through traditional business assumptions. No one seemed to know what was going on; the internet economy seemed to upend every well-established principle of economic theory, and corporate leaders had to deal with the seismic shifts with no precedent to guide them.

In his autobiography, *The Age of Turbulence*, former Federal Reserve Board Chairman Alan Greenspan recalls a 1995 meeting of the Federal Open Market Committee, the powerful group that controls the federal funds rate, the primary lever of US monetary policy, a few months after the dotcom stock market boom officially began with the Netscape IPO in August 1995. As the Committee prepared to vote on a proposal to continue easing the federal funds rate, Greenspan told the members that he 'wanted to step back... I told them: "I want to raise a broad hypothesis about where the economy is going over the longer term, and what the underlying forces are." My idea was that as the world absorbed information technology and learned to put it to work, we had entered what would prove to be a protracted period of lower inflation, lower interest rates, increased productivity and full employment. "I've been looking at business cycles since the late 1940s," I said. "There has been nothing like this." The depth and persistence of such technological changes, I noted, "appear only once every fifty or hundred years." My point was that monetary policy might now be operating at the edge of knowledge where, at least for a while, time-honoured rules of thumb did not apply.'

The New Economy affected McKinsey in several ways. One, large corporate clients needed more advice than ever before, as they tried to figure out whether they were equipped to deal with the altered realities that the spread of the internet was thrusting upon them. Two, though the overall attrition rate did not rise significantly, the Firm lost some of its best people to the technology boom. In 1999 alone, the San Francisco office lost fifty people—fully one-third of its original strength. Three, there was serious internal debate among the Firm's senior partners about how to engage with the dotcom phenomenon. And this would have a far-reaching impact on the culture that Marvin Bower had so assiduously created and guarded.

On one side were arrayed the traditionalists, who scoffed at the 'irrational exuberance', the term coined by Greenspan in 1996 to describe the business landscape. They wanted McKinsey to stay the way it had always been, above the hurly-burly, its consultants more monks than mercenaries. But it became increasingly difficult to keep the mercenary instincts in check. Young McKinsey partners were seeing their ex-colleagues and friends set up dotcoms and become millionaires almost overnight. Everyone all around seemed to be making more money than they had ever dreamt of. The stock markets were on fire. At the very least, should not the Firm go public? That would unlock enormous value and certainly make the partners extremely wealthy. There were even suggestions that McKinsey should start its own venture capital fund, or its own dotcoms.

As the boss, Gupta had to manage this conflict of worldviews, and align the factions in one direction. This was something he was very good at, as he has admitted himself.

'One of the things a managing director has to be good at is to be a very quick study, because I have colleagues who will run circles around me in arguments,' he told the *Academy of Management Executive* interviewer. 'But I have to be very, very quick and have the counter [argument], why a different perspective is also valid. Most of my colleagues would say that I am a quick study in those things. It is not easy for them to run circles around me, and therefore they respect my intellect and they know that they will not get around me. So then we get down to talking: now let's really talk about what is on your mind, instead of trying to convince me that what you're saying is absolutely the right and only perspective on a particular issue.'

Under Gupta's leadership, the senior partners finally took a call that attempted to balance both the fears of the traditionalists and the financial ambitions of the newly restless. No, McKinsey would not go public. That would destroy the intensely private and excellence-over-profits culture of the Firm, which was so precious to employees and so crucial to the McKinsey mystique. But the Firm would certainly change some other long-standing policies to stay in tune with the times and reap the benefits.

One of the most important decisions McKinsey took was to offer clients a fee structure linked to client satisfaction. Bower had always believed that such an approach would make the consultants focus on short-term gains for the client rather than long-term health. This now changed. McKinsey started striking deals which involved a performance bonus at the end of the assignment if the client was satisfied with the results of the 'engagement' (McKinsey-speak for a client assignment).

Start-ups were clamouring for advice at McKinsey's gates. The trouble was that they wanted guidance but did not have the cash to pay the Firm's fees. In a complete departure from all past policy—and in total violation of Bower's philosophy of always maintaining outsider status—McKinsey began taking fees in client stock rather than cash. The stock was put in a blind pool to be liquidated as soon as possible, with the profits to be shared by the partners. In at least one case, McKinsey even linked its fee to the rise in the stock price of the client. In all, the Firm did more than one thousand e-commerce-related assignments during the peak years of 1998 and 1999.

Obviously, many of McKinsey's dotcom clients eventually went bust, and it is impossible to know how much money the Firm made out of selling start-up stock at the height of the euphoria. But various reports suggest that at least for the Firm's senior partners, 1998 and 1999 were quite a bonanza. The minimum Gupta would have been making annually in those years would have been $5-6 million.

Looking back, after the bubble had burst and the dust settled, Gupta told *BusinessWeek* magazine in an interview published in the 7 July 2002 issue: 'Maybe we should have been a little more circumspect than we were. But I don't think we made any big errors or excesses.'

However, by this time there were tough questions being asked in many quarters about the role McKinsey had played in the rise of Enron, the energy trading major whose 2001 collapse had been as scandalous as its rise had been spectacular. McKinsey had consulted for Enron for eighteen years. Its last CEO, Jeffrey Skilling, was ex-McKinsey. As head of energy practice at the Firm, he had been an Enron consultant for years before joining the company. In 2006, he would be sentenced to twenty-four years in prison, after having been found guilty on nineteen counts, ranging from conspiracy to insider trading.

Over the years, McKinseyites had very openly championed Enron at every opportunity as one of the world's most innovative corporations. (It must be mentioned here that McKinsey was hardly alone in its assessment. *Fortune* magazine named Enron 'America's most innovative company' for six consecutive years. However, it may be argued that McKinsey would surely have had deeper knowledge than *Fortune* journalists of what was going on inside Enron.) In the end, it was clear that the corporation had, to a very large extent, focused its much-vaunted powers of innovation on systematic institutionalized accounting fraud.

McKinsey partners had sat in on Enron board meetings regularly, and had claimed credit for many of the energy trader's bold strategies. It was in fact impossible to deny that McKinsey's role had been crucial, perhaps even the driving force, behind Enron's transformation from a gas pipeline company to a near-science-fictional trading entity—at the height of its (apparent) success, Enron had even boasted of one day creating a futures and options marketplace for human intelligence.

As Enron went down in flames, taking its lead auditor Arthur Andersen with it, many observers expressed surprise that no McKinsey employee was even called for questioning by the investigators.

When asked about this in 2002 by *Business Week*, just months after Enron had filed for bankruptcy (at that time, the biggest in US corporate history), Gupta said: 'I won't specifically talk about our work at Enron. The broader answer is it's very sad to see an institution like Enron go through what it has gone through... In all the work we did with Enron we didn't do anything related to financial structuring or disclosure or any of the issues that got them into trouble. We stand by all the work we did. Beyond that, we can only empathize with the trouble they're going through. We have clients who are friends.'

But Enron had not been the only large McKinsey client that had bitten the dust while Gupta was at the helm. From 1994 to 2000, the Firm consulted for retail giant Kmart as it slowly and steadily imploded. Swissair, once one of the world's most respected airlines, was another victim of some disastrous advice from McKinsey. As recommended by the Firm, it spent $2 billion buying stakes in many small and struggling European airlines. The idea was that Swissair would do much more than just carry passengers and cargo: it would become a full-service aviation outsourcing company, offering everything from maintenance services to food to other airlines. The strategy proved suicidal, and Swissair filed for bankruptcy in 2001. Gupta told *Business Week*: 'In these turbulent times, with our serving more than half the Fortune 500 companies, there are bound to be some companies that are clients of ours that get into trouble... Good news is reported less often than bad news.'

As Gupta's third term drew to a close in 2003, there were indications that the 'conservative' faction among the partners was readying to seize control of the Firm once more. A week before the partners were slated to vote in the next global head, the British weekly *The Economist*, ran a piece in its 27 February 2003 issue asking: 'Can [Gupta's successor] restore McKinsey to its former glory?' The anonymous commentator noted: 'Mr Gupta's long stint saw big changes at McKinsey, notably greater enrichment of partners relative to up-and-coming associates and a belated rush to join the "new economy" boom. McKinsey is still dealing with the after-effects of a hiring spree in the late 1990s that tested the ability of its culture to absorb large numbers and also created unprecedented tensions when lay-offs followed the pricking of the technology bubble.' Gupta, the magazine summed up, 'has proved the adage that good consultants do not necessarily make good managers'. However, one should also bear in mind here that, as a magazine (or 'newspaper', as it eccentrically refers to itself), *The Economist* wears its British conservatism on its sleeve, and the man who seemed most likely to win the election for succeeding Gupta as managing director was McKinsey's London chief, Ian Davis, an Englishman, and a Bowerist to the core. *The Economist* writer even mentioned the possibility that if Davis got the top job, the Firm would possibly be managed out of London.

Davis was elected and, as expected, made it clear from day one that McKinsey needed to go back to its core values, stopping just short of saying that Gupta's almost single-minded focus on revenue growth had led the Firm astray. In fact, under Davis, McKinsey once again started refusing clients. Gupta had aggressively driven growth in China and India. Davis clamped down, mandating that the Firm should take on new clients only if it thought they were worthy and ready. His successor Dominic Barton has continued down the path that Davis charted, insisting that McKinsey's top priority should be quality and not size. It is almost as if the Firm looks back at the Gupta years as a mistake.

◆

Gupta stayed on in McKinsey as a senior partner after stepping down from the top job, but spent more and more of his time on his philanthropic and charity work. In time, he seemed to have become the archetypal global éminence grise on issues ranging from the world economy to corporate social responsibility and problems dogging developing nations.

However, it has later come to light that as a consultant and a McKinsey employee, Gupta may not have been fully committed to the Firm in the last few years he spent there. Anil Kumar, the McKinsey partner who would be arrested on the same day as Rajaratnam, and would plead guilty to the charge of passing insider information to the hedge fund boss for years in return for cash, seems to have been closer to Gupta than any other McKinseyite. Their shared Indian origins and IIT education may have been a factor in this, though the Firm has had dozens of Indians and IITians as partners for years. Whatever the reasons, Gupta and Kumar had been close enough to start a consulting firm on the side, officially owned by their wives, Anita Gupta and Malvika Kumar.

This firm, Mindspirit LLC, set up in 2001 while Gupta was still head of McKinsey, had at least one client, the database company infoGroup (earlier known as infoUSA), founded by IIT alumnus Vinod Gupta (no relation of Rajat Gupta), based in Omaha, Nebraska. According to an SEC filing by infoGroup, Rajat Gupta and Kumar advised Vinod Gupta on strategic matters. Mindspirit was compensated through 200,000 stock options, which the firm exercised for an undisclosed amount.

'It has always been a clear violation of our values and professional standards for any firm member to provide consulting or advisory services outside of McKinsey for personal monetary gain,' Michael Stewart, McKinsey partner and director of communications, told *Bloomberg Markets* magazine in July 2011.

In 2005 Gupta and Rajaratnam set up Voyager Capital Partners, an investment venture, along with investment banker Ravi Trehan, a friend of Gupta's. Rajaratnam put in $40 million, and Gupta and Trehan $5 million each. But Trehan, who ran his own debt fund Broadstreet LLC, soon started having problems with Rajaratnam and pulled out in 2006. Gupta took over Trehan's stake with a loan from Rajaratnam, bringing his investment to $10 million.

However, the story turns murky after this. Rajaratnam managed Voyager's investments, and seems to have made some uncharacteristically poor ones. It is quite clear that by mid-2008 he knew very well that Voyager was in deep trouble. In September, he took out $20 million of his money from the fund, without informing Gupta. Within days of this, Lehman Brothers collapsed, precipitating a stock market crash that effectively destroyed Voyager's entire portfolio. Gupta had lost his $10 million. He was aghast and furious with Rajaratnam. According to a document filed by the prosecution during Gupta's trial, in a conversation with fellow Goldman Sachs director Claes Dahlback a few days after Rajaratnam's arrest in October 2009, Gupta called his former friend 'a bad man'.

But the question which turned out to be crucial to Gupta's fate in his trial was: when did Gupta come to know that Rajaratnam had taken out $20 million from the fund, and when did he realize that his $10 million had gone down the drain? Gupta's defence team contended that he had come to know about it before the phone calls he made to Rajaratnam after the Goldman Sachs board meetings in September and October. In fact, he had spoken to his lawyers about suing Rajaratnam. So it was quite impossible that Gupta would be supplying Rajaratnam inside information.

Yes, the prosecution agreed, Gupta was angry with Rajaratnam and had thought of suing him. But all this happened much after the Goldman Sachs phone conversations. In a court filing, the government stated: 'Gupta's efforts in September 2009 and October 2009—months after the charged conspiracy—to collect information and consider whether to file a lawsuit against Rajaratnam has no relevance with respect to whether Gupta committed the charged crimes months and years earlier.' It also claimed that it had witnesses and evidence to prove that when Gupta made the two phone calls, both of them less than a minute after Goldman Sachs board meetings had got over, he was still on good terms with Rajaratnam.

The witness the prosecution was relying on to prove this was Anil Kumar.

It is quite amazing how in the later years of his career, Gupta associated himself with a number of highly successful businessmen of Indian origin (though Rajaratnam is a Sri Lankan Tamil), all of whom had one thing in common: they had been accused of dishonest dealings at some time or the other. Vinod Gupta, for quite a few years the poster boy of against-all-odds Indian entrepreneurial spirit in the US, faced a shareholder suit in 2006 that accused him of using company funds for personal pleasures. According to the suit, Vinod Gupta had twenty-eight club memberships, twenty cars, a yacht with an all-female crew, and infoGroup's private jet which he used to fly his family and friends around the world, all paid for by the company.

'Friends' included former President Clinton and his wife Hillary. The suit alleged that between 2002 and 2006, Vinod Gupta had used the infoGroup jet to fly the Clintons on personal, business and campaign trips at a cost of nearly a million dollars, which was a 'waste of corporate assets'. In 2008, Vinod Gupta resigned from the company he had set up in a garage and grown to nearly half a billion dollars of annual revenue, and repaid it $9 million.

In 2006, Rajat Gupta co-founded private equity firm New Silk Route Partners (NSR), along with Rajaratnam, investment banker Parag Saxena, and former Citigroup Senior Vice-Chairman Victor Menezes (Rajaratnam quit before NSR started operations, but the firm's founders initially worked out of his Galleon Group headquarters in Manhattan). NSR reportedly raised $1.3 billion to invest in India and other emerging economies. Anil Kumar was also supposed to be a founding partner, but finally did not join because he felt he was not getting a good enough deal. He was also not ready to quit McKinsey and work for NSR full-time.

In 1994, Parag Saxena was fined $250,000 by the SEC for failing to disclose conflicts of interest on stocks recommended to clients. Saxena, then a managing director at Chancellor Capital Management Inc., was charged with receiving unregistered stock at low prices in three companies that were just being formed— the Icos Corporation, the Neurogen Corporation and Ariad Pharmaceutical Inc.—and then recommending these stocks to clients when the companies were going public.

In 2006, the SEC charged Victor Menezes, then still a top Citigroup executive, with selling nearly $30 million of Citigroup stock just before the company announced a giant quarterly loss related to the Argentinian debt crisis. He settled with the SEC for $2.7 million. Both Saxena and Menezes paid up without admitting or denying wrongdoing.

And as we will see, Gupta was aware, while he and Anil Kumar were McKinsey staffers, that Kumar was on the take from Rajaratnam. Even if Gupta did not know the details of the specific services Rajaratnam was paying Kumar for, it is impossible to imagine that someone of his intelligence would not have figured out that whatever Kumar was doing was unethical, if not downright illegal. At any rate, he was certainly not following his employer's clearly enunciated code of conduct. And Gupta had been the Firm's worldwide head, the chief custodian of all that McKinsey stood for.

The Protégé

ANIL KUMAR WAS BORN IN 1958 IN CHENNAI (AT THAT TIME, Madras) to Kusum and Virendra Kumar; his father worked in multinational oil major Shell India (later nationalized and renamed Bharat Petroleum). A brilliant student right from his schooldays, Anil Kumar's academic achievements rival those of Rajat Gupta's. He graduated in mechanical engineering with top grades from IIT Bombay in 1980, and was accepted by Wharton Business School for its MBA programme. He was also the only student chosen from all the IITs that year for the prestigious DeBeers scholarship for post-graduate engineering studies at Imperial College, London.

Since the Imperial College course was of two years' duration, Kumar asked Wharton for an equivalent deferment of his admission. Wharton agreed to only a year. But Kumar was undaunted. Not only did he become the first student in Imperial College's history to finish the two-year applied mechanics course in ten months, he even topped his class. He then moved on to Wharton and decided to specialize in technology management, an area where his extraordinary record in engineering education would carry weight.

Graduating from Wharton in 1983, Kumar joined Hewlett-Packard as product manager for engineering application software. In 1986, he joined McKinsey's San Francisco office. By the mid-1990s, he was definitely being seen as a protégé of Rajat Gupta. When Gupta wanted McKinsey to prepare a roadmap for the IIT system, it was Kumar who worked on the project. When Gupta conceived the Indian School of Business, it was Kumar who was by his side and took charge of much of the execution of Gupta's vision. And of course, they set up Mindspirit LLC in their wives' names.

Kumar and Rajaratnam had been classmates at Wharton, but had moved in different circles. In fact, in the only interview he gave after his conviction, to *Newsweek* magazine (23 October 2011), Rajaratnam recalled a conversation he had had with Kumar after a statistics test at Wharton. According to Rajaratnam, Kumar asked him how he had fared in the test. Rajaratnam answered honestly that he had got 97 out of 100, and inquired how Kumar had done. Kumar bluntly replied that he would not tell him how much he had scored.

The two men met again in 1989, when Kumar was an associate at McKinsey's Silicon Valley office and Rajaratnam was an analyst at Needham Capital. Since Rajaratnam focused on technology stocks, he would visit the Valley regularly, and on one such trip he met up with Kumar. The context was microprocessor-maker AMD, which Kumar consulted for, and whose stock Rajaratnam tracked closely as part of his portfolio. They continued to meet two or three times a year, till Kumar was sent off to India in 1993 to set up the Firm's New Delhi operations. They renewed their acquaintance once Kumar came back to the US for good in 1999. By this time, Rajaratnam had set up Galleon and was on his way to becoming a mover and shaker in the hedge fund world.

Soon after Kumar returned to the US, he introduced Rajaratnam to Rajat Gupta at a social gathering. Gupta was just the sort of person whose contacts Rajaratnam wanted to have in his rolodex. Gupta moved around with heads of state, and counted men like Bill Gates as friends. Rajaratnam was merely a very wealthy man. He readily donated $1 million to the personal project that Gupta was passionately pursuing: the setting up of the Indian School of Business.

In his post-conviction interview, Rajaratnam told *Newsweek*: 'I gave [the school] a million dollars. I later found out they [Gupta and Kumar] never contributed any of their money, and are listed as the school's founders. And I'm not even a fucking Indian.'

Kumar had been the key prosecution witness at Rajaratnam's trial and his lengthy testimony had made it absolutely certain that the Galleon boss was found guilty. It was thus quite understandable that Rajaratnam referred to Kumar as a chut, a Hindi equivalent of female genitalia, when he spoke to *Newsweek*. He, however, claimed to still have the highest regard for Rajat Gupta, and said that the FBI had promised him that if he wore a wire when he next spoke to Gupta, he could get away with as little as five years in prison. Rajaratnam had refused.

By the early 2000s Galleon had become the biggest technology hedge fund in the US, and McKinsey was repeatedly sending him feelers through Kumar to get business from him. But Rajaratnam was not interested.

In September 2003 they met at a charity event in Manhattan, and Kumar brought up the topic—Galleon, he said, should hire McKinsey. Rajaratnam replied that he didn't want McKinsey as a consultant, he wanted Kumar. He drew Kumar aside and told him that he was grossly underpaid for the amount of work he put in and the amount of travelling he had to do. Kumar deserved better. He made an offer: he would pay Kumar half a million dollars a year if the consultant would call him once a month and discuss his 'ideas' about the technology sector.

In all probability, Kumar initially refused, saying that taking money for an occasional chat with Rajaratnam would violate McKinsey rules. But Rajaratnam was nothing if not persuasive. And, as his career amply demonstrates, he seemed to have an instinct for identifying the corruptibility potential in a man. He told Kumar to his face that he knew Kumar would maintain a list of his 'ideas' if he was paid for it, and he would not, if he was not paid for it. Besides, Rajaratnam would take care of all the arrangements: the money would be moved via a Galleon account set up in some frontman's name and transferred to a Swiss bank; no one would ever get an inkling.

Kumar has claimed that Rajaratnam caught him at a particularly vulnerable phase in his career, when he had begun to feel that his contribution was not being recognized and rewarded adequately by McKinsey. He has also claimed that he thought Rajaratnam merely wanted some 'intellectually oriented technology industry insights and market trend information'— purely harmless stuff. But this certainly did not prevent him from agreeing to receive payment from Galleon in a Swiss bank account opened in the name of his domestic help, Manju Das.

As Kumar and his lawyers put it, Kumar started off by giving Rajaratnam broad strategic information, but this did not interest Rajaratnam much. However, he did not press Kumar overtly for what he really wanted—material non-public information. Instead, the hedge fund boss played on Kumar's frustrations with his job, and worked subtly on his weaknesses, often taunting him that he knew more about what was going on with Kumar's client AMD than Kumar did (Rajaratnam was getting information from Robert Moffat via Danielle Chiesi).

'These not-so subtle gibes called into question the very essence of Anil's professional life—knowing his clients better than anyone else and helping shape their strategies,' claims the leniency plea that Kumar's lawyers masterfully crafted (this amazing document is analysed in detail in Chapter Thirteen). 'Mr Rajaratnam, to prove his point, revealed to Anil nonpublic information the former had acquired from his own sources. Anil fell prey to Mr Rajaratnam's manipulation and ultimately provided confidential information, in part, to prove to Mr Rajaratnam that he knew his clients as well or better than Mr Rajaratnam, and to validate his standing in Mr Rajaratnam's eyes.'

This was the version of events that Kumar presented in court: Rajaratnam targeted AMD information through Kumar, though he had other sources of information about the company. In 2004 Kumar began confirming information that Rajaratnam claimed to have received about AMD. As the months passed,

Rajaratnam started seeking more detailed information, and not simply confirmation of what he already knew. He wanted Kumar to reveal what AMD's top management was thinking and strategizing, especially big business deals that could affect the stock price.

In 2006 Rajaratnam received his first piece of windfall information from Kumar. As the lead consultant from McKinsey on the AMD account, Kumar knew that the firm was seriously thinking of acquiring graphics technology capability. The only way it could do so quickly was to buy a company already operating in that area. Kumar was privy to the entire process as AMD searched for the right firm to make an offer to. When it zeroed in on graphics chipmaker ATI Technologies, based in Markham, Canada, Kumar informed his benefactor. On 24 July AMD made its official announcement that it had acquired ATI for $5.4 billion in cash and stocks, leading to a sharp rise in ATI's share price. Rajaratnam had already built up a strong position on the stock. He sold, and is estimated to have made a neat profit of $23 million. A few days later, he called Kumar at home and said, 'Thank you. We're all cheering you. You're a hero.' So pleased was he that at the end of the year he paid Kumar a million dollars, double what he had promised him as his yearly fee.

However, by October 2008 the entire US financial and banking system was in deep crisis. And the FBI was listening to conversations between two men who seemed untouched by the panic. The following is an extract:

KUMAR: Ah Raj, eBay is gonna do massive layoffs on Monday.

RAJARATNAM: They're gonna do what?

KUMAR: Layoffs on Monday.

RAJARATNAM: OK.

KUMAR: Now the problem again, as usual, is will that mean everyone will say, shit, this company is in trouble...or will it be good news, right?

RAJARATNAM: Right.

KUMAR: But the only thing I do know is, I, I tried to get the percentage, I couldn't.

A year later, at six in the morning, Kumar opened the door of his East Manhattan apartment to find FBI agents with an arrest warrant and handcuffs. He fainted and hit his head against a wall. The agents had to take him to a nearby hospital for first-aid before they could book him for his crimes.

Less than three weeks earlier, Rajaratnam and Kumar had been on holiday in Miami with their families. One evening, according to Kumar, Rajaratnam received a phone call and told him that it was from an executive at networking equipment giant Cisco Systems, who was a Galleon informer. Cisco was going to buy Starent, a mobile infrastructure solution provider. Kumar had never heard of Starent, and nevertheless bought shares worth about $8,000 that night. A week later, Cisco announced the $2.9 billion deal.

Kumar was arrested on 16 October 2009. On 7 January 2010, he pleaded guilty to one count of securities fraud and one count of conspiracy. He had already agreed to cooperate with the government to the best of his abilities. He instantly became the prosecution's star witness.

This is the account of his cooperation that Kumar's lawyers presented in his leniency plea to the court: 'Mr Kumar understood that his decision to cooperate would have negative repercussions, not the least of which was that he would have to testify against his former classmate and friend Mr Rajaratnam and potentially his mentor Rajat Gupta, both of which came to pass. It meant too, the loss of his job, countless friends, the respect of peers and colleagues, and his carefully built and hard-earned international reputation. Nevertheless, in the aftermath of his participation in the instant criminal conduct, Mr Kumar wanted to right his wrong and to accept the consequences of his actions. He understood that the first step was to admit his illegal actions and assist the government in bringing the mastermind of the scheme to justice.

'Mr Kumar's cooperation began in late 2009 and continued until June 2012. During the course of this approximately thirty-month operation, Mr Kumar has been available to both the US Attorney's Office and the SEC on every occasion requested, whether in person, via telephone, or through his attorneys. Between proffer sessions, trial preparation, and days of testimony, Mr Kumar has met with the government on over twenty different days in person and an additional half-dozen on the telephone. During the course of his cooperation for the Rajaratnam trial, he spent over fifty days and hundreds of hours reviewing thousands of documents at the US Attorney's Office's request. In a case which had millions of pages of documents and emails, part of Mr Kumar's task was to identify for the government which documents he believes were relevant to the criminal scheme. He also listeneed to over fifty wiretaps associated with the case and the defendants, and helped the government interpret and correct the transcripts.

In March 2011, Mr Kumar testified in United States v Rajaratnam. Mr Kumar was the government's chief witness. He testified for four days and endured hours of relentless cross-examination while Mr Rajaratnam's attorney tried to destroy his credibility. Solely in preparation for his trial testimony, he met with the government on over ten different days, often doing so at 6.00 a.m. because early morning better suited the prosecutor's schedule.

His trial testimony was at the centre of the government's case against Mr Rajaratnam. Mr Kumar expertly explained to the jury how he had come to be a part of a criminal conspiracy, and spent many hours carefully and credibly interpreting emails and wiretaps for the jury.'

Later, the leniency plea goes on to say: 'The truthfulness, completeness and reliability of Mr Kumar's information and testimony was aptly demonstrated by the jury convicting Mr Rajaratnam. Moreover, Mr Kumar's cooperation was not the kind in which the truth emerged slowly and painstakingly, as is often the case in such matters, and which can unduly waste resources. Mr Kumar cooperated as fully and truthfully on day one as he did in month thirty...Mr Kumar has been a model cooperator and much more. He has excelled at every aspect of his cooperation.'

In 'A Dirty Business', a nearly 11,000-word piece on the Rajaratnam trial which appeared in the 27 June 2011 issue of *The New Yorker*, the writer, George Packer, describes Kumar's days in court: 'On the first day of testimony, in the courtroom of Judge Richard J. Holwell, Anil Kumar, the McKinsey consultant, walked to the witness stand, where he stood for a moment, in a dark suit and tie, and bowed his head, his hands clasped before him. He looked like a prisoner waiting to be sentenced. Rajaratnam sat, not with his lawyers but, rather, on a bench behind the defence table, the shiny wave of his hair almost touching his hunched shoulders. He was not as bulky as he looked in photographs. His lower lip jutted slightly, and he stared through rimless glasses with undisguised contempt at his former friend.

'As [Jonathan] Streeter (who led the prosecution team) led Kumar through the story of his descent into crime, Kumar's sombre penitence lifted and gave way to the didactic precision of a consultant. His memory was astounding, and his explanations to the jurors, whom he often addressed directly, were so smooth that they came across as almost smug. He gave crisp lectures on the difference between private-equity and hedge funds, and on the purpose of a board of directors. Kumar could not help contrasting, with a slight smile, his own interest in the long-term condition of American companies with Rajaratnam's focus on short-term payoffs. Then a question about a breach of trust, or a lie, brought Kumar back to why he was in the courtroom, and his face sagged.'

John Dowd, Rajaratnam's attorney, was at his bullying best when he rose to cross-examine Kumar. He accused him of peddling a 'monstrous lie'. Going into the details of how Kumar forged documents to set up the Swiss bank account for his domestic help Manju Das, Dowd asked, 'Your wife didn't know how adept you were at faking paperwork, did she?'

The question angered Kumar. 'Do you want an answer to that, sir?' he asked.

'I sure do,' replied Dowd.

'Yes, my wife did not know how adept I was.'

Later, Streeter took his witness back to the first days of his collusion with Rajaratnam. 'At the very beginning,' Streeter asked Kumar, 'you thought he was asking for legitimate information?'

Kumar said yes.

And then, once he started paying Kumar, Rajaratnam started asking him for confidential information, asked Streeter.

Kumar said yes.

'And, once he was paying you, you started giving it to him?' said Streeter.

'Yes, that is correct, sir,' said Kumar. 'To my eternal regret.'

When it came to testifying against Rajat Gupta, Kumar has claimed that it caused him great distress. His leniency plea states that when he was informed in October 2011 by the government that he would have to be a witness in the Gupta trial, he 'was crushed because he had worked for Mr Gupta, was a friend of Mr Gupta and his family, and had held him in high esteem as the CEO of McKinsey. However, Anil had an obligation to cooperate with the government and planned on fulfilling that responsibility without complaint.'

If one studies the chronology of events and reads between the lines, it becomes clear that once Kumar had agreed to cooperate with the government on the Rajaratnam case, the prosecutors intended to extract every useful drop of information from him. Kumar's sentencing had originally been scheduled for December 2011. But this had been decided when Rajat Gupta was a peripheral blip on the FBI's radar. It was when the SEC filed a civil administrative action against Gupta, and Gupta countersued, demanding a jury trial, that he suddenly became the focus of attention. On 26 October 2011, Gupta was charged and arrested by the FBI. And the government was not going to let go of Kumar with such a high-profile target as Gupta in its crosshairs. At some point, it must have been made clear to Kumar and his lawyers that if he did not testify against Gupta, there would be no leniency deal when it came to Kumar's own sentencing.

'On 1 June and 4 June 2012, Mr Kumar testified against his former boss and mentor Rajat Gupta,' his lawyers submitted to the court. 'It was gruelling in a different way than his testimony against Mr Rajaratnam, not because the cross-examination was as long as in the previous trial, but because Anil knew that he would be partially responsible for helping to convict someone with whom he and his family had deep and long-lasting ties.'

When Kumar was called to the witness stand during Gupta's trial, he walked up, according to a Reuters report, with his 'hands held in front of him and eyes cast slightly downward; Gupta's gaze followed him.'

His testimony during his two days in the witness stand would considerably strengthen the prosecution's case against Gupta.

Kumar's sentencing finally took place on 19 July 2012. He got away almost scot-free: two years on probation and a paltry $25,000 fine. He would, of course, also have to forfeit the $2.9 million that he had made from Rajaratnam for passing him inside information and parked in Manju Das's Swiss bank account. He had cooperated, and he could not have been rewarded more handsomely for his cooperation.

The Phone Call

THE ONLY PHONE CONVERSATION BETWEEN RAJARATNAM AND Gupta that the US government was able to tap took place in the early evening of 29 July 2008. It lasted eighteen minutes. The conversation is, to say the least, revealing. Gupta sounds unsure and confused at times, and is looking to his friend for career advice. He is also lobbying for a bigger role in the Galleon Group—and more money.

It is obvious from the conversation that Gupta is well aware that his long-time protégé, and McKinsey employee, Anil Kumar is working on the sly for Rajaratnam and is getting paid for it. Gupta has now been retired from McKinsey for about a year, but the conversation implies that it is very likely he knew about the arrangement between Rajaratnam and Kumar while he was still working at the Firm.

After the usual pleasantries, Rajaratnam, who is suffering from a cold, mentions that he has called because he is meeting Gary Cohn, president and chief operating officer of Goldman Sachs, in two days, then goes on: 'And there's a rumour that Goldman might look to buy a commercial bank.' Gupta is initially non-committal, but Rajaratnam asks him point blank: 'Have you heard anything along that line?' He mentions Wachovia, at that time the fourth-largest bank holding company in the US in terms of assets, but in deep trouble.

'Yeah,' says Gupta. 'There was a big discussion at the board meeting.' During Gupta's trial, the prosecution would establish that the Goldman board meeting he refers to was one held at St Petersburg in Russia about a month before this conversation. Rajaratnam waits for him to reveal more. 'Uh, whether we, uh…

buy a commercial bank. And, you know it was a uh, divided discussion in the board...I think more people saying why, because in essence it's a low-return business and while, yeah, it may be interesting to develop a deposit base which is a low-cost source of funding.'

Gupta has thus apparently given Rajaratnam information about what went on in a board meeting, information that can certainly be termed 'privileged' and 'nonpublic'. But has he really? Gupta's defence lawyers will have their own answer to that question during the trial.

'Uh, you know,' Gupta continues, reporting how the discussion went during the meeting. 'What we should probably explore more is, I mean, we aren't having trouble funding ourselves but, you know, we should explore more global sources of funding. And perhaps even you know, uh, insurance or other things which also are a low uh cost, also...'

'Return,' Rajaratnam completes the sentence.

Gupta then goes on to speculate what Goldman Sachs may end up doing. 'They are an opportunistic group,' he says, 'so...if Wachovia was a good deal and, you know, it's quite conceivable they'd come and say let's go buy Wachovia.'

To the cynical or the suspicious, Gupta's choice of words— 'they', 'opportunistic group'—may seem inappropriate for a paid director of Goldman Sachs. In fact, to such an ear, he may very well be sounding like an inside man in the investment bank working for someone else.

However, a lot of conversations between friends discussing their work can sound sinister, if studied just by themselves, away from their context and history.

'Or even AIG, right?' Rajaratnam asks.

'Or even AIG, yeah,' Gupta agrees.

Rajaratnam broods over this, and then Gupta adds to what he has already let out about the board meeting. 'A, AIG, it was definitely on, in, in in, the discussion...' he says. Getting an interested grunt from his friend, he continues, 'Um, and you know, their view was actually, which has proven to be wrong, their view was very bearish on the commercial banks, but uh obviously, the commercial banks have had a pop in the last...'

'Yeah,' says Rajaratnam, 'that's maybe just a dead cat bounce.' (In Wall Street parlance, a 'dead cat bounce' is a small, brief recovery in the price of a declining stock. The expression derives from the idea that even a dead cat will bounce a bit if it falls from a great height.)

'Yeah, it could be that,' agrees Gupta. 'I mean, their view of credit losses and all that is [that there's] still more to come, credit cards, retail, you know...? But you know, sometimes, that gets all factored into the market, as you know better than I do... Uh, so I would be extremely surprised if uh...'

'There was anything active,' says Rajaratnam.

'Anything imminent, yeah,' says Gupta.

Rajaratnam has got what he wanted, some clues to which way he should steer the dialogue and probe when he meets Goldman Sachs' Cohn. 'I'm gonna start by saying how do you see the future of financial services firms, the winners, right...? You know, can they (Goldman Sachs) just fund for short term? Commercial paper or do they need [longer-term sources of funds like] deposits and insurance and things like that... Because there are some values out there... AIG and Wachovia, and see what [Cohn] says.'

(Wachovia edged to the brink of collapse by the end of September 2008, with not enough liquidity to meet its daily obligations. The US government decided that the bank was too big to be allowed to fail, and stepped in. After some bitter financial wrangling between Citigroup and Wells Fargo, and intervention by the government, Wachovia was finally bought by Wells Fargo and merged with its own financial services operations. Goldman Sachs stayed away.)

The two friends now get down to the nitty-gritty of the payment that Gupta needs to get from Galleon, presumably earnings from the Voyager hedge fund. Gupta says he has already done the calculations and would be grateful if Galleon can pay him what is due to him till 30 June. Rajaratnam agrees and then says: 'Anything else? Anything interesting?'

Yes, there is. Because now Gupta introduces Anil Kumar into the discussion.

GUPTA: No. No, that's it. Otherwise, you know, uh, uh, I saw (sighs) you know, Anil, how, how is, I mean, he seems, seems a little unsettled yesterday. I don't know. (The rest of what he says is unintelligible.)

RAJARATNAM: He seemed unhappy.

GUPTA: Yeah.

RAJARATNAM: Because he did come to me and asked me, do you have [a] deal with Rajat on Galleon International.

GUPTA: Yeah.

RAJARATNAM: And I just said, nothing concrete. I didn't want to get into [it] with him?

GUPTA: Yeah, yeah.

RAJARATNAM: I sort of dismissed it, without getting him into it.

GUPTA: Yeah.

RAJARATNAM: Because (coughs) I'm getting a feeling that he's trying to, just do a mini, you know, be a mini Rajat, right?

GUPTA: Yes. Yes.

RAJARATNAM: Without bringing anything new to the party, right?

GUPTA: Yeah, yeah.

RAJARATNAM: Because then he was talking about whether he can participate somehow in Galleon International and, you know, at some point, you know, I'm also running a business for people who work hard and uh...

GUPTA: Yes.

RAJARATNAM: You don't need to be compensated and you know, you can't just keep on giving, right?

GUPTA: Yeah, yeah. Yeah.

RAJARATNAM: And I, you know, honestly, Rajat, I'm giving him a million dollars a year for doing literally nothing. Just because…

GUPTA: I know, you're being…you're being very generous.

Let's stand back a bit and consider what is happening. Even Gupta's greatest admirers may feel uncomfortable with this exchange. This is the former head of McKinsey, the most respected management consultancy firm in the world, which makes him one of the most respected names in the corporate world. He is discussing a man who has been his close associate for years, working with him not only as a colleague but also on his personal projects like the Indian School of Business: a man close enough to Gupta for the two of them to set up a consultancy firm on the side, in their wives' names. And the man Gupta is speaking to is someone who won't be allowed entry into the sort of circle that he moves in—a Bill Clinton or a Bill Gates or a Kofi Annan would not give their time of day to Rajaratnam. But Rajaratnam is much wealthier than Gupta, and that seems reason enough for Gupta to agree almost cravenly with anything he says. He wants to be in Rajaratnam's good books.

Now begins a bitching session that lasts several minutes.

RAJARATNAM: Yeah, but you know, I sometimes…

GUPTA: But he should sometimes say thank you for that, you know?

So, not only does Gupta approve of the relationship between Rajaratnam and Kumar, he in fact disapproves of Kumar not exhibiting overt gratitude.

'Yeah, but he's never ever said,' starts off Rajaratnam, then suddenly seems to realize that in his position, he can afford to be magnanimous. He shifts gears. 'I mean, look, he is my friend, so [I] take [it] in that spirit, right?' he says.

This seems to blindside Gupta a bit. He appears unsure which way to go. 'Yeah, yeah, I, I…' he hedges his bets. It seems that he thinks he needs to agree with his billionaire friend.

But Rajaratnam makes it easy for him by going back to grumble mode. 'But he just seemed, uh, I don't know what, he just seemed, I don't think he's...' he says. 'I mean, that's why I asked you, uh, I've never seen him laugh and be really happy, you know?'

GUPTA: Yeah, because...

RAJARATNAM: He's constantly sche...no, scheming is not the right word, but constantly trying to figure out what other people's angles are.

GUPTA: Right.

RAJARATNAM: And then he seems to know what everybody else is worth. You know, he leads with, 'Oh, Sunil Mittal (chairman of the India-based Bharti business group) is worth 20 billion dollars.' You know, when you start thinking like that...

GUPTA: Yeah.

RAJARATNAM: You know, 'And this guy wants to make 500 million' and...

GUPTA: Yeah.

RAJARATNAM: And (unintelligible) wants to make 300 million dollars, and this guy...

GUPTA: Yeah. Yeah. Yeah.

RAJARATNAM: And you know, he'll tell me Vin Gupta (of infoGroup, for which Mindspirit LLC consulted) wants to make 100 million dollars on this deal and, you know, if you start thinking like that...

GUPTA: Yeah.

RAJARATNAM: It...you know, you build the business and the money will come, right?

GUPTA: Yes. Yes. Yes.

RAJARATNAM: And...

GUPTA: Add value, and, and leave it to, you know, I, I, look at how hard he was fighting for this 2 per cent and NSR (New Silk Route) equity. I mean, it was just kind of, you know...

RAJARATNAM: You know, without, without a leg to stand on. I mean, you know, I think he (coughs) everybody was doing it (coughs) because they were magnanimous good people.

GUPTA: Look, his overall deal is NSR, as you were agreeing. It is very good. I mean, you know, gets 400,000 in cash, 10 million in, in, you know...

RAJARATNAM: Carry.

GUPTA: Carry.

RAJARATNAM: Uh, hum..

GUPTA: And you know, 6 per cent equity, I mean...

RAJARATNAM: Right. And I don't know, um um, I can argue that, that I did more for NSR than he did.

GUPTA: I, I, he, I... Absolutely right. Absolutely right. (Unintelligible)

RAJARATNAM: He, he, he coordinated the, he coordinated those uh telephone meetings, right?

GUPTA: Yeah, yeah, yeah... Absolutely right.

RAJARATNAM: And that's about it, right?

GUPTA: Yeah. Yeah. Yeah.

RAJARATNAM: I put in 50 million bucks, whatever.

GUPTA: Yeah, yeah.

RAJARATNAM: I went on the trips. Whatever, but...

GUPTA: Yeah. Yeah. Yeah.

RAJARATNAM: And I, look, I'm happy with, you know...

Does Gupta see this as an opportunity to ingratiate himself with Rajaratnam? For he says: 'You're happy. You're in a different place.'

RAJARATNAM: Yeah, I'm happy with it, but, you know, there's a fairness, right?

GUPTA: Yeah.

RAJARATNAM: Now, from, for the last three or four, I mean, four or five years, I've given him a million bucks a year, right?

GUPTA: Yeah.

Gupta's response indicates that he knew about the Rajaratnam-

Kumar nexus when Gupta was still employed at McKinsey and Kumar was a colleague.

RAJARATNAM: After taxes, offshore cash.

GUPTA: Yeah. Yeah.

So Gupta knew that that the payment methods were hardly kosher.

RAJARATNAM: Right? And then he comes to me and tells me, 'You know, moving to New York is going to be expensive and I'm only moving to be with NSR and you guys, and, you know, is there anything more that we can expect?' And you know, and it's like, I, I, and I felt, between you and [me], I felt like he was putting a stake through my...

GUPTA: Yeah.

RAJARATNAM: ...you know, stomach, because instead of saying thank you for giving me 5 million dollars after taxes...

GUPTA: Yeah, other, other thing is I don't understand why he doesn't...OK, you mention it once, and if people want to do it, they will come. I mean, like the NSR thing, you mention it once, if people want to do it, they'll do it for you. Otherwise, you just say OK, you know, fine.

RAJARATNAM: No (unintelligible). If he comes and does a big deal, and he's instrumental in orchestrating a deal and getting it done, right? People might say, hey, here's a bonus, you know?

GUPTA: Yeah.

RAJARATNAM: So, I don't know.

GUPTA: Yeah.

That closes the Anil Kumar chapter as far as this particular phone call is concerned. Gupta now asks for advice from Rajaratnam on what he should do about a job offer he has had from private equity fund Kohlberg Kravis Roberts (KKR), and about his engagement with New Silk Route (NSR). On NSR, Rajaratnam advises that Gupta should make it clear to Parag Saxena that his 'value-added is not to do cash flows', that his 'value-added is to bring people together, at the right time make the call, introduce people and so on and so forth'. 'If anybody complains that you are not spending one day or two days or you promised that, then they are not understanding your value,' he says. 'I think you're instrumental in uh, architecting this NSR in raising capital… And in giving it huge credibility in India.'

Rajaratnam then goes on to give Gupta broad career advice. Gupta should, he recommends, do 'a portfolio of things you enjoy doing and you want to do and that you, you can add value at, right?'

Gupta agrees. 'So,' says Rajaratnam, 'Galleon International can be one…'

This is the opening Gupta has been looking for, because he wants more than a role in the Galleon International fund (which Rajaratnam has promised him, as will be revealed during the trial), he wants a role in the larger entity, the whole Galleon Group. He starts off awkwardly, and as the conversation progresses, a pleading note creeps into his voice that is painful to hear.

GUPTA: By the way, on that, I want you to keep, us to keep having the dialogue as to what…

RAJARATNAM: Yeah.

GUPTA: You know, I can be helpful in Galleon International. By the way, not Galleon International, Galleon Group. I mean, you've given…

RAJARATNAM: Galleon Group, right.

GUPTA: …a position in Galleon International. That's good enough. I, I…

Evidence presented at Gupta's trial will show that while both Rajaratnam and Gupta will tell the world that Gupta is the chairman of Galleon International, the designation will never be made official on paper.

Rajaratnam knows what Gupta is angling for, and he seems to take evasive action by buying time. 'Yeah, but you know what,' he says, 'I, I am now at the point where I, in the last couple of years, I'm building, right?'

GUPTA: Yeah.

RAJARATNAM: Rather than just making returns, just and not building, right?

GUPTA: Right. Right.

RAJARATNAM: So I'm putting the structure in place and all of that, right? So we will build this into a 10-billion-dollar company, hopefully by the end of 2009.

GUPTA: Yes. Yes, you will.

RAJARATNAM: So and that's sort of the goal, right?

GUPTA: Yeah. Yeah. Yeah. Yeah.

RAJARATNAM: And so I, my goal, what I told people was, 2010 we enter with 10 billion dollars.

GUPTA: Right. And there, you know, I do want to, I, I, I, will now next week, I'll, I mean I've been having periodic meetings with these guys (Galleon International executives).

RAJARATNAM: Right.

GUPTA: On the fundraising side, and I'll continue to do that and, you know, they pulled me in, but I'm, you know, please keep telling them they, they should pull me in wherever they think I can add value, and, you know?

RAJARATNAM: Yeah. And I think, yeah...

GUPTA: And you should do...feel the same. Any meeting you want me to come...

That is clearly another attempt by Gupta to push his case for a role across the Galleon Group.

But Rajaratnam doesn't want to get into that. He now cleverly kills the Galleon topic by moving back to broader issues. 'So, so that thing,' he says. 'So I think, you know, having a portfolio of opportunities, right? To really leverage your, you know, experience, is the right way to do it, right?'

'Uh, hmm,' Gupta mumbles, perhaps disappointed. They go on to talk about other things.

The power hierarchy is quite well-defined in this conversation. Rajaratnam is on a higher rung. Gupta wants something from him, and hopes that Rajaratnam will consider his request favourably. Rajaratnam would rather not commit immediately, but keep Gupta dangling, confident that the man isn't going to go away, and will, as the prosecution at Gupta's trial will allege, be good for useful information from boardrooms, from time to time.

But why is the relationship skewed in favour of Rajaratnam? Everyone who has some idea about who these two people are, and listens to this conversation, will almost certainly come to the same conclusion: that the skew comes from Rajaratnam being much wealthier than Gupta. Gupta is worth $130 million, but Rajaratnam is a billionaire.

The cruellest cut for Gupta, however, was that while Rajaratnam was discussing Anil Kumar with Gupta, he was also discussing Gupta with Anil Kumar. Gupta would not know that till the wiretapped conversations were played in court during the hedge fund boss's trial.

Less than three weeks after Rajaratnam had complained to Gupta about Kumar's ingratitude, on 15 August 2008, he was telling Kumar about Gupta: 'There's also this sort of lost soul, type of lost, there's no...focus. There's a lack of focus and lack of clarity and what is it that [Rajat] really wants, and it seems like he retired too early.'

In another conversation, Rajaratnam explains the details of the deal that KKR is offering Gupta, and says 'it was about $5 million a year with upside'. Kumar expresses surprise at the choices that his McKinsey mentor is making. 'Is it really that he is so greedy for the money that KKR has offered him?' he asks. Rajaratnam's reply: 'My analysis of the situation is he's enamoured with Kravis, and I think he wants to be in that circle. That's a billionaire circle, right? Goldman is like the hundreds of millions circle, right? And I think here he sees the opportunity to make $100 million over the next five years or ten years without doing a lot of work.'

Both appear concerned about Gupta's emotional health. 'At

some point, what I worry about is that there can be this massive implosion in him,' says Kumar.

Rajaratnam muses: 'He didn't seem comfortable. He seemed like he was tormented, right?'

So, Gupta thinks Kumar is 'unsettled', and Rajaratnam thinks he is 'unhappy'. Kumar thinks Gupta could implode, and Rajaratnam thinks he is 'tormented'. Both the Indians seem to be in way above their heads, pathetically looking for affirmation from the confident Rajaratnam for their confused ambitions.

Something Good

PREETINDER SINGH 'PREET' BHARARA WAS BORN IN FIROZPUR in Punjab, but his parents migrated to the US when he was two. He grew up in Eatontown, New Jersey, and like several other players in the Galleon insider trading drama, had a brilliant academic career. He was valedictorian for his high school class—the student who has the honour of making the closing or farewell statement at the graduation ceremony.

He graduated magna cum laude ('with great honour', just short of the highest distinction, summa cum laude—'with highest honour') from Harvard University in 1990 and moved on to Columbia Law School, where he was a member of the Columbia Law Review. He went into private practice, and in 2000 was appointed a Southern District of New York prosecutor. Major cases in his five years on the job involved organized crime, narcotics and securities fraud.

In 2005 Bharara became chief counsel to Democratic Party Senator Charles E. Schumer, and played a crucial role in the Senate Judiciary Committee's investigation into the firings of prosecutors around the country by the George W. Bush administration. The investigation uncovered evidence that the sackings were politically motivated, enough to finally force the 2007 resignation of US Attorney General Alberto R. Gonzales. Yet so fair and apolitical had been Bharara's handling of the entire process that he earned the respect of both Democrats and Republicans. Michael M. Purpura, a senior lawyer in the Bush Justice Department at the time of the investigations and later an associate White House counsel, told *The New York Times*: 'To the extent that Preet was the driving force of the investigation, it was conducted in a completely fair, thorough and professional manner.'

In August 2010 the Senate confirmed him as the US Attorney for the Southern District, and he hit the ground running, successfully prosecuting terrorists, corrupt public officials, organized crime syndicates and fraudsters. But it was only after he led perhaps the most ferocious attack ever by the US government on insider trading and securities fraud, at a time when millions of US citizens were still in shock from the financial markets collapse of 2008, that he became a media star. In February 2012, *Time* magazine put him on the cover of all its editions, with the line: 'This man is busting Wall Street'. Two months later, the magazine named him one of the '100 most influential people in the world'.

In the accompanying profile, Viet Dinh, former Assistant Attorney General and close friend of Bharara, wrote: 'Without drama, [Bharara's] Manhattan team has battled terrorism, convicting the Times Square bomber Faisal Shahzad; crippled international criminal networks run by Russian arms dealer Viktor Bout, Jamaican drug trafficker Christopher Coke and Colombian rebel group FARC... For years, as others clamoured for scalps after the global financial crisis, Preet resisted the temptation of a sloppy kill and instead waited for the facts. His 58-0 record for insider-trading cases bodes ill for the bankers whom his office has charged with reckless lending practices or inflating mortgage values. Preet...is the Platonic ideal described by his hero (former US Supreme Court Justice and chief prosecutor at the post-World War II trial of Nazi leaders at Nuremberg) Robert H. Jackson: a prosecutor "who tempers zeal with human kindness, who seeks truth and not victims, who serves the law and not factional purposes and who approaches his task with humility"'.

But Bharara has also been accused of going after easy targets rather than the big fish who would be much harder to net. In April 2011, exactly a year before *Time* would anoint him one of the world's 100 most influential people, *New York* magazine carried an article titled 'The Next Best Crooks'. 'Three years after Lehman Brothers collapsed, no one responsible for the greatest financial calamity since the Great Depression has gone to jail, and a meaningful remedy for the transgressions of 2008 clearly isn't forthcoming from Congress or the White House,' commented author Robert Kolker. 'Bharara may be winning his share of insider-trading battles, but unlike [Rudy] Giuliani or [Eliot] Spitzer (former Southern District US Attorneys who went after Wall Street fraudsters), he doesn't seem to be hauling in the biggest bad guys of his time. Whatever satisfaction comes from seeing Rajaratnam and company squirm, and possibly go to jail, there is still a sinking feeling that they're only the most expedient, not the biggest, targets. "Preet's smart," says one friend and fellow prosecutor. "White-collar cases are difficult. The one area where they're less difficult is insider-trading cases."'

A month after the *New York* article appeared, when George Packer of *The New Yorker* asked Bharara about the allegations, 'his even manner gave way to pent-up annoyance at "ideologues".' 'It bothers me a little bit when people suggest, without knowing anything, that we're not even bothering to look,' he said. 'We have grand-jury secrecy—I don't go out and announce my investigations. But I got to tell you something: where there's smoke, we take a look. Do you have any idea how much people want to bring the case if it exists? So what could be the reason we haven't? Sometimes people say, "It's because you're beholden to these guys", which doesn't make any sense. Do we *look* like we're afraid to prosecute anyone?' Later, in a 'defensive flurry', he said that a lot of people do 'bad things' but that 'doesn't mean it's a criminal act. There are lots of bad people out there who I can't charge criminally.'

Obviously, he believed that Rajat Gupta had done a bad thing which was also a criminal act.

◆

The skirmishes between the prosecution and the defence began long before the case was scheduled to come up on trial. Both sides were hell-bent on getting as many concessions as they could prise out through a series of pre-trial briefs.

In January 2012, four months before the case would come up for trial, Gary Naftalis and his defence team made several filings before Judge Jed Rakoff.

The first one asked the court to dismiss some of the charges against Gupta: 'The indictment focuses on just two instances in which Mr Rajaratnam is said to have traded on inside information he supposedly received from Mr Gupta, but improperly uses those instances to create five purportedly separate substantive securities charges.'

The second filing pleaded that the court should force the government to provide a 'bill of particulars', which would specify the benefits Gupta had allegedly received. As Wayne State University Law School professor and *The New York Times* columnist Peter J. Henning put it: 'The indictment is vague about what Mr Gupta received in exchange for disclosing the confidential information, only stating that he "benefited and hoped to benefit from his friendship and business relationships with Rajaratnam in various ways, some of which were financial". To the extent the defence can pin down exactly what prosecutors believe was the quid pro quo, the easier it will be to dispute the claim. The government no doubt prefers to keep the allegation as broad as possible so that a wide range of evidence can support a jury finding of a quid pro quo exchange between the two men.' The prosecutors had submitted literally truckloads of documents— more than 2 million pages—but this, said Gupta's lawyers, was no 'bill of particulars'. 'The indictment reflects, and attempts to mask, the weakness of the case against Mr Gupta,' they argued.

Another filing requested the barring of wiretap evidence in the trial. After all, the government had already admitted that there was no direct wiretap evidence that Gupta had been involved in insider trading. The prosecution was going to build its case on phone call timings and trading records—purely circumstantial evidence.

However, the prosecution did have in its possession tapes of at least three conversations that it definitely wanted to use in the trial. In these conversations, Rajaratnam told colleagues that he had a friend on the Goldman Sachs board who was supplying him with inside information. The conversations took place soon after Galleon took major trading decisions on Goldman stock.

In the Rajaratnam trial, the judge had allowed the use of wiretaps despite objections from the defence. Gupta's lawyers argued that the ruling had been incorrect, that US law did not permit federal authorities to use wiretaps in insider trading cases (Rajaratnam's was the first insider trading case where the authorities had tapped phones, leading to widespread criticism on Wall Street. Bharara had responded that when white-collar criminals were using sophisticated technology to make their ill-gotten profits, it was only right that the investigators use the same means to catch them.)

But even at this pre-trial stage, Judge Rakoff made it more or less clear that he would not bar the use of wiretapped conversations. 'Looking at it realistically, if I were the defence, I would not be optimistic on this particular motion,' he said.

This would hardly have surprised Gupta's lawyers, but they had needed to raise the issue now. If Gupta was convicted, they would still have recourse to this argument at the appeal stage. In fact, Rajaratnam's lawyers were already preparing to press the point once more at the appeals court.

Under US law, prosecutors must provide the defendant with all 'exculpatory' information that might 'negate evidence of a person's guilt or mitigate the severity of the punishment'. Therefore, Naftalis's team asked for all evidence 'in which the government expressed its own doubts about Rajaratnam's veracity—or simply that he is not to be trusted, even if stopping short of calling him a liar—[because it] would obviously be helpful to the defence, and equally obviously is known to the government'. That is, if the government had evidence that Rajaratnam played around with the truth, Gupta's lawyers could use that to try to convince the jury that the claims that the hedge fund manager made about having a man on the board of Goldman Sachs was just an empty boast.

In effect, while Gupta's lawyers were, on the one hand, saying that using wiretaps as evidence in insider trading trials was unconstitutional, they were ready to accept any wiretap evidence that suggested that Rajaratnam was untrustworthy. Some might have termed this an attempt to have one's cake and eat it too, but, under the circumstances, this was a perfectly valid legal strategy.

On 30 April the US Attorney's Office filed a brief before Judge Rakoff, requesting that the wiretaps of three conversations that took place between Rajaratnam and two of his colleagues, on 24 September and 24 October 2008 must be allowed as evidence. 'Rajaratnam's statements in these three recorded conversations are essential evidence of the insider trading charges against Gupta in this case,' it argued. 'There are no recordings of the conversations between Gupta and Rajaratnam on 23 September and 23 October in which Gupta is alleged to have tipped Rajaratnam (as there was no wiretap over Rajaratnam's work phone or any of Gupta's phones). And because there were no other participants in these conversations, there are no witnesses to testify about the content of the calls between Gupta and Rajaratnam. Thus, Rajaratnam's statements in the subsequent wiretapped calls with (his colleague Ian) Horowitz and (another colleague David) Lau provide indispensable evidence that *(a)* Gupta tipped Rajaratnam during unrecorded phone conversations between Gupta and Rajaratnam on 23 September and 23 October, and *(b)* Rajaratnam purchased and sold Goldman stock on 23 September and 24 October, respectively, on the basis of these tips by Gupta. Particularly in light of certain arguments that Gupta has already made, and has proffered the Court he intends to pursue at trial, the importance of this evidence cannot be overstated.'

In other words, the government was conceding that those tapes were the best evidence it had that Gupta passed on confidential information to the hedge fund billionaire. As Alison Frankel put it in her column for Thomson Reuters on 16 May 2012: 'Without Rajaratnam's fleeting recorded references to tips about Goldman Sachs, the government's case against Gupta was all inference, requiring jurors to draw lines between phone records and Rajaratnam trades.'

However, the critical legal question was: when one person on a recorded phone call tells another about a conversation he had with someone else, is that evidence or hearsay?

The prosecutors had argued in their brief that the recorded conversations fell under exceptions to the bar on hearsay evidence. The government had asked Judge Rakoff for a ruling that the tapes were admissible because they were made in furtherance of a conspiracy involving both Rajaratnam and Gupta. They also argued, in a bit of circular reasoning, that Rakoff should admit the hearsay evidence because the government really needed it to prove its case. The tapes 'are the most probative evidence available that Rajaratnam traded Goldman shares based on a tip from Gupta', the government's brief said. 'The introduction of these statements would be consistent with the rules of evidence and advance the interests of justice.'

In reply, Gupta's lawyers asserted that Rakoff could not rule on the admissibility of the tapes until the government had 'established by a preponderance of evidence at trial' that Gupta was part of the insider trading conspiracy. 'The government seeks to dispense with the inconvenience of a trial—and Mr Gupta's testing of its trial evidence—by asking the court to admit alleged co-conspirator statements before trial, with virtually no evidence in hand, based largely [or perhaps even entirely] on bald statements in its brief that are unproven and, in many instances, unprovable.'

What were these tapes? In two conversations on the morning of 24 September 2008, the day after the Goldman Sachs board members had been informed that Warren Buffett's Berkshire Hathaway was investing $5 billion in the bank, Rajaratnam, speaking with Galleon trader Ian Horowitz, referred to 'something good' he had learned about Goldman that led him to load up on the bank's shares just before close of trading the previous day. The prosecution alleged that the 'something good' was Gupta's tip-off about the Berkshire investment. The following month, Rajaratnam had told Galleon Asia Chief David Lau that he had 'heard yesterday from someone who's on the board of Goldman Sachs' that Goldman's earnings would be drastically lower than analysts expected. Rajaratnam dumped 150,000 shares of Goldman after receiving that tip.

Gupta's lawyers argued that, to bring in the tapes under the hearsay exception for conspiracy, prosecutors had to show that Gupta knew Horowitz and Lau were part of Rajaratnam's insider trading ring. But not only did Gupta not know that Rajaratnam was involved in insider trading, he also had no idea who Horowitz was—and, to cap it all, Horowitz had not even been indicted by the government on any charge. And anyway, how could the prosecutors possibly prove that Rajaratnam's statements to Horowitz and Lau furthered the conspiracy?

According to Gupta's lawyers, the Galleon chief's 'vague and generalized statements about "something good" actually suggested that Horowitz was not part of any conspiracy and that Rajaratnam was not tipped about Berkshire'. 'It makes no sense that Rajaratnam would use such vague and indefinite words with Horowitz if he had, in fact, received a valuable tip the day before,' they asserted. 'Likewise, Rajaratnam's complete failure in two separate conversations to supply Horowitz with the name of the person from whom he purportedly heard the "something good", or even some identifying information concerning that person, further confirms that Rajaratnam's statements were not part of any insider trading conspiracy.'

On 24 October 2008, Rajaratnam told David Lau, who was

based in Singapore: 'I heard yesterday from somebody who is on the board of Goldman Sachs that they are going to lose $2 per share. He was telling me that the quarter is really bad.' But, said Gupta's lawyers, this 'merely described supposed past events without requesting action by Lau, [so] settled law precludes any finding that they were in furtherance of a conspiracy'. Like Horowitz, Lau had also not been indicted.

'Even if Rajaratnam's statements on 24 October were not inadmissible hearsay, which they are, the Court still should exclude them from evidence, because they pose a danger of unfair prejudice to Mr Gupta, substantially outweighing any probative value they may have. At trial, the government will invite the jury to conclude that, on the 24 October recording, Rajaratnam was referring to Mr Gupta (albeit not by name) as the person who told him the prior day that Goldman Sachs had a quarter-to-date loss of two dollars per share,' contended Gupta's counsel.

'That conclusion, however, requires a number of logical steps, including inferences that Rajaratnam spoke truthfully to Lau on 24 October about having received a tip; that Rajaratnam in fact received that tip from Mr Gupta (as opposed to a source within Goldman Sachs); that Mr Gupta in fact learned the two dollars per share number on the 23 October board posting call; and that Mr Gupta conveyed that number to Rajaratnam in an unrecorded telephone call later that day. The long chain of inferences necessary to ground the relevance of Rajaratnam's 24 October statements demonstrates that those statements have, at best, attenuated probative value.

'Balanced against that low probative value, the danger of unfair prejudice is substantial. In order to make the logical journey the government will suggest, the jury will have to ignore contrary evidence…at every step of the way. There is real risk they will do so… The serious risk here is that jurors will place undue weight on the 24 October recording, and use it to draw conclusions that are unsupported by, or even contrary to, the evidence. The

Court should not permit the government to unfairly exploit the 24 October recording in this fashion.'

Besides, Rajaratnam was a known braggart who lied about and exaggerated his access to inside information, argued Gupta's lawyers. Nothing he said was trustworthy. In fact, the government itself had acknowledged that he was a liar.

'First, the government has argued that Rajaratnam "was an organizer and leader of insider trading schemes" at Galleon. Similarly, the government has argued that Rajaratnam encouraged insider trading at Galleon, judged the value of employees by their ability to obtain unlawful tips and frequently pressed them to do so. In that context, Rajaratnam had every reason to build up his own value and set an example by mis-stating or exaggerating his own access to inside information. For example, Rajaratnam learned in a wiretapped call at 2.32 p.m. on 23 July 2008 about a source of inside information that his co-conspirator Anil Kumar had developed, and then claimed that source as "my guy" in another wiretapped call twenty minutes later with his brother Rengan. Rajaratnam's motive to exaggerate to fellow Galleon employees about his access to information undercuts the truthfulness of his statements about Goldman Sachs on the 24 October recording.

'Second, the government itself has publicly and vigorously attacked Rajaratnam's credibility. After his conviction, Rajaratnam gave an interview to *Newsweek* magazine in which he described his treatment by federal agents at the time of his arrest, including pressure tactics designed to obtain a confession and persuade Rajaratnam to falsely implicate Mr Gupta. In response to that interview, a number of government representatives made unusual public statements concerning Rajaratnam. A spokesperson for the United States Attorney's Office stated that "[a] number of his assertions [were] inaccurate". An FBI spokesperson said that statements Rajaratnam attributed to the agents who arrested him "were never uttered".

'The government's own accusations of mendacity flatly contradict any attempt it may make to show Rajaratnam's trustworthiness.'

And in the 24 September and 24 October conversations, 'Rajaratnam had an incentive to brag and exaggerate, in conversations with Galleon employees, that he had access to superior information, whether or not he believed his conversations were private.'

However, in spite of the valiant efforts made by Gupta's defence, Judge Rakoff allowed the tapes to be used as evidence.

The trial, originally scheduled for April, finally began on 21 May.

The $5 Billion Deal

IN THE COURT, GUPTA SAT WITH HIS DEFENCE TEAM. IN THE row behind him sat his wife Anita, the woman whom he had met more than four decades ago at IIT Delhi while rehearsing a play, and their four daughters. As Judge Jed S. Rakoff waited for lead prosecutor Assistant US Attorney Reed Brodsky to begin his opening arguments, one of Gupta's daughters wiped tears from her eyes.

Judge Rakoff, who had been a federal judge for sixteen years, had in recent times become a sort of hero by demanding greater accountability in cases of alleged Wall Street fraud. The SEC had long preferred to agree to settlements with companies accused of such crimes. The companies neither accepted nor denied guilt, paid a fine, and were let off. According to the SEC, prosecuting each case to its fullest extent would put great stress on its budget, and would mean that it would be able to pursue far fewer offenders. Rakoff disagreed vehemently and, in a December 2011 ruling that shook Wall Street, rejected a $285 million settlement that SEC had made with Citigroup after the bank was accused of selling a $1 billion investment product to investors in 2007, without telling them that it was actually using the instrument to bet against them. Rakoff pointed out that if Citigroup had actually done so, then, according to the SEC deal, the guilty executives would go scot-free, and the bank would pay the fine using shareholders' money—people who were in no way involved in or even aware of what the bank had done.

But Judge Rakoff is much more than just a white-collar criminal's worst nightmare. He wrote his master's thesis on Mahatma Gandhi. A champion of civil liberties, he said in a commencement speech in 2003, referring to the draconian post-9/11 laws passed by the Bush administration to counter terrorism: 'If, in the name of combating terrorism, we so restrict our own freedom, have we not thereby lost part of the very battle we seek to win?' He has come out strongly in opposition to the death penalty, commenting in a ruling that it 'is tantamount to foreseeable, state-sponsored murder of innocent human beings'.

Judge Rakoff also worried about the concentration of wealth and economic power in the hands of a few. In an interview to huffingtonpost.com on 27 December 2011 he said: 'It is disturbing to many people that there is such a concentration of wealth in a relatively small percentage of the population today. Many years ago you had the so-called robber barons, and the fear that it is not healthy for a democracy to have so much economic wealth, so much economic power, concentrated in relatively few hands... In the 1990s, of course, free enterprise, capitalism and so forth were glorified to a degree. Some of that was political. We had finally won the battle against the Iron Curtain, and part of the reason we won was because our economic system was a lot better than theirs. But I think maybe it was an over-glorification of capitalism.'

However, his personal views did not matter when he sat in the judge's seat, he emphasized. 'We take an oath to administer justice for rich and poor alike, and that means that Daddy Warbucks gets the same justice from us as Little Orphan Annie,' he explained. 'So most judges—and I like to think I'm one of them—are pretty good at excluding those kinds of considerations from their determination of a case.' (Daddy Warbucks, a character in the popular comic strip *Little Orphan Annie*, represents the greedy capitalist.)

Rakoff was a man who elicited both respect and fear. In a profile of Rakoff in *The Washington Post* (on 20 January 2012) David S. Hilzenrath wrote: 'His reputation for cross-examining lawyers and his widely acknowledged intellect lead them to prepare anxiously for appearances before him. One boiled it down to this: "He thinks he's the smartest guy in the court, and in almost every instance he's right.'"

Hilzenrath had asked him about his close friendship with Gary Naftalis, Rajat Gupta's defence lawyer. Many judges routinely recuse themselves from cases that involve lawyers close to them. Rakoff never does that. 'When I put on the robe and go up on the bench, I could[n't] care less whether it's my best friend or my worst enemy,' he said. Later, he elaborated in an email: 'Whenever any lawyer (close friend or just acquaintance) has a case before me, I cut off all social contact with that person throughout the duration of the case. Thus, for example, I have not had any out-of-court contact whatsoever with Gary Naftalis for over a year [since when his initial Gupta matter came before me].'

Jed S. Rakoff was no ordinary judge. A *Washington Post* reader had even proposed that this blunt, fearless and fair man should stand for President.

◆

The jury consisted of eight men and four women, mostly working-class New Yorkers. A few minutes after lead prosecutor Brodsky began speaking, Preet Bharara quietly entered the courtroom and sat down in the last row, close to the door.

Brodsky started off by telling the jury that this was a straightforward case of insider trading: 'Gupta threw away his duties, threw away his responsibilities and broke the law.' Gupta and Rajaratnam had been friends and business associates: 'Together they offered each other far more than they could achieve individually.' Brodsky repeatedly emphasized that insider trading was something that the rich and powerful indulged in to rook the ordinary investor. '[For Rajaratnam], getting tips from Gupta was like knowing the outcome of a game before it ends or getting tomorrow's business news today.'

He referred to the phone call Gupta had made to Rajaratnam seconds after the close of the Goldman Sachs board meeting that approved Warren Buffett's $5 billion investment in the bank, and how, within minutes of that call, Galleon bought $43 million of Goldman shares.

In his opening remarks, Naftalis, referring to Gupta as 'one of America's most respected business leaders', said that 'it defies common sense that in the twilight of an illustrious life, [Gupta would] decide knowingly, wilfully and deliberately to suddenly become a criminal and do it for no benefit.' Moreover, at the time when Gupta was on friendly terms with Rajaratnam, most of Wall Street viewed the fund manager as respectable.

Also, he pointed out, the government had no wiretapped evidence that Gupta had ever provided any secret information to Rajaratnam, and in the conversations with his colleagues in which the hedge fund boss had mentioned a source at Goldman, he had never named Gupta. The government, said Naftalis, was giving the jury a 'cropped photograph', not the full picture.

'Rajaratnam was in a secret and separate world concealed from Rajat Gupta and concealed from every other law-abiding person,' he said. 'There will not be any direct evidence that Rajat Gupta was part of that secret insider trading world, because he wasn't.' The government case was based on hearsay. 'They're presenting a case based on speculation, a case based on guesswork, a case based on suspicion. There is an absence of real, hard, direct evidence.'

Besides, Gupta was hardly the only Goldman insider that Rajaratnam knew. Galleon, after all, was one of Goldman's biggest customers, and three Goldman executives were already under investigation for leaking information. Even Gary D. Cohn, Goldman's co-president, had visited Galleon's headquarters around the time that Gupta was allegedly passing on information to Rajaratnam. 'The No. 2 guy at Goldman Sachs doesn't make house calls for every Tom, Dick and Harry,' said Naftalis, in case anyone had not fully grasped the point he was making.

'There may be a crime here, but Rajat Gupta had nothing

to do with it,' he said. 'You've got the wrong man on trial here. The evidence will show that Raj Rajaratnam had sources all over town; he had other sources at Goldman Sachs.'

And then, of course, there was Gupta's philanthropic work. Judge Rakoff had already warned Naftalis that this was of no relevance to the case, but Naftalis was hardly going to let the jury remain unaware of Gupta's deep commitment to making a difference to the lives of people across the world, through improved healthcare and education. But Rakoff was implacable. He ordered the jury out of the courtroom and warned Naftalis not to spend time on his client's philanthropic record. The lawyer replied that the prosecution had accused Gupta of being motivated by greed, and he needed to counter that argument; he should be allowed to mention Gupta's role in the war against 'AIDS, malaria and tuberculosis'.

'Or the bubonic plague,' said Rakoff, a rejoinder wry enough to make even Gupta smile. Rakoff refused to permit Naftalis to mention specific diseases.

The opening arguments over, the court adjourned. The prosecution would now start calling its witnesses to testify.

The first witness was Caryn Eisenberg, who had been Rajaratnam's executive assistant at the Galleon group for two years beginning in 2008. She revealed that one of the very first instructions she received upon joining was that she was never to bother her boss during the first half-hour or the last half-hour of the trading day. Unless…unless it was one of five people calling, and she was a given a list of those five names, which she noted down in her red notebook.

The names were Rajat Gupta, Rajiv Goel, Parag Saxena, Stanley F. Druckenmiller and Anil Kumar. Goel and Kumar had pleaded guilty of providing Rajaratnam with inside information and had testified against him at his trial. Saxena ran the private equity fund New Silk Route that Gupta and Rajaratnam had helped set up, and in which the Galleon boss had invested $50 million. Druckenmiller, who had once been legendary investor George Soros's right-hand man, had gone on to be one of the world's most successful hedge fund investors. He had shut down his fund, Duquesne Capital Management, in 2010. But no connection had ever been found between him and Rajaratnam's illegal activities.

Reading from her notebook, Eisenberg said that Gupta was identified as a 'good friend'. She said that Gupta called often and visited the Galleon offices, sometimes without making a prior appointment.

Brodsky now zeroed in on the 23 September phone call. Eisenberg had received the call and recognized the voice at the other end as belonging to one of the men on the 'important people' list, though he did not identify himself. The man told her that he needed to speak urgently to her boss. It was just a few minutes before the markets closed, a time when Rajaratnam was not to be disturbed, but since it was one of the people from the list, Eisenberg put the call through. Rajaratnam was not at his desk, but Eisenberg located him. The Galleon boss ran back to his office, closed the door and took the call. And as soon as he put down the phone, he called one of his traders, Gary Rosenbach, into his office. The door was closed again. When Rosenbach went back to his desk, Eisenberg heard him shouting on the phone: 'Buy Goldman Sachs! Buy Goldman Sachs!'

Afterwards, she told the jury, she noticed that Rajaratnam 'was smiling more'.

She said she had a clear memory of the events because the next morning she had learned about Buffett's investment in Goldman Sachs and had connected it to the excitement of the previous afternoon.

Later, David Frankel, the lawyer from Naftalis's team who cross-examined Eisenberg, established that Rajaratnam had flown to Atlantic City with a group of people including David Heller, then the co-head of Goldman Sachs' securities division, and Michael Daffey, another Goldman executive, for the annual celebration of a high-end fantasy football league in which they had participated. Obviously, the aim was to emphasize to the jury once more that the Galleon boss was close to various Goldman executives who could have supplied him with inside information. Gupta was hardly his only Goldman contact.

Indeed, Eisenberg testified that during her two years with Galleon, the list of important people grew to about ten names. Among the additions was David Loeb, Goldman Sachs's head of Asia equity sales in New York and a managing director. 'He would call throughout the day, but not as frequently as some of the other callers,' Eisenberg said of Loeb. Loeb has not been accused by the government of any wrongdoing.

If someone had indeed leaked Rajaratnam the news of Buffett's investment, it need not necessarily have been Gupta.

In fact, by the end of the day, some people may have been left wondering why Loeb had not been charged.

Moreover, the mere fact that Gupta was included on Rajaratnam's list of 'important people' meant nothing by itself. As columnist Walter Pavlo pointed out on forbes.com on 23 May: 'While Gupta was on Raj's shortlist, I am certain he was also on other shortlists. I am confident that executive assistants at a number of firms were told to escalate a call from Rajat Gupta. Lloyd Blankfein, CEO of Goldman, might put someone like Gupta on his "shortlist" since Gupta was on the firm's board of directors. Billionaire Bill Gates may have Gupta on his list since he was on the board of the Bill & Melinda Gates Foundation. But being on those lists does not help the government's case.

'Cases like this, circumstantial cases, depend on portraying the defendant as someone encircled by evil while avoiding the direct evidence, the DNA that puts them at the scene of a crime,' wrote Pavlo. 'Being on a list where a number of people have already pled guilty is persuasive and effective on a jury when the goal is to get a guilty verdict. There is more circumstantial evidence to come, and much of it will not favour Mr Gupta. However, the jury, and the public, who cast quick judgement in cases like this, need to consider the circumstantial evidence that puts Gupta outside a circle of convicted felons and on a shortlist that many of us would want to be on.'

Frankel also used his cross-examination of Eisenberg to show that Rajaratnam was certainly not above lying when it suited him. In answer to his questions, Eisenberg testified that Rajaratnam sometimes directed her to lie to Gupta about his availability when Gupta called or made unannounced visits to the office. 'Lying, as in saying he wasn't in the office,' Eisenberg said, adding, 'he may have snuck out of the building to avoid him.' Frankel showed jurors excerpts of an instant message exchange dated 29 February 2008 between Eisenberg and Anita Teglasi, another Rajaratnam assistant. 'Raj made me lie to Rajat,' Eisenberg wrote. 'He doesn't want to see him.'

Since the prosecution was expected to use wiretaps of Rajaratnam's conversations to prove Gupta's complicity in his insider-trading activities, Gupta's defence team had decided to show up the hedge fund manager as a liar at every opportunity it got.

But the prosecution was far from finished with the events of 23 September 2008. On the third day of the trial, it called to the witness stand a young Indian-origin former Galleon trader. Ananth Muniyappa testified that just before close of trading on 23 September, Rajaratnam had told him and Rosenbach to buy about $24 million of Goldman stock. But Leon Shaulov, a top portfolio manager and trader at Galleon, had known nothing about this. Two hours later, when Goldman announced the Berkshire investment, Shaulov was distraught, because he had been betting big against financial stocks. And when he learnt that Galleon had bought a chunk of Goldman stock on that very day, without informing him, he was, according to Muniyappa, enraged.

The prosecution then showed the jury a couple of emails that substantiated what Muniyappa recalled about Shaulov's fury. At 6.16 p.m. an angry Shaulov wrote to Rosenbach: 'Thanks for the heads up btw. I'm short 170mm fins. Not one word from anyone. Thanks very much. All I get is sick dilution. 0 help. 0. What I give versus what I get back is disgusting.' The next morning, Rosenbach emailed Rajaratnam at 6.23 a.m: 'I spoke to Leon and believe I diffused him.'

The point the prosecution was attempting to make was that Galleon had not had a bullish outlook on Goldman: Shaulov was one of its senior-most traders and had been shorting Goldman stock. But the phone call from Gupta caused Rajaratnam to change his mind. Why was Shaulov not informed? After all, he was about to lose a lot of money (nearly $170 million) on the position he had built up on financial stocks, almost definitely with Rajaratnam's knowledge and approval. It is quite possible that Galleon's top dog forgot to inform Shaulov in the heat of the moment—after all, by Eisenberg and Muniyappa's account, he ordered the purchase of Goldman shares barely three minutes before the markets closed. Alternatively, he might have decided to keep Shaulov in the dark because he was apprehensive that if he got the trader to do a dramatic volte-face on the stock, it could have attracted the notice of a lot of other traders on Wall Street, and started tongues wagging.

The man who followed Muniyappa to the witness box was Byron D. Trott, former vice-chairman of Goldman Sachs, part of whose job had been to handle some extremely high-net-worth clients of the bank (he quit Goldman in 2009 to set up his own investment firm). Among the men whose wealth Trott helped manage for Goldman was Warren E. Buffett. In fact, so pleased had Buffett been with Trott that he had mentioned him in two of his investor letters—the annual sharing of thoughts with shareholders of Berkshire Hathaway that is eagerly awaited and meticulously read by the global investment community. In 2003, a year after Trott started advising him, he wrote that Trott 'understands Berkshire far better than any investment banker with whom we have talked and—it hurts me to say this—earns his fee'. In 2008, Buffett called his trusted confidant 'the rare investment banker who puts himself in his client's shoes'.

When asked by a prosecutor to tell the jury who Buffett was, Trott said: 'He's the most respected businessman and investor in America.'

When Gupta's lawyer objected to this glowing tribute, Judge Rakoff smiled and commented: 'I didn't think that was in dispute.' However, for the benefit of the jury, he asked Trott: 'Is he a very large and well-known investor?'

'Yes,' said Trott.

The prosecution wanted Trott to tell the court how the Buffett-Goldman deal was struck.

The story that Trott recounted was extraordinary. For, according to him, the entire process, from the germ of the original idea to getting the board's approval of this $5 billion covenant, happened in just twenty-four nerve-wracking hours.

Trott, who lives in Chicago, was meeting a client on 22 September 2008 when Goldman's co-president Jon Winkelried called him on his cell phone and told him that the investment bank was planning to raise $10 billion in a common stock offering. Given the ongoing financial crisis, if Goldman could pull it off, it would boost all-round confidence in the bank and also have a salutary effect on the markets. Even as Winkelried spoke, Trott's brain had started ticking. How about, he asked, if he pitched Buffett to be a 'cornerstone investor' on this? Winkelried agreed immediately, and Trott took the next available flight to New York.

The next morning, in Goldman's headquarters, Trott presented the top managers with a proposal that he thought Buffett would buy. He had discussed investing in Goldman with Buffett a few months earlier, but the world's smartest investor had not been interested. So Trott knew he had to come up with something special, and he thought he had managed to do that. 'I know

Warren very well,' Trott told the court. 'We had done numerous deals together and I knew the structure that he would want.'

For Goldman, of course, the upside was obvious: if Buffett could be persuaded to invest, others would follow, and the bank would be able to raise the rest of the $10 billion easily. A thumbs-up from Buffett would be, as Trott put it, 'hugely credentializing'.

Once he got the go-ahead from his top management, Trott called Warren Buffett. He offered a complex deal that ensured Buffett 10 per cent annual interest on a $5 billion investment plus the option to buy additional Goldman stock at a set price. And, as he had hoped, Buffett liked what Trott was offering and accepted the terms.

Trott went back to his bosses and told them that Buffett was on. It was now nearly lunchtime, and two more steps would carve the deal in stone. Trott had to inform Buffett that the deal was officially agreed upon, after which the Goldman board had to approve it formally. But Buffett had already told Trott that he had promised to take his grandchildren for a meal and did not want to be disturbed till half past two. So Goldman scheduled a board meeting by phone at 3.15 p.m.

Trott called Buffett after he had dropped his grandchildren home. Less than an hour later, the Goldman board approved the investment.

How hush-hush was the whole process, asked the prosecuting lawyer. 'This was about as top secret as you can get,' replied Trott. Even the chief financial officer of Berkshire Hathaway had not known about it; Buffett had not bothered to inform him. When Trott called Buffett in the afternoon to tell him that Goldman's top management was fine with the deal, Buffett told him to ring up the Berkshire CFO and explain it to him. Only a few top Goldman executives had been privy to the proposal, and it had all happened so fast that chances of leakage were extremely low. And the independent board members had come to know of it only at the board meeting.

Trott's testimony seemed to add to the evidence piling up against Gupta. But Gary Naftalis wanted a hearing with Judge Rakoff without jury presence. At the hearing, Naftalis complained that the prosecution was withholding evidence against David Loeb, which could be 'exculpatory' for Gupta. Brodsky admitted that Loeb was heard on a government wiretap passing information to Rajaratnam. Loeb had passed on tips about Apple, Intel Corporation and Hewlett-Packard to the Galleon boss.

Naftalis remarked angrily that it should be Loeb who should be on trial, not Gupta.

Brodsky retorted that Loeb had not had access to information about the Buffett deal nor about Goldman Sachs' earnings. 'There is no evidence, zero, none from the government that Loeb had access to material nonpublic information about Goldman's earnings,' he said. 'The defence wants to blow this up and confuse the jury.'

As the court adjourned for the day, Gupta must have felt particularly lonely. His daughter Aditi was graduating from Harvard Business School, his own alma mater, the next day, but he would not be around to watch the ceremony. Anita, his wife, would have to attend without him.

The Chairman Who Wasn't

THE FIRST WITNESS THE PROSECUTION CALLED, ON 24 MAY, the fourth day of Rajat Gupta's trial, was Carolann Shields, an IT security manager at McKinsey, in charge of phone and email records at the firm.

To prove to the jury that Gupta and Rajaratnam were close, the government presented several emails written by Gupta over the years. Shields' role was to establish the authenticity of the emails. The earliest mail was from March 2005, in which Gupta said he wanted to move his money to Goldman Sachs' private wealth management group. In this mail addressed to Jeffrey Klein, a Goldman executive in New York, he mentioned: 'I understand that you also handle accounts for Raj Rajaratnam and (investment banker) Ravi Trehan, who are close friends of mine.'

Another mail had Gupta responding to a February 2007 note from Marshall Lux, then a managing director of McKinsey. 'Joined the board of the Harlem Children's Zone,' Lux had written, referring to the charity run by Geoffrey Canada, who had stood guarantee for Rajaratnam when he had been granted bail. 'Raj Rajaratnam said hello.' Gupta wrote in reply: 'Raj is one of the most outstanding hedge fund managers and a very close friend.'

The prosecutors got Shields to validate phone records showing that Gupta placed calls to Rajaratnam shortly after two Goldman Sachs telephonic board meetings. They also played the three secretly recorded conversations between Rajaratnam and his Galleon colleagues that the prosecution and defence had fought over at the pre-trial stage—the 'something good' chat, and the one about Goldman losing $2 per share.

The jury was also shown a series of calendar entries for

Gupta that confirmed the dates and times when he participated in Goldman board meetings. In his cross-examination of Shields, David Frankel reviewed the calendar notes, entry by entry. What became obvious was that Gupta's days were chock-a-block with meetings. It would be quite natural for him to make telephone calls immediately after meetings.

The next witness was Mark R. Belgya, chief financial officer of J.M. Smucker, the Orrville, Ohio-based maker of fruit spreads, ice-cream toppings, natural peanut butter and other food products. Smucker had purchased the Folgers coffee business from Procter & Gamble in June 2008 for $3.3 billion. The government was accusing Gupta of passing on information about the deal before it became public knowledge. The allegation was again based on phone records that showed that Gupta had called Rajaratnam after attending a Procter & Gamble meeting in which the sale of Folgers was discussed and approved. The call had not been recorded.

Belgya testified that it was the largest transaction Smucker had ever undertaken. He said that the company secretly contacted Procter & Gamble after the consumer products giant had announced that it wanted to sell off Folgers. Project Moon, as the deal was code-named by Smucker, involved months of negotiations, and finally the Smucker board approved it on 2 June 2008. On the same day, Rajaratnam told a colleague during a tapped phone conversation that he had learned from a director of Procter & Gamble that Smucker was buying Folgers. The deal was announced on 3 June, after the markets closed.

According to Belgya, only a few people knew about Project Moon, but that handful included Procter & Gamble Director Gupta.

However, during cross-examination, Naftalis read out from the press release issued by the company to announce the acquisition. The note listed many banks and law firms that advised on the deal—firms like Morgan Stanley, the Blackstone

Group and Weil, Gotshal & Manges. As he named each firm, Naftalis asked: 'I take it they were also knowledgeable about the transaction?' Belgya agreed. Naftalis had scored a point. There were actually dozens of people who knew about the negotiations. Indeed, Smucker had intended to make its announcement on 4 June, but had to bring it forward by a day because *The Wall Street Journal* published a story on 3 June about Smucker being all set to buy Folgers. Obviously, people were leaking information, and not only to Rajaratnam.

After lunch, William George, Harvard Business School professor and independent director of Goldman Sachs, took the stand. He testified about the duty of a Goldman director to keep confidential the board's discussions about the bank's strategy and finances. Prosecutors then asked him about a two-day strategy meeting of the Goldman board in St Petersburg, Russia, in June 2008. The government alleged that the next month Gupta improperly discussed the specifics of the meeting with Rajaratnam.

This was the only Gupta-Rajaratnam conversation that was on tape, dated 29 July 2008, in which Gupta had told Rajaratnam that the Goldman board had discussed the option of taking over either a commercial bank or an insurance firm (see Chapter Seven).

The prosecutors took George through the minutes of various Goldman board meetings held in 2008 and presentations made to the directors in painstaking detail. Both Judge Rakoff and the jury were visibly bored—a few jury members were seen trying to stifle yawns. For Goldman chairman Lloyd Blankfein had called board meetings very often as the financial crisis had deepened.

'There were a very large number of meetings called on very short notice, typically by telephone, said George. 'They included a range of things.' Most of these were, George said, 'posting calls', Blankfein briefing the board members about what was going on inside the bank and how it was planning to react to the growing mayhem in the financial sector and capital markets. By

September, as Lehman Brothers slid into oblivion, Blankfein was calling meetings several times a week, and sometimes twice a day, even on Sundays. Directors had barely two hours' notice before they had to dial in.

On 14 September Blankfein told his board about the Federal Reserve's talks about Lehman Brothers, the risk that insurance giant American International Group (AIG) was going under, and Goldman Sachs' own liquidity position. Blankfein told directors that AIG 'was experiencing severe liquidity stress, and it wasn't clear how long it could continue'.

The next day, Blankfein updated the independent directors about Lehman's bankruptcy and Bank of America Corp's acquisition of Merrill Lynch. The day after that, Blankfein discussed Goldman's third-quarter results. On 17 September the board met again over a conference call, to consider the options Goldman had of raising money. The bank could go to the capital markets, or turn to sovereign wealth funds. But, recalled George, the board liked neither of these routes. However, when the option of getting an outsider like Warren Buffett to invest in Goldman was mooted, 'the board seemed very open to that'.

Six days later came the critical board meeting when independent directors were informed about Buffett's investment and a plan to sell an additional $2.5 billion in shares to the public. 'There was a discussion of whether this would open the markets and Goldman Sachs could go into the market [to raise more funds],' George told the jury.

The other board meeting crucial to Gupta's case was the one on 23 October. Goldman Sachs was about to report a loss for the first time in its history and board members were hastily summoned to dial in.

George remembered that meeting vividly since he had a class to teach at Harvard before he could join the meeting. He rushed out as soon as class was over, went to a courtyard to seek out a private spot and took the call on his mobile phone. He was already thirty minutes late.

The jury perked up a bit when George spoke about an email Gupta had sent him in September 2007, when he and Rajaratnam were involved in setting up New Silk Route. Gupta's mail, which had a PowerPoint presentation on the fund attached, was essentially a sales pitch, asking Gupta to invest in the fund. 'Bill, I don't know whether New Silk Route is a good fit with your investment portfolio, but I thought some Indian and Asian exposure may be good,' he wrote. 'It would be a privilege to have you as an investor, and I hope you will consider it seriously. I will follow up with you next week at the Goldman board meeting.' George thought about it and finally declined to invest.

This had been just another piece of evidence that the prosecutors were presenting to the jury to build up the case that Gupta and Rajaratnam had had close business ties. The many hours that the prosecutors had kept George in the witness stand was an indication that they also intended to justify the mountain of documents they had submitted to the court: that it was a case of sheer overwhelming quantity substituting for quality. They intended to go about their business with extraordinarily bloody-minded meticulousness. The heaps and heaps of details they piled on the jury, they hoped, would make up for the fact that they had nothing other than circumstantial evidence against Gupta.

But the next witness they produced livened up proceedings somewhat.

If William George had represented one end of the US corporate spectrum—former CEO, Harvard professor, independent board member—Michael Cardillo perhaps was a good exemplar of the other end. The next morning's edition of *The New York Post* began its report on Cardillo's testimony with the telling sentence: 'The rats are coming out of the woodwork.'

The thirty-five-year-old Cardillo, a former Galleon employee, had been charged with insider trading in October 2009. He had pleaded guilty to one count of conspiracy and one count of securities fraud, and had been cooperating with the government ever since. He had worn a wire for the FBI and taped conversations he had had with his former Galleon friends and colleagues. He had also testified against former colleague Zvi Goffer, who was subsequently convicted of insider trading.

Cardillo began his career at Galleon as a $40,000-a-year back-office clerk and ended up as a portfolio manager overseeing $125 million. Now a pariah as far as jobs on Wall Street were concerned, he was making his living by trading on the markets with his own money.

In Judge Rakoff's court, Cardillo said that he bet on Procter & Gamble's stock price in January 2009 after getting a tip from Rajaratnam's brother Rengan ('RK'). Cardillo said that RK told him P&G was going to announce a decline in organic sales, which could have a negative effect on the company's stock price. According to Cardillo, RK told him that the tip came from 'Raj's guy on the P&G board'.

RK's information turned out to be correct. The next day P&G disclosed that organic sales growth would decline by 2 to 5 per cent, the first such drop in two years. By then, Cardillo had already punted on the share price dropping. 'I remember making a lot of money,' he told the jury.

Phone records presented by the government showed that Gupta had called Rajaratnam from a hotel in Davos, Switzerland, a few hours after participating in a P&G board call in which sales figures were discussed.

The prosecutors also wanted Cardillo to testify on the Smucker deal. Cardillo had told investigators that RK had also tipped him about the company buying Folgers. But Gupta's lawyers were opposing this tooth and nail. Before Cardillo was called, Naftalis told Judge Rakoff: 'As they can see, they have no phone call. We would say there is no evidence connecting us, or Mr Gupta, to Smucker at all.' The government's insistence was based on the fact that there had been a call made to Rajaratnam's office from an unassigned phone line at McKinsey less than an hour after the Procter & Gamble board meeting that approved the sale.

Later, with the jury sent off, Naftalis continued his argument. Cardillo would testify to anything the prosecution wanted, he said. After all, here was a man who had pleaded guilty and had avoided going to prison as part of a deal with the US Attorney's office. Besides, what Cardillo was saying was certainly pure 'hearsay'. Under the rules, witnesses can testify about conversations they participated in, but they cannot generally tell jurors what they heard second-hand about discussions they were not directly involved in.

The information that Cardillo was claiming to have received was, by his own admission, third-hand. He had heard from RK who had heard from Rajaratnam that he had an insider on the Procter & Gamble board. Cardillo had admitted that no names had been mentioned. He had never met or spoken to Gupta. Under cross-examination, Belgya of Smucker had testified that dozens of people had known in advance about the Folgers transaction. Moreover, anyone in McKinsey could have used that phone line to call Rajaratnam's office, and there was not a shred of evidence that the call had anything to do with Smucker.

But Judge Rakoff demurred. He ruled that he would allow Cardillo's recollections because they were statements made in furtherance of an insider trading conspiracy and that there was sufficient circumstantial evidence to allow for their admission.

So, the next day, Cardillo testified that he'd bought Smucker shares after RK told him that the company was going to buy Folgers, and that the tip had come from 'Raj's guy at P&G'. However, he did not know the identity of 'Raj's guy'.

To support Cardillo's testimony, prosecutors showed the jury records of Galleon buying large amounts of Smucker stock before the public announcement of the Folgers purchase. They also produced documents to offer a timeline of when certain information had become available to Gupta, and when it became available to the public.

Naftalis sought to discredit Cardillo by asking about cash that he had received for helping former Galleon trader Craig Drimal to execute trades on his personal account, based on tips from Goffer. Cardillo said he'd once accepted $50,000 in cash for helping Drimal. Drimal had already been convicted and sentenced to sixty-six months in prison in August 2011 for conspiracy, securities fraud and insider trading.

At one point, the prosecution's insistence on producing a seemingly endless line of documents—minutes of board meetings, letters, emails and news articles—finally got on Judge Rakoff's nerves. He noted: 'Counsels, I am in awe of our jury because they have managed to remain attentive even though the vast bulk of the day could be described as "Mr Witness, I show you document X. Let's put it up on the screen." The notion that the jury is going to peruse carefully several thousand documents shows a naïvety.'

Naftalis had another go at Cardillo the next day. With reference to Cardillo's claim about RK telling him about 'Raj's guy' on the Procter & Gamble board, he showed the jury several analyst reports from December 2008 and January 2009 speculating that the company might need to revise and lower its organic sales growth forecasts. Interestingly enough, the prosecution allowed Naftalis to present the first analyst report without raising any objections, but objected when he introduced the second one. Judge Rakoff overruled the objection, telling the prosecutors that since they had not objected to the first report, they had 'waived' their right to keep the other reports out of evidence.

Naftalis had used the analyst reports as the foundation for his next attack on Cardillo. This time, it was about claims that Rajaratnam and his traders had made to colleagues. He asked Cardillo whether they 'exaggerated' and 'bragged' about having sources of inside information. 'Were there others at Galleon who claimed to have sources of inside information that they did not have?' Naftalis asked. The prosecutors objected, and Judge Rakoff barred Cardillo from answering.

Naftalis rephrased his question. 'At morning meetings with Raj Rajaratnam, did people talk about or exaggerate their sources of inside information from time to time?' he asked.

'There were rare occasions when it happened,' Cardillo said.

Naftalis then asked if Cardillo had ever heard Rajaratnam, his brother RK or other Galleon traders talk about sources of illegal tips concerning companies such as Kraft Foods or Chico's FAS.

Cardillo said he'd once witnessed the brothers discussing the possibility of Kraft's acquiring chocolate maker Cadbury. 'Raj had said to RK, "You'll get the heads-up if this is coming together. You'll get the heads-up on that." I didn't know if it was feasible or probable.'

'You were sceptical?' Naftalis asked Cardillo.

'Yes, I didn't think he was ever going to get that information.'

After protracted and often acrimonious negotiations, Kraft bought Cadbury for $19 billion in 2010, several months after Rajaratnam had been arrested by the FBI.

Naftalis asked Cardillo if he had heard that Raj Rajaratnam had given inside information about Intel's financial results to George Soros. Cardillo said he remembered something about that, but could not recollect the details. Did Mike Fisherman, a former Galleon analyst, tell Cardillo that he had got a tip from the chief financial officer at women's retailer Chico's, and that Cardillo could make some money by short-selling the company's shares. And didn't Fisherman later admit to Cardillo that he had just made up his inside source at Chico's? Cardillo admitted that this was so.

Naftalis then told the jury that Cardillo had clearly made a deal with the government. He had been charged with six counts of securities fraud, relating to six stocks. He had pleaded guilty to only one, and had been let off the hook on the others. It had been a simple trade-off, and Cardillo as a government witness would say and do anything to stay out of prison.

He asked Cardillo if he wore a wire to secretly record conversations with former Galleon colleagues in order to lure them into making incriminating statements.

Cardillo acknowledged that he had worn a wire to at least five meetings with Fisherman, who Cardillo had described as a close friend. Upon prodding from the lawyer, he revealed that he'd recorded a conversation with Fisherman just ten days before Fisherman's wedding in January 2010.

'You didn't wear a wire to the wedding, did you?' asked Naftalis acidly.

Cardillo replied, deadpan, that he could not recall whether he had.

◆

After Naftalis had put Cardillo through the wringer, the prosecution called an executive for a company that provided electronic swipe cards to Galleon offices. Caryn Eisenberg, Rajaratnam's executive assistant, had told the court that her boss had given Gupta an electronic key card to enter the Galleon headquarters whenever he wanted.

Reed Brodsky showed jurors data about the card's use, which indicated that someone using the card assigned to Gupta swiped into Galleon's Madison Avenue office on 12 March 2007 at 11.36 a.m. Brodsky then produced Gupta's calendar for that day, which showed that Gupta had scheduled a teleconference of the audit committee of the Goldman Sachs board of directors in which first-quarter earnings would be reviewed from 11.30 a.m. to noon. From noon till 2.30 p.m, according to the calendar, Gupta had an 'NSR Partners Meeting, Location: Galleon Office'.

This supported the government's claims that Gupta was at the Galleon office when he participated in the Goldman Sachs teleconference during which the bank's earnings for the first quarter of 2007 were discussed. Prosecutors said Gupta then passed on the information he'd learned about Goldman to Rajaratnam. Galleon bought 350,000 Goldman shares that day, twenty-five minutes after the audit committee meeting call ended. The next day Goldman announced earnings that exceeded analyst estimates.

Throughout the day, the first two rows in the courtroom had been filled with Gupta's family and friends. Much of the proceedings had seemed to go well for Gupta, but the swipe card evidence, introduced just before the court adjourned at 5 p.m., was clearly a setback.

The next day would be worse.

◆

On 31 May the prosecution started proceedings at the Federal District Court in Manhattan by trying to make a case that Gupta had played an active role in Galleon's business. Ayad Alhadi, a former managing director of marketing at Galleon, was called to the witness stand. His testimony led to *The New York Post* headlining its day's story on the trial: 'Gupta A Secret Raj Exec'.

Alhadi said that Gupta began helping Galleon raise money in 2008. The two of them travelled to the United Arab Emirates for meetings with potential investors such as the Abu Dhabi Investment Authority and the Emirates Bank on 31 March and 1 April that year.

Alhadi liberally dropped Gupta's name in his requests to set up meetings. In an email to a banker, he had written: 'I will be in the Emirates with Rajat Gupta, a friend and adviser to Galleon. He's a highly respected global business leader and I know a meeting with him would be very worthwhile.' In a mail to Gupta, he jubilantly reported the reaction of an executive at the National Bank of Abu Dhabi when he heard about Gupta's Galleon connection: 'When I told him about your affiliation with Galleon he was extremely impressed. He said it would be an "honour to meet you".

Later, the defence would claim that Alhadi had told government investigators in a pre-trial interview that for some investors, meeting Gupta was like meeting a rock star. However, Ahladi said he did not recall saying that.

When asked what he introduced Gupta as to potential investors, Ahladi replied: 'I introduced him the way he was introduced to me, the new chairman of Galleon International.' He said that Rajaratnam called him into his office a few days before the trip and told him that Gupta was the new chairman of Galleon International.

This was mysterious, since the wiretapped conversation between Gupta and Rajaratnam on 29 July, nearly four months after the Middle East meetings—and which the jury had already listened to—makes it quite clear that while Gupta wanted the job of chairman, Rajaratnam had not given it to him yet. So Rajaratnam had clearly lied to Ahladi when he told him that Gupta was the new chairman of Galleon International.

During cross-examination by defence lawyer Robin Wilcox, Alhadi admitted that he 'never received notice that [the appointment as chairman] was consummated'.

However, it is also obvious that Gupta went along with the fiction in his meeting with the Arab investors, perhaps believing that it was only a matter of time before his role was made official.

Brodsky asked Ahladi whether Gupta had said anything about Rajaratnam during these meetings. 'Yes…it was a positive opinion of his investment capabilities,' replied Ahladi.

Within four days after Gupta's Middle East marketing trip, the Abu Dhabi Investment Council promised to invest up to $75 million with Galleon. Brodsky asked whether an investment of this size within just four days of the sales pitch was common. 'That's pretty uncommon,' said Ahladi.

One of the pillars of Gupta's defence had been that he had no motive at all in passing on insider information to Rajaratnam;

there was no proof that he derived any benefit from his friend. But if Gupta was hoping that he would be made chairman and given a stake in the Galleon group, and was therefore helping raise funds from investors, the no-benefit argument was weakened. There certainly was some expectation of benefit.

As the government was alleging, Gupta and Ahladi had made the trip to the Middle East just a few months before Gupta had tipped off Rajaratnam on goings-on in Goldman Sachs and Procter & Gamble.

Next up was Stephen Pierce, a Goldman managing director, whose prosecution-envisaged role was to emphasize to the jury the level of confidentiality wrapped around the Warren Buffett $5 billion deal. Pierce was watching a baseball game on 21 September 2008 when he got a call on his mobile phone that a management committee meeting had been called.

The problem was that he was at the New York Yankees stadium, along with 50,000 cheering fans.

'What was the significance of being there on that day?' asked a prosecutor.

Interjected Judge Rakoff, a devoted Yankees fan: 'As opposed to the significance of being there on any other day?'

But there was some special significance, Pierce revealed. It was the last game that would be played at that stadium; the Yankees were moving to a new one.

Pierce had got up from his seat, run out of the stands and found an empty janitor's closet where he took the call. The committee discussed Goldman's $10 billion fundraising plan and various strategic options. 'It was extremely confidential,' Pierce said on the witness stand.

When the call was over, he said, he walked out of the closet and went back to his seat to tell his cousin (who had accompanied him to the game) that he had to leave. He caught a taxi back to Goldman's offices. The next two days, he said, were spent working round the clock to get the deal done.

During cross-examination, the defence showed the jury an email, to bolster its argument that the Buffett investment may not have remained as secret as Pierce was claiming. At 5.08 p.m. on 23 September, nearly an hour before Goldman went public with the news, Pierce sent an email to his lawyer, David Scherl at the firm of Morrison Cohen, telling him that he should keep an eye on the financial wires for a major announcement. 'Watch the tape,' he wrote. 'Hard work pays off.'

Moments after Goldman made its announcement, at 5.50 p.m, Scherl replied: 'I am psyched for YOU, STUD […] well done. Well done. Feel proud, Buddy.'

The Most Outrageous CEO

IN APRIL 2008, A FEW DAYS AFTER GUPTA RETURNED FROM his trip to the Middle East to raise funds for Galleon, Heather Webster, managing director, JP Morgan Private Client Services, visited him at his home in Wesport, Connecticut, for a routine review and estate planning session. Gupta had been her client for quite a few years. Five months after the visit, the September 2008 issue of *Institutional Investor News* magazine would list thirty-five-year-old Webster as one of the twenty rising stars of wealth management in the United States. According to the magazine, she was at that time handling about $500 million of assets for forty high-net-worth clients and had increased the value of their assets by about 20 per cent in three years.

The prosecution at Rajat Gupta's trial wanted Webster to tell the jury how wealthy Gupta was at the time he was allegedly indulging in securities fraud with Rajaratnam.

According to Webster's notes from the meeting, Gupta's personal net worth at that time was $84.1 million, including $11.2 million in cash. He had also set up an irrevocable trust worth $38.6 million. Gupta had received quarterly payments totalling $6 million from McKinsey in 2008 and was set to receive $2.5 million a year in 2009, 2010 and 2011 from the firm. In addition to this, he was receiving about $700,000 a year at the time as a member of Goldman's board, as well as $300,000 a year each from two other companies where he was a director. He was also slated to receive $500,000 a year for serving on the board of a Russian bank, Webster said.

Webster's testimony was no surprise to anyone in the courtroom. It was common knowledge that Gupta was an extremely wealthy man (though nowhere near as stratospherically wealthy as Rajaratnam had been). One of the main arguments of Gupta's defence team right from the beginning had been that, given his wealth, he could have no financial motive in passing on insider information to the Galleon boss. But the prosecutors were less interested in Webster's calculation of Gupta's assets than in one particular sentence of the notes she had taken that day at his home.

The lines read: 'Chairman Galleon International, $1.3 billion, 15 per cent owner, invests in long/short equity in Asia, entitled to performance fees.'

Again, as we know, Gupta was certainly not chairman of Galleon International at that time—nor, for that matter, ever. But Webster's notes seemed to indicate that Gupta was certain that he would get the chairmanship and a hefty equity stake in the fund.

The prosecution presented this to the jury as further proof that Gupta hoped to gain financially from his association with Rajaratnam. Even if he had not made any money out of Rajaratnam, he thought he would, in the future. So there was a motive for his alleged crimes, and a quid pro quo.

Gupta's defence team had tried to prevent the government from using Webster as a witness. It had argued—outside the presence of the jury—that Webster's notes should not be admitted because they could give the jurors a false impression about Gupta's dealings with Galleon. Gupta's lawyers' stand had always been that he had an informal association with Galleon and no formal arrangement was ever reached. Judge Rakoff, however, ruled that the testimony could be introduced.

During cross-examination, Webster told the jury that at that meeting Gupta had revealed to her his intention of giving away 80 per cent of his assets to charity. But when the defence tried to raise the issue of Gupta's many philanthropic activities once more, Judge Rakoff prohibited any testimony on that, saying evidence regarding that would be prejudicial. 'The annals of white collar crime in this district are filled with people who wanted to make themselves respected, powerful members of society by giving to charity,' he said.

◆

In the afternoon, it was time for Anil Kumar to take the stand.

According to a Reuters report, as Anil Kumar walked to the stand, 'Gupta…raised his eyebrows as he turned to his wife and daughters in the gallery.' This was his protégé and family friend, and he would now be testifying against Gupta.

Kumar said he began working closely with Gupta in 1997 when they started work on setting up the Indian School of Business. He said he introduced Gupta to Rajaratnam, who made an anonymous donation of $1 million to the school.

In 2006, according to Kumar, Gupta told him that he wanted to start an investment fund after he retired from McKinsey the following year. Gupta 'wanted to create the best asset management company in Asia, as good as the ones in America, but this would be focused on India,' Kumar said. It was Gupta, then, who suggested that Rajaratnam would be an obvious person to contact about the new venture, since he was South Asian and was running one of America's biggest hedge funds.

Kumar got Gupta and his former Wharton Business School classmate together, and Rajaratnam was excited by the proposal. 'They both had a joint aspiration to raise about $2 billion for the fund,' Kumar said.

Then Kumar told the jury that in 2007 he, Gupta and Rajaratnam met many times to discuss the fund. The meetings took place behind closed doors in Rajaratnam's office, which was separated from Galleon's trading floor by a sliding glass partition. A prosecutor asked Kumar to describe the trading floor.

'It was noisy, a lot of people screaming and shouting,' said Kumar, 'and sounding pretty high-testosterone.'

The fund that they were hoping to start was to be called

Galleon Global Group, or G3, which would be an arm of Galleon, with one unit dedicated to making private equity investments and another that would operate as a hedge fund focusing on South Asia. According to Kumar, Gupta's planned role in the venture was seen as that of 'a sponsor, a wise man, a strategy person, a raiser of funds, those kinds of things'. But G3 never saw the light of day. Instead, it became Taj Capital, which later morphed into New Silk Route.

New Silk Route managed to raise just around $1 billion in capital. According to Kumar, this dissatisfied Rajaratnam, who pulled out of the venture. However, he had invested $50 million of his own money in the fund, and New Silk Route began operations from Galleon's offices.

The lawyers were not finished with Kumar when court adjourned. However, his testimony the next day would be drowned out in the media because it was also the day that Lloyd Craig Blankfein, chairman and CEO of Goldman Sachs, made his appearance in the courtroom as a prosecution witness. Since the financial crisis of 2008, the fifty-six-year-old Blankfein, born into a lower middle class Jewish family in New York City and currently estimated to be worth at least $450 million, had been the most visible face of US investment banking. Depending on whom one spoke to, he represented either the worst of Wall Street greed, or was the smartest financial operator on the planet.

However, what Kumar told the court on his second day in the witness stand, as the media throngs waited outside to catch Blankfein arriving, would turn out to be a significant factor for the jury to bring a guilty verdict against Gupta. Gupta's attorneys had consistently argued that Gupta and Rajaratnam had had a falling out after Gupta had lost his entire $10 million investment in the Voyager Fund in the September 2008 stock market crash.

As mentioned in Chapter Five, Gupta squarely blamed Rajaratnam for this debacle. And the knowledge that Rajaratnam had pulled out a significant chunk of his own money in Voyager just before disaster struck, without informing Gupta, had disillusioned him about his 'close friend' and made him bitter. Therefore, Gupta's lawyers contended, Gupta would hardly be passing on inside information to Rajaratnam just days after he had seen his money vaporize.

But Kumar testified that according to what Rajaratnam had told him, the falling out between the two had happened in February or March 2009. If what Kumar was saying was true, the two would have still been on the best of terms when Gupta called Rajaratnam after the Goldman Sachs board meetings. Gupta would have been unaware at that time of Rajaratnam's betrayal and the fate of his investments.

Later, the testimony of defence witnesses would contradict what Kumar said about this crucial timeline—when Gupta fell out with Rajaratnam. The exact timing of the break-up of the friendship would remain somewhat of a mystery. The only aspect of this matter that would be beyond all doubt would be that even if Gupta had passed on tips to Rajaratnam, he had never made any money out of it. Indeed, his association with the Galleon boss had seen him lose a lot of money.

Kumar left the courthouse virtually unnoticed. It was now time for Lloyd C. Blankfein to take the stand.

Blankfein took over as Goldman CEO in 2006 after President George W. Bush chose Henry Paulson as US Secretary of the Treasury. (As mentioned earlier, Paulson and Gupta had worked together to set up a business school in China; everyone in this elite circle seemed connected to one another in some way.) Blankfein had been ranked No. 1 by *Forbes* magazine (25 November 2009) in its list of 'The Most Outrageous CEOs of 2009' (Rajaratnam came in third). 'And last but not least: the divine Lloyd Blankfein, chairman and chief executive officer of Goldman Sachs,' read the magazine's acerbic comment on its chosen top dog. 'Despite bearing scant resemblance to, say, Mother Teresa, the Pope or the Dalai Lama, Blankfein told the *Sunday Times* of London in

November that he was just a banker doing "God's work". He later said he meant it as a joke, but he certainly pays himself as if he were accomplishing something greater than human. In 2007, he made $73 million, and only $25 million in 2008, as the economy tanked, but look for a recovery in his compensation this year as Goldman Sachs has recovered far ahead of the economy as a whole. In honour of the modesty of his pronouncement, we lift him to the celestial height of No. 1 on our list of CEO outrages of 2009.' Comedian Stephen Colbert pointed out that Blankfein never specified which god, and speculated that it was perhaps Shiva, Lord of Destruction.

But while *Forbes* was outraged, *The Financial Times* (23 December 2009) named Blankfein as its '2009 Person of the Year', explaining that 'his bank has...unashamedly taken advantage of the low interest rates and diminished competition resulting from the crisis to make big trading profits'. Obviously, these were the very reasons why Blankfein featured high on so many hate lists.

Testifying before the Financial Crisis Inquiry Commission, an independent body set up in 2009 by the US legislature to 'examine the causes, domestic and global, of the current financial and economic crisis in the United States', Blankfein said that he considered Goldman Sachs as primarily a market maker, not as a creator of the sub-prime mortgage-related securities that led to the US financial and housing market collapse. In other words, Goldman's job was to sell, not bother about what it was selling.

Indeed, as it later became public, Goldman went far beyond that. Not only did it create just such a product, it sold it even when fully aware that investing in the product could ruin the buyer. In April 2010 the SEC sued Goldman for fraudulent selling of a synthetic CDO (collateral debt obligation, a derivative that was a major contributor to the crash) that Goldman had developed and marketed.

According to the SEC, in early 2007 the bank created and sold a CDO called Abacus, linked to sub-prime mortgages, without disclosing to buyers that hedge fund Paulson & Co., a

Goldman client, helped pick the underlying securities and bet against Abacus. Paulson & Co. made a billion dollars, while other Goldman clients, who bought Abacus, were left holding the can. 'The product was new and complex but the deception and conflicts are old and simple,' the SEC stressed. 'Goldman wrongly permitted a client that was betting against the mortgage market to heavily influence which mortgage securities to include in an investment portfolio, while telling other investors that the securities were selected by an independent, objective third party.'

Soon after this, at a hearing before the US Senate, Blankfein shrugged it all off by saying that he did not believe Goldman had any moral or legal obligation to inform its clients that it was betting against the products which they were buying from the bank. In reply to Senator Carl Levin's question whether the bank would disclose its position 'when they're buying something you solicit them to buy, and then you're taking a position against them', Blankfein said: 'I don't believe there is any obligation [to tell investors]. I don't think we'd have to tell them, I don't think we'd even know ourselves.'

Goldman Sachs received $10 billion of US taxpayer aid during the financial crisis (it paid the sum back with interest in June 2009), and also $12.9 billion as part of the government rescue package for collapsing insurance firm AIG. As profits soared in 2009, the media keenly reported on how much the bank was stashing away at the end of each quarter in its bonus pool for staff. The amounts—it had $16.7 billion in its bonus kitty by the end of the third quarter, translating to an average of more than half a million dollars per employee—seemed staggering in the midst of the worst economic crisis that had hit the US in eighty years.

Naturally, there was widespread public outrage. 'Is Goldman Evil?' asked *New York* magazine on its cover (26 July 2009). Earlier in the month, in *Rolling Stone* magazine (13 July 2010), writer Matt Taibbi had described Goldman Sachs as a 'great vampire squid wrapped around the face of humanity, relentlessly jamming its blood funnel into anything that smells like money'.

Goldman posted a record $13.4 billion profit in 2009. But faced with a public relations disaster, it slashed bonuses for the fourth quarter, pegging the aggregate sum at $16.2 billion (expectations had risen to $22 billion), and made a $500 million contribution to Goldman Sachs Gives, the firm's charitable arm.

In November 2011, Blankfein was listed as No. 43 on *Forbes* magazine's list of The World's Most Powerful People. But Taibbi's 'vampire squid' label had stuck. In December 2011, Occupy Wall Street protesters dressed up like giant squids and marched on the bank's New York headquarters, bearing signs that read: 'Goldman Sachs consumes'.

On 14 March 2012, Greg Smith, a Goldman Sachs executive director who had worked at the bank for twelve years, resigned through an open letter published in *The New York Times*. Citing a 'decline in the moral fibre' under 'the current chief executive officer, Lloyd C. Blankfein, and the president, Gary D. Cohn, [who had] lost hold of the firm's culture', he spoke of a 'toxic and destructive environment' where the only thing that mattered was making money. Senior executives referred to their own clients as 'muppets' and went out to 'hunt elephants'—which in the bank's lingo meant: 'get your clients...to trade whatever will bring the biggest profit to Goldman'. Smith added: 'It makes me ill how callously people talk about ripping their clients off' and hoped that his letter 'can be a wake-up call to the board of directors'.

While Goldman Sachs issued a public statement saying that it disagreed with Smith's portrayal of the firm and that 'in our view, we will only be successful if our clients are successful', Blankfein and Cohn sent out a mail to all employees, expressing their disappointment at reading 'the assertions made by this individual that do not reflect our values, our culture and how the vast majority of people at Goldman Sachs think about the firm and the work it does on behalf of our clients'.

So, here was Lloyd Blankfein at the United States District

Court for the Southern District of New York. To avoid the media, he had obtained special permission to drive his car into a parking garage below the building and enter through the basement. This was his second visit to the courthouse as a witness in fifteen months. The first time had been at Rajaratnam's trial, in a courtroom three floors up, directly above the one where Gupta's trial was being conducted.

At Rajaratnam's trial, the prosecutors had played the tape of Gupta's conversation of 29 July 2008 with Rajaratnam, in which he told the Galleon boss that the Goldman Sachs board had discussed the acquisition of a bank or an insurance firm. Blankfein had testified that by doing so, Gupta had violated the investment bank's confidentiality policies. He had said that it was important for Goldman directors not to disclose private discussions about the publicly-traded bank's business. 'We don't want information about our company to get out until it's appropriate,' he had told the jury. Premature disclosure, he had explained, inhibits the free exchange of ideas among directors, who might otherwise fear that what they say privately could become public.

There was no doubt in anyone's mind that he would say the same today.

'But Judge Rakoff, who has grown increasingly frustrated over the slow pace of the trial, tried to liven up the proceedings,' reported *The New York Times*. 'After the judge's deputy swore in Mr Blankfein, a prosecutor took him through a series of biographical questions. Mr Blankfein, the son of a postal worker, said he was raised in East New York, Brooklyn, and attended Thomas Jefferson High School before graduating from Harvard. The prosecutor then turned to his career at Goldman, skipping over his stint as a lawyer.

'Judge Rakoff seized upon the omission and interrupted the questioning. "I'm sure you want to hide the fact that the witness is a lawyer," Judge Rakoff said to the prosecutor. He turned to Mr Blankfein.

'"Did you go to law school?" the judge asked the witness.

'Mr Blankfein said that he had, and that he had once worked as a corporate tax lawyer for four-and-a-half years. (He graduated from Harvard Law School in 1978 and practised at Donovan, Leisure, Newton & Irvine in New York.)

'"But then you got religion and moved on," said Judge Rakoff, eliciting laughter in the courtroom.

'"It was a mutual decision," said Mr Blankfein, breaking into a smile.'

That was about all that the court had time for on that Monday. In fact, right from the day the trial began, the two sets of lawyers had perhaps spent more time arguing with each other than in examining witnesses. They had repeatedly had the jurors removed from the courtroom so they could present their disputes on minor details and technical issues to the judge. At several points during this endless quibbling, Judge Rakoff had lost his patience and complained angrily about the lawyers 'arguing every point to the nth degree'. He had tried as best as he could to hurry up the proceedings, but the lawyers were intractable. So Blankfein would have to come back to complete his testimony.

This caused a bit of a problem. The court was taking a day off on Tuesday because Judge Rakoff was scheduled to deliver a speech in Washington. And the day after, Blankfein wanted to attend his daughter's high school graduation ceremony and then have a celebratory lunch at the town of Yonkers in Westchester County bordering New York City. It would be hard, he said, to get to the courthouse in time. So it was agreed that the trial would resume on Wednesday, but Blankfein would return to the witness stand on Thursday.

◆

The questions that the prosecution put to Blankfein on Thursday ran along the expected lines, as did his answers. He reconfirmed the confidentiality of board meeting discussions, because they were 'potentially market-moving with respect to our stock'. He reiterated that Gupta talking about Goldman Sachs considering buying a bank was a violation of that confidentiality. He was then handed over to Gary Naftalis for cross-examination.

Naftalis started off on a light note, going over ground that the prosecution had already covered about Blankfein's career, ending with him becoming chief executive of Goldman in 2006. 'You became the No. 1 person at Goldman Sachs,' said Naftalis.

'Chairman and chief executive is my official title,' Blankfein replied with a smile. 'No. 1's not an official title.'

Naftalis then asked Blankfein whether Gupta had planned to resign from the Goldman board in September 2008. Blankfein confirmed this. He also confirmed that Gupta had told him that he planned to join private equity firm Kohlberg Kravis Roberts and that this could lead to conflicts of interest. In fact, Blankfein had initially accepted his resignation, he told the jury, and Goldman had prepared a news release on Gupta's departure, praising his contribution to the bank as a board member. Goldman even gifted Gupta a pair of cufflinks as a token of its gratitude for his service.

Then suddenly, everything changed. Lehman Brothers went bankrupt and the US financial markets were plunged into deep crisis. It became extremely important for Goldman, Blankfein testified, to project a sense of stability. The resignation of a board member, even if entirely unconnected with the bank's financial health or the larger market problems, could send out just the sort of signals that Goldman did not need. Blankfein persuaded Gupta to stay on. This was what Naftalis had been leading up to. He wanted, in effect, Blankfein to acknowledge to the jury that Gupta had been a valued member of the board.

The lawyer had more questions to ask Blankfein, but it was five in the evening and the court had to break for the day. The most powerful investment banker in the world would have to postpone his return to his perch on Wall Street for another day. But he managed to maintain a cheerful façade. Which was not true of Judge Rakoff, who looked like he was close to boiling point.

Naftalis spent much of the next day cross-examining Blankfein. However, as had become the norm in the trial, there were a myriad technical issues raised by the prosecution team, and much time was spent on sorting these out.

The defence's aim was to establish that what Gupta had told Rajaratnam about the Goldman board discussing the possible purchase of a commercial bank was not 'material nonpublic information' under the insider trading laws. Naftalis produced two July 2008 reports by analysts at investment banks Merrill Lynch and Oppenheimer. In both cases, the authors had met top Goldman executives while preparing their reports. Both mentioned the prospect of Goldman buying a retail bank. The Merrill Lynch report was headlined: 'Goldman Sachs Bank and Trust? Don't Rule it Out.'

The point Naftalis wanted to stress to the jury was that what Gupta had told Rajaratnam on 29 July 2008 was hardly a secret. Analysts were writing about it, quite possibly based on what Goldman Sachs executives had revealed to them.

'Items that your senior management [discuss] are no longer confidential under Goldman's confidentiality agreements?' asked Naftalis.

'Yes,' Blankfein had to agree.

Naftalis then came to the next Goldman board meeting whose proceedings Gupta had allegedly tipped Rajaratnam about. In fact, it had been a 'posting call', one of those that independent director William George had referred to in his testimony a few days before. Naftalis said that on that same day (23 October 2008) Goldman Sachs had also announced that it was firing more than 3,000 people, a full 10 per cent of its workforce. Blankfein testified that he could not recall anything about that.

Naftalis produced a copy of *The Wall Street Journal* that carried a story about the dramatic downsizing. 'I don't even know that it's true, I just know the article says that,' Blankfein said blandly, after taking a look at the paper. He had played into

Naftalis's hands. The lawyer presented a transcript of a voicemail Blankfein had sent Goldman employees the day of the newspaper report (23 October 2008), confirming the layoffs. What Naftalis wanted to suggest to the jury was that Blankfein's memory of events was unreliable, so his testimony could be flawed.

By the time Blankfein was allowed to leave the court, he had spent nearly three whole days there, without access to his cell phone or BlackBerry. 'It had to have been among the least productive weeks of Lloyd C. Blankfein's six-year tenure as the chief executive of Goldman Sachs,' commented *The New York Times* (8 June 2012). 'Though Mr Blankfein appeared at ease in the courtroom, he had to clear his busy calendar. He could not monitor the volatility in the financial markets. He could not even check his BlackBerry, to which he has acknowledged something of an addiction. In short, he could not do his job. Instead, Mr Blankfein, who has spent most of his career in the fast-paced environment of a trading floor, had to sit still on the witness stand and respond to hours of often-monotonous questions. Lawyers on both sides had him discuss Goldman's inner workings, from the contents of board meetings to his relationship with his lieutenants.'

On the same day, columnist David Levine wrote in huffingtonpost.com: 'At times during his days in court, Blankfein was left sitting on the witness stand while the judge, prosecution and defence lawyers engaged in lengthy sidebar conversations to decide procedural matters. These moments were particularly awkward, since Blankfein—with cell phones banned from the courtroom—had no choice but to sit on the stand, silently facing the jury and audience. At times, Blankfein would sit for upwards of fifteen minutes, looking around the room and grinning widely. On his way out of the courtroom on Friday, the Wall Street titan said he was happy to have finished. "There's only so many times you can count the number of stars [on the courtroom flags]," he said.'

The Unluckiest Man in the Whole World

DURING THE ONE DAY OF THE TRIAL BETWEEN BLANKFEIN'S first and second appearance in the court (when he was attending his daughter's graduation), the prosecution had focused on Gupta's involvement in Voyager Capital Partners. He had invested $5 million when Voyager was set up in 2005 and later exercised an option he had had and put in another $5 million. But the 2008 market collapse wiped out his investment. The prosecution called several witnesses, including former Galleon employees, to testify and piece together what happened at Voyager.

Voyager was a so-called fund-of-funds that invested in several Galleon funds. Some of these funds had investments in Goldman Sachs. Therefore, the prosecution was implying, Gupta stood to gain financially by passing on secret Goldman information to Rajaratnam.

Voyager performed brilliantly at first, returning about 41 per cent annually in its first couple of years. But in the months before the crash of 2008, the $400 million fund had badly overextended itself by taking bets on future movements of stocks worth far more than the cash it had. The bets turned sour as the financial crisis hit, and the fund collapsed because it just couldn't pay up.

At the end of 2007, Gupta and Rajaratnam got into a dispute over the value of Gupta's stake in Voyager. Rajaratnam felt that the profits on Gupta's second $5 million investment should be calculated from the day he had exercised his option to up his stake and put in the money. Gupta, however, insisted that his share should be computed from the date of the inception of the fund. If one used Rajaratnam's methodology, Gupta's stake worked out to about $12.5 million, while by Gupta's logic it was

$16.4 million. In the end, Rajaratnam gave in and agreed to the higher figure.

The prosecution was determined to cover every detail in the dispute, including the complex calculations. Many documents were produced, witnesses were asked to validate them and explain their arcane nuances to the jury. This took up the entire day. By the time court adjourned, the jury's eyes had glazed over, and Judge Rakoff had described the proceedings as 'excruciating'.

The next day, before Blankfein was called to the stand, government witness James Barnacle Jr, an FBI agent, took the jury through a long series of charts that summarized all the evidence that the prosecution had presented—the timelines, the phone call records, the trades made by Galleon and the supposed illegal profits that it had made on these trades, the dates when the information Galleon was alleged to have traded on the basis of became public, and so on.

During cross-examination, defence lawyer David Frankel produced the details of two money-losing Goldman and Procter & Gamble trades that Galleon had made after Gupta had allegedly tipped off Rajaratnam. Frankel pointed out that the FBI's charts were misleading, since they did not document any loss-making trades that Galleon had made. 'So you made charts for trading profits but not for losses, correct?' Frankel asked Barnacle. 'No, I did not,' the FBI agent said.

Once Blankfein's testimony was over, the government had no more witnesses to call. But as a final set of evidence, the prosecution played several secretly recorded voicemail messages left by Gupta on Rajaratnam's cell phone. In one of these messages (on 10 October 2008) Gupta says: 'Hey Raj, Rajat here. Just calling to catch up. I know it must be an awful and busy week. I hope you are holding up well. Uh, and I'll try to give you a call over the weekend just to catch up. All the best to you, talk to you soon. Bye bye.'

Gupta's lawyers had been arguing from the outset that by

October 2008, his relations with Rajaratnam were extremely strained, following the Voyager fiasco. Why then was Gupta sounding so friendly on the voicemail?

Lead prosecutor Reed Brodsky now rested the government's case.

◆

There was still about an hour of court time left. Rajat Gupta's defence used that to show the jury the videotaped deposition of Ajit Jain, a top Berkshire Hathaway executive. There were several similarities between the stories of Gupta and Jain. Both were India-born, had studied engineering at IIT and then done an MBA from Harvard Business School. Like Gupta, Jain had also joined McKinsey from Harvard. Today, he runs Berkshire's massive reinsurance operations, and is widely tipped to succeed Warren Buffett at the helm when the Sage of Omaha, who is now in his eighties, decides to retire.

Describing his relationship with Gupta as 'completely social', Jain spoke about a lunch they'd had in January 2009 at Stamford, Connecticut, where Jain is based, during the course of which Gupta had told him about his falling out with Rajaratnam. 'He told me that he had $10 million invested and he had been gypped, swindled and cheated by Raj and had lost his $10 million,' said Jain. He said he was 'shocked' to hear of this and the conversation 'left [him] with the impression' that it was not just a bad investment or loss of money but 'deliberate hanky-panky on the part of Rajaratnam'. He also acknowledged, in response to a query by Gary Naftalis, that it was 'unusual' for Gupta to tell him about his investment losses.

Naftalis had now established for the jury the acrimony between Gupta and Rajaratnam, and from an unimpeachable source. But the conversation Jain had reported had taken place in January 2009, several months after the last time Gupta had allegedly tipped off Rajaratman. Anil Kumar had testified that

Rajaratnam had given him the impression that the falling out occurred sometime in February or March 2009. Clearly, it had taken place earlier. But the defence had not yet been able to present any evidence that it had happened early enough to exonerate Gupta.

Late in the evening, after court had adjourned, Gary Naftalis told the media that it was 'highly likely' that Gupta would testify in his own defence in the coming week.

On the next day of hearings, Gupta's defence team produced several witnesses to testify to his character. Ashok Alexander, a former McKinsey colleague who now headed the Bill & Melinda Gates Foundation in India, had flown in from Delhi. Another witness was Anil Sood, a former senior World Bank executive who had known Gupta for more than half a century, having been his classmate in school since fifth grade and then at IIT Delhi. Soon after Gupta was indicted, Sood had written a long piece on friendsofrajat.com, expressing his confidence that 'Rajat will emerge successfully from this totally uncalled-for ordeal and go on to do what he has done all his life—being a good human being, helping others, and contributing to make the world a better place.'

'I have admired Rajat—always—and my admiration for him has grown over the years,' he wrote. 'His respect for all human beings comes through in every aspect of his personal and professional life… He has always been a person of the highest integrity and stood up for what is right… What Anita, Rajat and the family have endured in recent months is grossly unfair and unjust—a lifetime of achievement maligned by unproven hearsay. The picture of him that has been painted by some is simply NOT of the Rajat I have known well for half a century. The situation has been very difficult for his family and also for all of us friends who care for him deeply. Rajat, supported by his family, has shown tremendous grace and dignity in the face of this most difficult challenge of his life.' In his testimony in Judge Rakoff's court, he said that Gupta 'inspires trust and confidence'.

During cross-examination, prosecutor Reed Brodsky asked both Alexander and Sood if they had known about any investments or business dealings that Gupta had had with Rajaratnam. They said they had not.

More important, in terms of pure information, was the testimony of Suprotik Basu, a public health specialist who is a UN envoy on matters related to malaria, and who had been with Gupta on 23 September 2008, the day he allegedly called Rajaratnam and told him about Warren Buffett's investment in Goldman Sachs.

How did he first meet Gupta, asked Naftalis.

'[In January 2008] I got an urgent call that a businessman wanted to end all childhood deaths from malaria by 2025,' said Basu.

A prosecutor jumped to his feet and objected. The objection was sustained.

Naftalis used Basu to walk the jury through Gupta's busy calendar on that fateful day. Gupta and Basu had met at five in the evening, an hour or so after the Goldman Sachs board meeting had wound up. They'd had a conference with Julian Schweitzer, the World Bank's head of health nutrition, and Raymond G. Chambers, the United Nations special envoy for malaria. Basu then accompanied Gupta to a dinner honouring the health minister of Ethiopia at a midtown Manhattan restaurant.

Basu told the jury that he had seen Gupta many times with a 'earpiece in his ear, constantly returning phone calls between meetings'. This fitted in with Gupta's lawyers' argument that given the packed schedule that characterized a typical day for Gupta, it was his normal practice to use breaks between meetings to make and return phone calls. So there was nothing unusual or suspicious about him calling Rajaratnam right after the Goldman board meeting ended.

Naftalis asked Basu whether he had heard Gupta referring to Goldman Sachs or Warren Buffett that day. He had not.

The prosecution now went over the phone records again for the jury—the records showed that Gupta and Rajaratnam had spoken to each other at least six times on that day, including the fifty-six-second conversation right after the Goldman board meeting.

Brodsky asked Basu if he was present for that call. Basu said he wasn't.

Late in the day, Gupta's eldest daughter Geetanjali took the stand.

The thirty-three-year-old Geetanjali told the jury that she was an alumnus of Harvard College, Harvard Business School and Harvard Law School, and worked for the Harvard Management Company, which oversees the investment of the university's endowment.

But that was about all that she could tell the jury that day. Naftalis began asking her about a conversation she had had with her father in 2008 about his troubles with Rajaratnam, and the prosecution objected to the line of questioning. After some bickering, Judge Rakoff decided to hear out the defence and prosecution in a private conference. Geetanjali would have to continue her testimony the next day.

After listening to the arguments from both sides about what she could say, Judge Rakoff ruled that Geetanjali could testify about her observations of her father's reaction to his Galleon involvement, but she was not permitted to recount statements Gupta had made to her.

The defence had by now clarified that Rajat Gupta would not testify. *The Financial Times* quoted Judge Rakoff as saying, of the defence's decision to call Geetanjali instead: 'It's a bit of a gimmick.' However, he then added that 'it's within their tactical right'.

Of Geetanjali's testimony, a *The New York Times* (12 June 2012) journalist noted admiringly: 'Geetanjali Gupta's education at Harvard Law School may not have included a class on how to testify, but she was poised and articulate in answering questions on the witness stand on Tuesday at her father's criminal trial.'

Geetanjali told the jury that she was at her parents' house at Westport, Connecticut, on 20 September 2008, three days before the Goldman Sachs board meeting on the Berkshire investment. She was sitting in the library with her father when he spoke to her about his problematic $10 million investment in Voyager. 'He was upset,' said Geetanjali. 'He was running his hand through his hair, as he often does when he is stressed… He is usually a very calm and collected person.'

The defence showed the jury an email from October 2008 that she had sent her father asking for his help in landing her friend a job at the Dell family foundation. In the mail, which began 'Hi Baba', the Bengali word for 'father', she asked: 'How bad are things with the Raj fund?'

By Thanksgiving—or late November that year—Geetanjali said, the whole family was discussing the investment. She said that her father was 'depressed, withdrawn and not himself'.

This is how *The New York Times* described her cross-examination:

On cross-examination, Reed Brodsky, a prosecutor known for histrionics in the courtroom, reduced his voice to almost a whisper. He asked her two questions.

"Do you love your father?"

"Yes," she replied.

"Would you do anything for your father?"

"I would do anything for my father, but I would not lie, though, on the stand," she said.

Brodsky retreated. Geetanjali returned to her seat in the first row of the visitors' gallery. When the jury left the courtroom, she went up to her father. For nearly three weeks, Rajat Gupta had sat with his lawyers, his ruggedly handsome face never betraying any emotions. But as he stood up to gather his daughter in his arms in a loving embrace, his eyes welled up with tears.

Over three days, the defence had summoned a dozen witnesses, but most of them had been called to tell the jury that they believed Gupta to be a person of unshakeable integrity, and to mention his tireless commitment to a dizzying number of philanthropic causes. In the final analysis, other than Geetanjali's testimony, the principal thrust of the defence's case had been that a jury could not convict a man of such impeccable credentials in personal, professional and public life on the basis of evidence that was, whichever way you looked at it, circumstantial.

◆

For the prosecution, Assistant US Attorney Richard Tarlowe did the summation of arguments. He told the jury the government's story all over again, distilled from phone records, minutes of board meetings, trading records, and masses of email. He displayed charts that showed the sequence of events—Gupta participating in board meetings of Goldman Sachs and Procter & Gamble, Gupta calling Rajaratnam, Galleon buying or shorting shares to make quick profits. These were not coincidences, he told the jurors.

On 23 September 2008 there was only one call made to Rajaratnam's work phone in the final ten minutes of trading, 'and that call was from Gupta,' said Tarlowe. 'That evidence is devastating.'

He replayed the wiretapped conversation of 24 September in which Rajaratnam gloats to a colleague that he was told at 3.58 p.m. that 'something good might happen to Goldman'.

Gupta was going to be chairman of Galleon International, Tarlowe said. In fact, he had started telling potential investors that he was chairman, even before the appointment had been officially made. He was going to start a new fund with Rajaratnam, where he would have a stake and a share of the 'extraordinary profits' that the fund would make, based on insider trading. 'Rajaratnam offered Gupta many benefits,' Tarlowe said. 'What was good for Rajaratnam and Galleon was good for Gupta.' Indeed, when they had a dispute about Gupta's stake in Voyager, the fund they had already set up together, Rajaratnam acceded to his demand and 'bumped up' his stake by $4 million. This was actually Gupta's reward for informing Rajaratnam about what went on at the board meetings he attended.

The witnesses whom the defence had called had known nothing about Gupta's relationship with Rajaratnam. 'Those witnesses shed absolutely no light,' said Tarlowe.

The defence would argue, Tarlowe told the jury, that this was all circumstantial evidence, but in this case circumstantial evidence was as strong as eyewitness testimony. The defence had been claiming that Gupta would never pass on tips to Rajaratnam after he had lost his $10 million investment in Voyager. The defence was wrong. There was even more incentive for Gupta to engage in an illicit relationship with the Galleon boss, said the prosecutor. It was simple. Gupta would want to recoup his losses, make his money back.

'Gupta abused his position as a corporate insider by providing secret company information to his long-time business partner and friend, Raj Rajaratnam,' said Tarlowe, his voice rising towards the end of his speech as he tried to impress upon the jury the seriousness of Gupta's crimes. These leaks allowed 'Rajaratnam and his criminal associates at Galleon' to make millions of dollars through illicit trades, he said, and there was 'overwhelming evidence' to support this.

In the defence summation, Naftalis repeatedly pointed out to the jury, as he and his team had throughout the trial, that the government had not been able to present any direct evidence. 'With all the power and majesty of the United States government, they found no real, hard, direct evidence,' he said. 'They didn't find any because it didn't happen.'

'The prosecution failed here to prove that Mr Gupta acted knowingly and wilfully and with any specific intent to defraud,' he said, going back to the essence of what Gupta had been charged with. No one had accused Gupta of trading illegally; there was no evidence that Rajaratnam was paying Gupta anything secretly; there was no witness at all to any of the tips the prosecution was claiming Gupta had given the hedge fund manager. 'No cash changing hands here,' Naftalis said. 'No dishonest dimes ending up in Mr Gupta's jacket.'

'As they say in that old commercial, where's the beef in this case?' the lawyer asked. 'If you put in a lot of paper, you give the illusion that you might have something more than you actually have—an illusion of making something out of nothing. That is a gambit that can bamboozle people into thinking something was proven when it wasn't.' Heaps of pointless paper and 'a parade of meaningless witnesses' was how Naftalis described the prosecution's case.

'We don't punish people for making mistakes, for being negligent, for trusting people, for not being smart enough to see through somebody that it took eight months of wiretaps for the government to find,' he said. Till his arrest, Rajaratnam was a star, a man admired by the business community for his success. No one knew that he was using dishonest means. Gupta had been deceived too, just as the rest of the world was. 'There was a secret world of Raj Rajaratnam that was unknown to Rajat Gupta,' said Naftalis. 'Our law does not make people criminals based on guilt by association.'

In the eight months that the FBI had tapped Rajaratnam's phones, the agency had not been able to catch a single conversation that in any way indicated that Gupta was involved in Rajaratnam's illegal activities. All the government had was some phone records, and 'there was no evidence of what was said in any conversation. There is not a single wiretap recording out of those thousands of wiretapped calls where Rajat Gupta gave any inside information. None, zero.' The most that the government had was some unreliable 'boasting' by Rajaratnam and 'second-or third-hand hearsay'.

What were the facts? One, that Rajaratnam had cheated Gupta on the Voyager deal; Galleon records showed that Rajaratnam had withdrawn a large sum of money from the fund without telling Gupta. Two, Gupta had wanted to step down from the Goldman Sachs board on 12 September 2008. This was before the phone calls Gupta made to Rajaratnam to supposedly give him insider tips. In fact, it was Goldman Sachs Chief Executive Officer Lloyd Blankfein who had convinced Gupta to stay on.

'This resignation drives a stake through the heart of the government's case,' Naftalis said. 'He resigned. They begged him to come back. The only reason that he stayed is because Goldman Sachs panicked, because Rajat Gupta is a prominent and respectable business leader. His resignation might cause panic in investors in a volatile market.'

And what about Blankfein? He was 'a man with no memory of anything' and had been 'less than candid'. Naftalis added: 'I suggest to you that no one could be that cold and callous and not remember that he fired 3,000 people, as if it happens every day. If you can't remember firing 3,000 people without any kind of notice, how can you pretend to remember anything about some posting call?'

Throughout his closing, Naftalis stressed that the government had the burden of proving its case beyond a reasonable doubt. If the government did not meet that high burden, he told the jury, 'It's your duty to say not guilty, or, as they say in Scotland, not proven.'

He ended his summation by talking about his visit to one of the oldest courthouses in England. Written on the walls of the basement, he recalled, were the words: 'In this hallowed place of justice, the Crown never loses because when the liberty of an Englishman is preserved against false witness, the Crown wins.'

'The United States,' Naftalis said, 'always wins when justice is done.'

The prosecution's rebuttal of the defence's closing arguments was done by Reed Brodsky. 'No one is above the law; neither his positions, power, money or good deeds give him the right to violate the law or give him a free pass for having violated it,' he said, describing Gupta and Rajaratnam as 'two men with public sides of success; but hidden, concealed from the public, was a different side, a side that committed crimes'.

If the jury had to believe what the defence had been saying, Brodsky contended, 'you'd have to believe that Gupta was the unluckiest man in the whole world'.

♦

The jury deliberated for slightly less than ten hours over two days. On 15 June it announced its verdict: Rajat Gupta was guilty of conspiracy and securities fraud on three counts of leaking confidential information relating to Goldman Sachs on three occasions in 2008. He was found not guilty of two charges of tipping Rajaratnam on Procter & Gamble.

After the verdict was read in the courtroom, Gupta maintained his stoic calm. His wife Anita buried her head in her hands. His daughters broke into tears.

What, however, was quite astonishing was that several jurors wept as they left the courtroom.

Naftalis immediately announced that his client would appeal the verdict. 'This is only Round One,' he said. 'Having lived a lifetime of honesty and integrity, he didn't turn into a criminal in the seventh decade of an otherwise praiseworthy life.'

Judge Rakoff set Gupta free on bail until his sentencing on 18 October (this was later brought forward by a day). Gupta was facing a maximum sentence of twenty-five years in prison.

Preet Bharara, US Attorney for the Southern District of New York, issued a triumphant statement that read: 'Rajat Gupta once stood at the apex of the international business community. Today, he stands convicted of securities fraud. He achieved remarkable success and stature, but he threw it all away. Having fallen from respected insider to convicted inside trader, Mr Gupta has now exchanged the lofty boardroom for the prospect of a lowly jail cell. Violating clear and sacrosanct duties of confidentiality, Mr Gupta illegally provided a virtual open line into the boardroom for his benefactor and business partner, Raj Rajaratnam.

'Almost two years ago, we said that insider trading is rampant, and today's conviction puts that claim into stark relief. It bears repeating that, in coordination with our extraordinary partners at the FBI, we will continue to pursue those who violate the securities laws, regardless of status, wealth, or influence. I thank the members of the jury for their time, attention, and service, and the dedicated career prosecutors from my office who so ably tried this case.'

Reported *The New York Times* on 15 June 2012: 'The case, which caps a wave of successful insider trading prosecutions over the last three years, is a significant victory for the government, which has penetrated some of Wall Street's most vaunted hedge funds and reached into America's most prestigious corporate boardrooms. It also demonstrated that prosecutors could win an insider trading case largely built on circumstantial evidence like phone records and trading logs. Previous convictions, as in the trial of Raj Rajaratnam, the hedge fund manager on the receiving end of Mr Gupta's assumed tips, have relied more heavily on the use of incriminating wiretaps.

'Mr Gupta is one of the sixty-six Wall Street traders and corporate executives charged with insider trading crimes by Mr Bharara since 2009. Of those, sixty have either pleaded guilty or been found guilty. Juries have convicted all seven defendants who have gone to trial.'

Yet, after having delivered the guilty verdict, some of the jurors seemed to feel emotionally drained. One of them, contacted by *The New York Times* over the phone, would only say that she was glad the trial was over. For, yes, the trial was over, but the central mystery remained unanswered in the heads of thousands of people, including some of the jurors. There was nothing at all in Gupta's life to indicate that he would knowingly commit a crime, indeed, knowingly even hurt another human being. Orphaned as a teenager, he had fought the odds to reach incredible heights, through sheer intelligence and hard work. And then he had devoted much of his formidable intellect and energy to solve the problems of the planet's underprivileged. Why would he do what he had now been pronounced guilty of?

As Richard Lepkowski, the jury's foreman, put it, Gupta 'was a wonderful example of the American dream'.

'We wanted to believe that the allegations weren't true, but at the end of the day the evidence was just overwhelming,' admitted Lepkowski. 'We looked at him and what he had done professionally. We were hoping he would walk out of this courthouse.' But, he said, 'on the counts we convicted, we felt there was enough circumstantial evidence that any reasonable person could make that connection.'

Lepkowski acknowledged that one of the questions that had troubled the jury was the crucial issue of motive. Gupta was already wealthy far beyond most people's dreams. He was respected across the world, both for his professional achievements and his unquestionable commitment to make the world a better place. Why would he throw it all away by passing on information like a sneak thief to Rajaratnam, a man who was intellectually, socially, culturally, indeed on every parameter other than net worth, inferior to him?

'I wouldn't say he was an unwilling participant, or that greed wasn't a part of this,' Lepkowski said. 'But I am saying that Mr Rajaratnam made it easy for Rajat Gupta to break the law.'

However, one of the jurors, Ronnie Sesso, was quite clear. 'What did Mr Gupta get by giving Raj this information?' she said. 'A need for greed.'

It all seemed bizarre.

In the course of writing this book, I spoke face-to-face, and over the phone, and communicated over email with more than a dozen people who had known Gupta well. Each and every one of them believed that Gupta was innocent. I personally know possibly another dozen who have met Gupta just once, maybe for no more than three minutes, and each had been struck by his unassuming demeanour. 'Amazingly down to earth' was the phrase I kept hearing when people spoke about him. Greed of any kind was something no one to whom I spoke could associate with him at all.

Had he really changed so much in the seventh decade of his life? Naftalis said that that was impossible—but the circumstantial evidence against him was quite phenomenal. In a wiretapped conversation, Rajaratnam had told Anil Kumar that he thought Gupta was 'tormented'. If so, what was he tormented about? Gupta's life had been distinguished throughout by a remarkable absence of moral confusion, of doubt about which was the righteous path at every bifurcation of the road. But after a lifetime of upright and courageous honesty, did he actually feel that the world had not rewarded him enough? Did he really, as Rajaratnam thought, want to join the billionaires' club?

Or was he the unluckiest man in the whole world?

The One That Got Away

IN A TELEPHONE CONVERSATION WITH GUPTA, RAJARATNAM had complained that he had never seen Anil Kumar laugh and 'be really happy'. But on 19 July, when Kumar came out of a New York court after his sentencing, he wore as wide a grin as is possible without tearing one's ears. Judge Denny Chin had sentenced him to two years on probation and fined him a paltry $25,000. He would, of course, also have to forfeit the $2.9 million that he had made from Rajaratnam for passing him inside information and that was parked in a Swiss bank account.

It was possibly the least punishment that could be handed out, without shocking the public, to a man who had done a deal with the prosecutors and sung like a canary.

While announcing the sentence, Judge Chin noted that he was 'persuaded that this was aberrational conduct and that Mr Kumar has led a law-abiding and productive life'.

The opening lines of the seventy-two-page document that Kumar's lawyers had filed in court, pleading for leniency were: 'Anil Kumar is a truly extraordinary man. But for his involvement with Mr Rajaratnam, he has led a life devoted to work, family and improving the lives of and opportunities for countless people in India and the United States.' It then goes on to detail how Kumar had, right from childhood, fought seemingly insurmountable odds to excel at everything he touched, how he had repeatedly sacrificed his personal happiness for the greater good, had bitten the bullet and soldiered on even after his employer McKinsey treated him unjustly, devoted his life to relentless philanthropy, and sought professional help to understand how he could have been led astray by an overweight Sri Lankan-origin criminal.

The document portrays a life beset with difficulties right from infancy. Unfortunately, many sections of this biography can only provoke a guffaw from any Indian, or lock-jawed amazement at the sheer misinformation or hypocrisy implicit in much of it.

Kumar's father worked for Shell India (which became Bharat Petroleum after it was nationalized in 1974) and as part of the job, had to frequently move cities. When the family found itself in Goa (which Kumar's lawyers described as 'an underdeveloped former Portuguese colony'), the ten-year-old Kumar 'persuaded his parents to let him apply for one of only a few openings available for gifted children at Doon School, a prestigious Indian boarding school'. Having been accepted, in 1970, he 'left his family to attend school almost a thousand miles from home'. Though all this is recounted as a sort of David Copperfield story, most Indians would recognize it as a pretty privileged childhood.

The document claims that, since Doon School at that time did not allow students to make phone calls, Kumar's only contact with his family in the five years he spent there was through mail. 'The school was so far from his parents' home' that his father came to visit him only once, and his mother and sister never. 'Yet, as would become a hallmark of his life, Anil embraced his circumstances and made the most of the opportunities offered him.' To say the least, it sounds rather strange that the family of an employee of a multinational company could not afford to visit their son for five years, nor have him over on vacations. If nothing else, surely, Kumar's father's job benefits included an annual leave travel allowance?

Kumar's lawyers quote from testimonials about his leadership spirit, integrity and compassion—'Anil provided us our moral compass'—from various schoolmates of his.

As we already know, Kumar was a brilliant student. He topped his class at Doon, got a double-digit rank in the IIT entrance test, and joined IIT Bombay. He worked hard at IIT and did very well academically. But that was hardly enough to satisfy his urge to better the world. 'During his IIT years, the world suffered through its first major energy crisis.' Well, actually, the first oil shock came in 1973, and Kumar was at IIT from 1975 to 1980, but let that be. 'At a relatively young age, Anil recognized that energy would be a major concern for the planet and that society needed to explore alternative means of providing energy. Thus, still embracing Doon School's call to be a "citizen of a global society", Anil aspired to do his share by studying and researching energy conservation during his senior years at IIT. He focused mainly on solar energy, believing it would be the most sustainable form of energy.' All of which, as any IITian would know, only means that his final-year project (mandatory for all engineering students) was on solar power.

When he was accepted by Wharton for its MBA programme, but without financial aid, 'Anil's family loaned him some initial tuition money'. Please remember, this is a family so impoverished that it could not visit him at his boarding school for five years. And one can be sure that if his parents had sold the family silver or their ancestral home to loan him the tuition money, Kumar's lawyers would not have failed to wax eloquent on that.

While at IIT, Kumar met his future wife Malvika. 'Malvika studied psychology in Bombay, thirty miles away from IIT. These thirty miles, which took Anil over two hours by bus, train and another bus, could not prevent Anil from trekking from IIT to Bombay to be with Malvika every single weekend for the five years he attended IIT.' This takes the proverbial cake, since that great heroic voyage of love has been performed by hundreds of thousands of Bombayites every day for decades. Besides, even if Malvika lived at the southern tip of Bombay, the distance from IIT would be twenty miles, not thirty. A 50 per cent error like that could have cost a McKinsey executive his job.

The lovebirds married in 1983, after Kumar graduated from Wharton, and had a son, Aman. The document, as released by the US government, has large sections blacked out here to protect

Aman's privacy, since he seems to have been a child with special needs. The next section that has been blacked out definitely alleges that Kumar's employer, McKinsey, made no concession for his family situation and slave-drove him. All we can read are fragments: 'McKinsey did not allow him time off and Anil had to work...', 'Anil balanced a highly demanding career at McKinsey...', 'Anil's 100-hour work weeks at McKinsey', 'Anil had straddled two stressful lives'. In 1993, Anil was given the option of going to New Delhi and starting McKinsey's India operations. The family moved to India, but Aman found it very difficult to adjust to the change. The Kumars returned to the US after five years. Malvika and Aman went first, but McKinsey insisted that Kumar stay back to complete his client commitments, and he could visit his family in California only semi-monthly in the nine months he had to stay on before he could relocate.

The details of Aman's childhood and later life have been censored out, except for the information that he turned out to be an exceptional student and joined Harvard Business School in September 2012. There is also a testimonial from Aman about what an extraordinary father Anil has been.

One of the most important hooks on which Kumar and his lawyers hang their plea for a lenient sentence is that Kumar's misdeeds have already hurt Aman enough, and a prison term for his father would cause him untold suffering. The sheer length of the sections relating to Aman that have been censored for the public indicates that Anil Kumar has tried to squeeze the maximum amount of sympathy for himself from his son's condition.

Nearly 15 per cent of the whole leniency plea document is about Anil Kumar's son, and how much he has suffered in his young life and how much more he will if Kumar goes to prison.

There is something distasteful about this.

A comparison may not be fair, but another defendant who pleaded guilty in the Galleon case, IBM executive Robert Moffat, did not bring up the fact that his wife has been suffering from multiple sclerosis for three decades and is nearly blind, to plead for leniency.

◆

After the Aman chapter, Kumar's leniency document moves on to the blame game. It claims that McKinsey gave him a raw deal for most of his career, repeatedly setting him near-impossible tasks, and then ignoring him even when he met those punishing targets. (The document also mentions that 'there is little in the way of letter documentation for the McKinsey years since once Anil was arrested, his former McKinsey colleagues were instructed to dissociate themselves from him'.)

First, Kumar was sent off to set up the firm's Silicon Valley business. He drove up and down the highways, noting down companies' names, pounded the pavements, made cold calls and expanded the office to thirty-five people in five years. After this, he was sent off to India. The document says that the offices were bare bones—a hotel room. The truth, however, is that McKinsey hired some of the most plush suites in one of New Delhi's most expensive hotels and the offices were exceedingly swanky.

'Projects in India were difficult to obtain because McKinsey partner rates were extremely high, especially by Indian standards. One week of a McKinsey engagement equalled the yearly salary of some Indian CEOs. Undeterred by what at times seemed like insurmountable odds, Anil worked long and arduous hours to develop the office. Slowly, but surely, Anil succeeded; he was able to prove his and McKinsey's worth to government agencies, multinational companies, and finally Indian companies themselves. As a result of his efforts, the New Delhi office began to flourish, eventually becoming McKinsey's largest Indian office.'

Independent observers have a very divergent view on this. Many believe that McKinsey's high rates were a careful strategy to create an uber-blue-chip image, and for many Indian business groups it soon became a status symbol to be a McKinsey client. Every week, in the mid- to late-1990s, financial dailies carried reports of a number of family-run business houses having hired McKinsey for developing long-trem strategies that were given titles like Vision 2020. The principal purpose seemed to have been to communicate to stakeholders and lenders that after the country's economic liberalization, Indian family-run businesses were changing their ways. The McKinsey stamp helped immensely in this essentially public relations exercise. It is very doubtful whether McKinsey's recommendations were either useful or even followed, in most cases.

'Anil believed his star was on the rise at McKinsey. He was, however, wrong. Although he had been promised his opportunity to run the Indian offices, McKinsey passed Anil over and chose a different partner to run India. This was a devastating blow to Anil's self-esteem amd professional future; he believed he had been deliberately misled by his superiors. Seeing no future in India, after working so hard for six years, in 1998, Anil returned to the United States. Had Anil received the promotion as promised, it is likely that the Kumar family would have relocated to Singapore, Hong Kong, or other neighbouring country (censored). Anil would have, essentially, commuted to and from India, a common practice among other Asian professionals at the time.'

This rather contradicts the argument presented previously, that the Kumars went back to the US because Aman could not adjust to India. And if Anil hated being away from his family for nine months, being able to visit them only semi-monthly, the Singapore/Hong Kong relocation would hardly have offered him a better family life.

Returning to California, Kumar found that McKinsey had no real job for him, so he 'characteristically envisioned the needs for the future and created his own opportunities'. With the dotcom boom in full swing, he created an e-commerce practice for the firm, which soon started contributing 25-30 per cent of

McKinsey's revenues. But he also saw the pitfalls of the business and repeatedly warned the firm against overexposure. His fears proved true. McKinsey was hit hard by the dotcom bust, and decided to blame Kumar for its lost revenues: 'almost overnight, he became a pariah'.

The 'pariah' claim, again, sounds somewhat dubious, since it is an indisputable fact that Kumar was very close to Gupta, who was heading McKinsey at that time.

'This was particularly difficult for Anil to accept because he had warned McKinsey about its overexposure and nevertheless received the blame. Once again, Anil had no leadership role at McKinsey. This made two serious career setbacks in just a few years. He felt both undervalued and wrongfully ostracized. In 2003, Anil was advised by the senior-most McKinsey partners that his future at McKinsey was limited and he should seek employment elsewhere. This was a crushing blow to his self-confidence and sense of self-worth after his decades of dedication to McKinsey.' If this is true, one wonders if it had anything to do with Gupta stepping down from his managing directorship in 2003. Did Kumar lose a top-echelon protector within the firm?

As detailed in Chapter Six, Rajaratnam is supposed to have cleverly used Kumar's state of mind to entrap him in a cycle of sin. 'In an otherwise law-abiding life, Anil Kumar was blind to Mr Rajaratnam's ability to manipulate. The professional disappointments for a man used to being among the highest of achievers, the personal uncertainties of his (censored), and (censored) has described, all contributed to an inability to say "no" to Mr Rajaratnam. Indeed, Mr Rajaratnam masterfully cultivated in Anil a kind of dependence, by reassuring Anil that he would always have a place with Mr Rajaratnam. This furthered the connection, deepened the manipulation and extended Kumar's indebtedness to Mr Rajaratnam.' So, in a way, it was McKinsey that was to blame for Kumar taking to a life of crime.

Poor Anil Kumar. Indeed, he did not even do it for money. As the plea document explains: 'Money, as such, was not a motivating factor in Anil's providing Mr Rajaratnam with material nonpublic information. To better understand his motivations and conduct, Mr Kumar sought medical help immediately after his arrest.' What the medical professionals diagnosed has, however, been censored for the public.

Among the reasons cited by Kumar's lawyers why the court should show leniency and give him a 'non-incarcerative sentence' is his cooperation with the prosecutors. The document provides a long account (described in some detail in Chapter Six) of how he had spent almost three years answering questions, helping the government, meeting lawyers at 6 a.m., and testifying against Rajaratnam and Gupta, and how guilty he felt standing witness against his mentor and friend.

And, of course, Aman needs his father. This argument was presented at great length (half a dozen pages) by Kumar and his lawyers. Of course, this has been censored and is not available to the public, to protect Aman's privacy. The by-product of this deletion from the public record is that we will never exactly know to what abject extent Kumar used his son's condition to save his own skin.

Anil Kumar's philanthropic activities—what his lawyers call 'life purpose of altruism and improving the lives of others'—would by themselves call for a fat tome. A much abbreviated list of what he did for his native India would be: helping raise money for Doon School, enabling IIT Delhi to double its student capacity without increasing fees, setting up the Indian School of Business (ISB) while letting 'others take credit for his significant contributions', and being a founding member of the Bharti Foundation which provides free education to children from impoverished families.

While Kumar surely worked very hard in setting up ISB, statements like 'But for Anil, the school would not exist today' and 'ISB, the first international world-class higher education institution in India, is one of Anil Kumar's great contributions to Indian society' are hyperbolic, to say the least. ISB was Rajat Gupta's brainchild, and it was his sterling reputation and stature that drew a number of Indian industrialists to support the project. Kumar's work would have been limited to the operational aspects of the projects, as in several other projects that Gupta spearheaded. But here is Kumar shamelessly attempting to take all the credit for the business school.

In the United States, Kumar was a volunteer consultant on a project to promote the arts in San Jose, California, and was on the boards of the Children's Discovery Museum in San Jose and the San Jose Civic Light Opera. He was a founding charter member of TiE (The Indus Entrepreneurs), an entrepreneurial organization 'deeply important in job creation and innovation' around the world. He founded the Indian American Council to better connect the Indian diaspora in the US to worthwhile causes in India that would benefit from the diaspora's expertise. This is perhaps a reference to the American Indian Foundation, which was again Gupta's initiative. It was Gupta who persuaded President Clinton to be a trustee of the Foundation, which brought the Foundation a unique prestige. Kumar hardly founded this charitable organization. Quite simply, Kumar is, as termed by John Dowd (Rajaratnam's lawyer), 'the worst liar ever'.

Post-arrest, Kumar has been working even harder in the area of philanthropy, at 'breakneck speed', as his plea document puts it. He is helping Max Healthcare in India to set up a state-of-the-art medical college and research campus, is working with the Hero Group to establish a multi-discipline university, has persuaded various Indian business groups to institute scholarships for meritorious students from underprivileged backgrounds and to employ deaf and mute people. He is mentoring two initiatives that will train deaf and mute people for employment in the hospitality industry, and is helping set up vocational training institutes to impart employability skills to dropouts from the Indian school system.

In the US, he has helped the Baylor College of Medicine, without charging any consultancy fees, to increase organizational effectiveness and initiate a global education outreach programme (Baylor is partnering Max Healthcare in its medical education project). He has agreed to become an unpaid faculty member at the Abramson Centre for the Future of Health at the University of Houston, with a mandate to develop strategies to improve the health of populations in under-resourced environments. He is also working with children from disdvantaged families in the Silicon Valley area to improve their social skills.

And we haven't even started on his 'small acts of kindness'. From being a mentor to younger students in Doon School, to rescheduling meetings when on a working trip to London to visit a friend in hospital, helping new Indian immigrants find accommodation, being a standing guarantor for them when they applied for their first credit cards, mending malfunctioning electrical fixtures and appliances for friends, taking care of children of sick neighbours...this man is clearly an angel in human form. (Indeed, one letter of recommendation attached to the plea document does call him an 'angel'.)

But the most interesting argument advanced in the plea memorandum is that if Kumar were sent to prison, it would harm countless people in India. The memorandum explains: 'The culture in India is vastly different from that in the United States. Former Federal District Judge (censored), who was raised in India, has family there, and regularly visits India, explains "it is particularly important to consider the enormous—indeed disproportionate—weight that is given in Indian culture to whether an individual is imprisoned for his wrongdoing. Imprisonment in India is almost entirely reserved for violent criminals who are a grave threat to society, and that cultural attitude is of significance, since Anil has and will continue to rely on his relationships in India to forward both his consulting and charitable activities."'

Two clear points emerge from this, other than the broader

absurdity about Indian attitudes. The first point that makes one sit up occurs in the memorandum just a few lines before the quote from the federal judge, which says: 'In the United States, Anil Kumar is regarded as so toxic that most companies and even non-profit institutions will not associate with him.' This, when Kumar hadn't even been sentenced—and Kumar and his lawyers have the gall to suggest that Indians have a 'cultural' problem with jailbirds!

The second point, the memorandum admits to is that 'the vast majority of work, both *paying* and charitable, that Mr Kumar has been able to obtain is in India'. The federal judge also mentions Kumar's consulting work in India. So all that work setting up medical colleges and universities in India may not be purely 'contributions to India', right? Even though the document classifies them under that heading. Kumar is obviously getting paid for doing that work!

So it appears that, though Americans are not willing to give Anil Kumar the time of day, Indians have been giving paid work to this convicted felon, and Kumar shows his gratitude by terming them 'unforgiving' as a race!

(Censored name), a long-time friend of Anil's, sees the same deep flaw in Indian character. 'I expect that incarceration will make it considerably more difficult, if not simply impossible, for Anil to continue pursuing the initiatives he is leading here, because Indian culture tends to ostracize and strip of social acceptance, individuals who are sentenced to prison. Simply put, senior leaders in business, education and other sectors with whom Anil works closely and whose support he needs for his initiatives, will not associate with an individual sentenced to prison.'

The audacity of the arguments keeps piling up. 'Incarceration, no matter how short, would cost Anil his ability to earn a living and support his family and more importantly, it would end his ability to perform life-transforming charitable work for countless people in need,' avers the memorandum.

In short, Anil Kumar must be kept out of prison for the sake of Indians, that irrational merciless bunch of underfed under-educated losers. And because—though we may of course be wrong—Indians are the only fools who will pay for Anil Kumar's services any more.

The US government has kept its part of the deal with the man who ratted on everyone—the naïve senior executive who was forced by Rajaratnam to open a Swiss bank account in his domestic help's name and assign all operating rights to the account to her employer; the man who can stoop low enough to use his son's disability to the hilt to keep his butt out of prison.

The leniency plea filed by this 'the worst liar ever' and ingrate beggars belief.

And, who knows, Judge Denny Chin may really want to see India as a poverty-free, fully literate nation. Anil Kumar's contributions will obviously be essential to achieve that dream of a billion people.

The Fall

THE SENTENCING DATE FOR GUPTA WAS SHIFTED ONCE MORE, this time to 24 October 2012.

US State Attorney Preet Bharara filed a thirteen-page sentencing memorandum to Judge Rakoff, 'respectfully [submitting] that a sentence within the applicable Guidelines range of ninety-seven to 121 months' imprisonment is appropriate'. As was the norm, Bharara's team had based their recommendations using United States Sentencing Guidelines (USSG), which set out a uniform sentencing policy for individuals and organizations convicted of felonies and serious misdemeanours.

This was how they had worked it out: According to USSG, the base offence level for insider trading was 8. According to the government's calculations, Rajaratnam had made illegal gains (and avoided losses) totaling $15.4 million based on Gupta's tips. This, as per USSG (which calibrated felonies by moneys involved), raised Gupta's offence level by 20. And since 'the defendant abused a position of public or private trust (and, in this case, both), in a manner that significantly facilitated the commission of the offence', the government added 2 to this, and came up with a total offence level of 30. This called for a sentence of ninety-seven to 121 months' imprisonment.

'[A] significant term of imprisonment is necessary to reflect the seriousness of Gupta's crimes and to deter other corporate insiders in similar positions of trust from stealing corporate secrets and engaging in a crime that has become far too common,' argued the government. '...The evidence at trial demonstrated that Gupta knew what he was doing was improper and unlawful. Indeed, Gupta had spent much of his career in a profession built on protecting the confidences of clients. He understood as well as anyone the important responsibility that comes with being in a position of trust. Moreover, as a member of the boards of Goldman Sachs and Procter & Gamble, Gupta personally participated in approving the internal policies at these companies that prohibited the disclosure of confidential information.'

The memo described the phone conversation on 29 July 2008 between Gupta and Rajaratnam, the only one that had been intercepted, as 'an extraordinary window into Gupta's state of mind and willingness to breach his duties to please Rajaratnam... After being asked by Rajaratnam about a rumour concerning Goldman's strategic plans, Gupta casually and without any hesitation or reservation disclosed to Rajaratnam the deliberations of the Goldman board.' It recounted, 'During that same conversation, Rajaratnam referenced the millions of dollars that he had been paying Anil Kumar offshore, in cash, for several years. Remarkably, Gupta did not even flinch upon hearing that Kumar, who was a senior official at McKinsey and had been Gupta's protégé, had this secret and almost certainly illicit arrangement with Rajaratnam.'

Referring to what Gupta had been convicted of doing as 'shocking' and 'extraordinarily serious and damaging to the capital markets', the government said that Gupta must receive exemplary punishment. 'Imposing a significant sentence for insider trading to deter others from participating in this kind of conduct is particularly appropriate in this case for several reasons,' it argued. 'First, Gupta's prominence in the business community means that the Court's sentence has the potential for a greater deterrent impact than a similar sentence in the average case. Second, a significant sentence will send a clear message to board members and other high-level corporate insiders—the very people who have the most access to material nonpublic information—that insider trading will not be tolerated or punished lightly, regardless of the status of the offender...

Third, a sentence that is not commensurate with the sentences imposed on other recent insider trading defendants who held lower-level positions and were not as successful, prominent, or well-connected as Gupta also runs a serious risk of undermining public confidence in the criminal justice system.'

The sentencing memorandum filed by Gupta's defence team ran to 225 pages, including annexures. In addition, Naftalis & Co. submitted more than 400 letters written to the Court requesting leniency. The writers ranged from luminaries to Gupta's family members, associates, friends, and many people who had not known Gupta well but had benefited from his generosity, kindness and guidance.

It's very important to note, however, that the defence memo, while asking for a lenient sentence, carefully steered clear of admitting Gupta's guilt. It avoided what law expert Peter J. Henning, writing in *The New York Times* (18 October 2012) called 'something judges always like to see: a measure of contrition for the misconduct... That posture protects Mr Gupta's position in case the convictions were reversed and a retrial ordered. It also means he is unlikely to tell the court that he accepts responsibility for what he was convicted of doing.'

As expected, the memo went to great lengths to emphasize that the 'convictions in this case represent an utter aberration in the life of the man...Rajat Gupta's life story does not merely include a record of charitable giving, or of caring for others and having a loving family. It is, instead, a life defined by helping others and one fundamentally at odds with the events of this case. That is, the events of this case are uncharacteristic in the most literal sense, inconsistent with the true character of the man.'

He had been the ideal husband, father and grandfather. In her letter to the Court, Gupta's wife Anita wrote: '[After] thirty-nine years and four daughters and two granddaughters, whenever I try to picture my husband in my mind, I see him tired and jet-lagged, sleeping on the family room couch with a baby, sleeping on his chest. That was always his favourite thing to do and his girls have always been the most important things in his life.' His third daughter Aditi wrote that despite his gruelling work schedule, he 'was more engaged and more "present"' as a father than he would have been 'simply [being] around on a day-to-day basis'. His eldest daughter Geetanjali recalled that, during times when Gupta's job required him to travel extensively, '[R]ather than being apart from us for too long, our father would take us on trips around the world with him as he worked...I lost my first tooth biting into an apple in Paris, spent my eleventh birthday in London, and helped afflict a poor restaurant full of people with endless rounds of "Old McDonald" as my family tried to keep my littlest sister entertained over dinner in St Petersburg.'

Others recounted numerous instances when Gupta had helped them with money and advice in times of need, very often spontaneously, and never asking for anything in return. According to these letters, Gupta simply did the right thing on every occasion throughout his life, whether in his personal or professional capacity, and embodied the highest principles of humanity.

Wrote Bill Gates: '[Gupta's] work in global health and promoting the well-being of the world's poorest people [has] made a real difference in the lives of literally millions of people around the world... Because of his remarkable business background, he brought a level of clear-headed thinking and focus on results, all the while remaining a dogged advocate for the world's poor who desperately needed the treatments [our] funds would support. There was every reason in the world for Rajat to back out of such controversial and time-consuming volunteer work, yet he remained steadfastly dedicated to the task. And many millions of people are leading better lives—or are alive at all—thanks to the efforts he ably supported.'

'In all of my interactions with him, my experience is of a caring, selfless, and dedicated person who worked to help those that were not as fortunate or economically privileged as others,' wrote Deepak Chopra. 'I think Rajat has tremendously contributed to humanity and has so much more to offer to the world... As a friend of Rajat's and his family's, I request that you take my letter into consideration during his sentencing and show leniency to Rajat and his family.'

'My name is Kofi Annan, and I was Secretary General of the United Nations from 1997-2006,' begins a letter sent to Judge Rakoff. 'I am writing this letter to tell you about his good work and to urge you to take that work into account in fashioning an appropriate sentence. I do not have any knowledge of the facts related to the case before you, and I cannot add or subtract from the evidence that relates to that case. But based on our work together over the years, I do have a certain knowledge and understanding of Rajat. He is a person who has conducted his life with an admirable sense of purpose and desire to improve the lives of people in trouble around the world. He has devoted his time, energy and talent—with no expectation of personal benefit or gain—to projects that are wholly admirable and worthy of praise. I urge you to recognize Rajat for the good that he has done in this world, to give him the credit that he deserves for helping others and to take into account his efforts to improve the lives of millions of people.'

'He always quoted the Bhagavad Gita, the verse that said: "You are entitled to do your duty, and not to the fruits of that duty", and he lived by that credo,' wrote Mukesh Ambani, the date of whose letter indicates that he was the first among the big names to write to the judge for clemency. 'He is a man of great character and his footprint on India is large. I respect Rajat for his dedication and humility and he will always be a friend of mine. I hope that you will consider this when you look at his sentence.'

Having established Gupta's stellar human qualities (and some of the events recounted by the leniency-seekers could bring a lump to the throat of a sensitive reader), the defence tried to demolish the government's reasoning on the specific prison term. It pointed out that the illicit gains that the government had mentioned (around $11.6 million), as directly resulting from Gupta's tips, was a highly bloated figure. This was the value realized by the Galleon funds as a whole. The true number that should be considered was the profits made by Rajaratnam alone, which, according to the defence's calculations, based on evidence given in the Rajaratnam trial, was at the most around $350,000.

The government's estimate of the losses that Rajaratnam avoided ($3.8 million) when he sold off Goldman Sachs stock, based on Gupta's tip that the investment bank was going to report poor earnings, also came under attack. This number, the defence argued, assumed that if he had not received the tip, Rajaratnam would have held on to the shares for two months, till Goldman officially announced its results. As was by now acknowledged by all, Rajaratnam was fundamentally a short-term in-and-out trader, and he would never have held on to the stock for so long in the face of increasingly negative analyst reports and Goldman's falling stock price. 'This assumption,' said the defence, 'in addition to being contrary to common sense, is purely speculative.'

On 31 October 2012, investment bank UBS published a report that Goldman Sachs seemed headed towards a loss in the fourth quarter. This report was immediately picked up by Reuters and widely circulated. So it would have been far more logical—and consistent with Rajaratnam's investment record—that he would sell his shares on that day. Then the losses-avoided figure was $1.2 million, which the defence said was a much more rational estimate than the $3.8 million the government had claimed.

If so, then Gupta's offence level, as per UGGS, dropped to at most 22, which yields a sentencing range of 41 to 51 months.

The defence then argued further, citing observations made by judges in other cases, that gains made should not be a factor at all in sentencing in insider trading cases. The tipper had only passed on information, and had no control over what the tippee did with that information—whether he did anything at all, or whether he made or lost money based on the tip. Also, in Gupta's case, he did not engage in any trading, and there was no evidence of any quid pro quo at all, 'only an attenuated (at best) inference of a potential business or relationship benefit [that he would be made chairman of Galleon International].'

By this logic, Gupta's offence level was 10, which should lead to 6 to 12 months in prison.

Top IBM executive Robert Moffat provided tips to Danielle Chiesi on three major public companies, IBM, Lenovo and AMD; so his crime was much more serious than Gupta's. Also, unlike Gupta, Moffat received tangible benefits, even though they were not financial (he was sleeping with Chiesi). And he got only six months. In fact, the Court had explained this lenient sentencing specifically, saying that 'Mr Moffat, though he breached his duty to his employer, did not provide information in exchange for money, and did not stand to make any monetary gains from his transgression.'

Anil Kumar, who provided Rajaratnam with inside information regarding a number of McKinsey clients in exchange for substantial cash payment—$2.1 million—which he hid in a Swiss bank account, received a non-custodial sentence, and during sentencing, was given credit by Judge Chin for his 'many charitable deeds both here and in India'. '[These deeds] are admirable,' pointed out Gupta's defence team, 'but represent a small fraction of the amount of time and energy Mr Gupta has committed to giving back to others around the world.'

Also, hadn't Gupta and his family already paid enough for what he had been convicted of? This was 'the quintessential case of a monumental fall that is, in and of itself, severe punishment'. Gupta's daughter Aditi, who had graduated from Harvard Business School while her father's trial was on, had described in her letter to the Court how she had been harassed on campus. She had received anonymous hate mail carrying news reports on Gupta's trial. There had been a mail going around asking Harvard to sever all ties with Gupta, who was on the business school's advisory board. 'Well-meaning' professors had even suggested that she take a year off to let things 'die down'.

So now the defence proposed what it felt should be the correct punishment. Given Gupta's lifetime of good work, it was clear that 'the conduct for which he was convicted represents an isolated aberration... Where the convicted conduct is dramatically at odds with the defendant's life and character, especially where he has devoted significant time to civic and charitable contributions, courts have found the defendant deserving of a non-Guidelines sentence substantially below the advisory range, including non-custodial sentences. We do not believe any of these individuals presented a record of contributions to the community matching, in scope or duration, that of Mr Gupta. We have not found any case comparable to this one, in which the defendant can point not only to a significant expenditure of time and effort, but further, that he or she was involved in founding and helping to sustain major initiatives improving and in some cases saving millions of lives.'

The defence requested the Court to impose a probationary sentence, with the condition that Gupta perform, for a significant period, a rigorous full-time programme of community service. It also suggested two such options.

The first was a course of service with the charity Covenant House, which provides emergency shelter and other services for homeless, runaway and at-risk youth. Gupta could provide direct services to these children at Covenant House's New York site, including working as part of the intake team at the Crisis Centre, and assisting participants in the transitional living programme and in job training. In addition, he could assist Covenant House in developing a plan to implement a set of strategic initiatives for the organization.

But the second proposal was the big one—unorthodox,

in fact completely out of left field. The East African nation of Rwanda had been devastated in the early 1990s by tribal wars that had left an estimated 800,000 people dead—or 20 per cent of the country's population. It has been a long and slow road to recovery since then, and Rwanda is still ravaged by problems, including extreme poverty, and a high incidence of AIDS and malaria. Rwanda had been selected for special consideration and funding from a six-year $63 billion US government health care initiative spearheaded by President Barack Obama. Gupta, the defence suggested, could live and work in rural districts there, helping implement the country's initiative to improve delivery of health care and agricultural development. He would work under the direction and supervision of the government of Rwanda, along with the humanitarian organization CARE USA.

'We recognize this is an unusual community service proposal, but one that could potentially provide great benefits to large numbers of Rwandans desperately in need of help, and which Mr Gupta is uniquely situated to perform,' argued the defence. 'Moreover, it would require Mr Gupta to confront significant hardships and would thus constitute punishment commensurate with the seriousness of the offence, as Mr Gupta would be thousands of miles from his family and friends, and would be living in basic accommodations in rural areas of the country.'

The defence team had already been in touch with the Rwandan government, which had responded enthusiastically to the proposal. It had agreed to accept 'responsibility for crafting a [specific] programme of work, for the terms imposed on Mr Gupta being carried out, and to ensure that regular reports are provided to the appropriate authorities in the United States by the Ministry of Justice/Attorney General's office'. 'We believe,' Justice Minister Tharcisse Karugarama had written, '[Gupta] can make a significant difference in helping us to accomplish the aforementioned objectives (i.e., ending HIV, malaria and extreme poverty, and ensuring food security) …The field conditions where

Mr Gupta would be spending the majority of his time living and working would be difficult but would match the need to punish but at the same time give the convict the opportunity to reflect and recant.' Emphasizing that the proposal 'has our full support', the minister wrote: 'It is our belief that this kind of arrangement would be a rare, unique but very important example of international legal cooperation and that it might provide future precedent to other situations of similar nature and that this would be good for international justice.'

This was an astonishing proposal, and media across the world discussed it avidly. Rajat Gupta's defence team had certainly given Judge Rakoff a lot of food for thought. Would he agree to this sort of exceptional mode of punishment for a case that was also in every way truly exceptional? No living businessman other than Bill Gates has perhaps contributed as much as Gupta has done to the service of humanity. Would his extraordinary story end in this distressed nation, which would definitely gain from his expertise and unquestionable commitment to the betterment of human life? In a way, many felt, that would be a fitting climax.

It would be a redemption hallmarked by the humility and grace that had been the essential themes of Rajat Gupta's life. To a large extent, it would also regain for him the inspirational status he had been endowed with by hundreds of thousands of people across the world.

But Judge Rakoff, with truly impeccable logic, made sure that a perfect ending eluded Rajat Gupta.

What Can One Say Now?

JUDGE RAKOFF'S SENTENCING ORDER IS A BRILLIANT STEP-BY-step exposition of how he arrived at what he believed was the right punishment for the crimes Rajat Gupta had been convicted of. He begins by saying that he would not follow the Unites States Sentencing Guidelines (USSG) for sentencing, and then proceeds to explain why.

Imposing a sentence on a fellow human being was a formidable responsibility that required careful and sensitive consideration of a large complex of facts and factors, said Rakoff. The USSG, however, was based on a notion that was anti-common sense, that 'this complicated analysis, and moral responsibility, can be reduced to the mechanical adding-up of a small set of numbers artificially assigned to a few arbitrarily selected variables... Whereas apples and oranges may have but a few salient qualities, human beings in their interactions with society are too complicated to be treated like commodities, and the attempt to do so can only lead to bizarre results.'

Nowhere was this more obvious than in Rajat Gupta's case, said Rakoff. 'The Sentencing Guidelines assign just 2 points to Mr Gupta for his abuse of a position of trust—the very heart of his offence—yet assign him no fewer than 18 points for the resultant but unpredictable monetary gains made by others, from which Mr Gupta did not in any direct sense receive one penny.'

Over the years, the Guidelines had become dramatically harsher when applied to white-collar crimes. A significant reason for this was the public outcry caused by the massive frauds by companies like Enron and WorldCom, and the subsequent Congressional mandate to the Sentencing Commission, which issues the USSG, to turn the heat on. But the Commission had focused largely on a single factor as the basis for enhanced punishment: the amount of monetary loss or gain occasioned by the offence. In doing so, said Rakoff, the Commission effectively ignored the statutory requirement that federal sentencing take many factors into account. United States Code, Title 18, Section 3553(a) clearly lays down these factors.

The Code mandates that while imposing a sentence, the Court should consider the nature and circumstances of the offence and the history and characteristics of the defendant. The sentence should be sufficient, but not greater than necessary, to make sure of the following: that it reflects the seriousness of the offence, promotes respect for the law, provides just punishment for the offence, and protects the public from further crimes by the defendant.

The USSG were particularly inappropriate in Gupta's case, argued Rakoff. Of the 30 Guideline points that the government said reflected the proper measure of Gupta's crime and punishment, 'no fewer than 20—or two-thirds of the total—are exclusively the product of Rajaratnam's and his companies' monetary gain, in which Mr Gupta did not share in any direct sense.' The heart of Gupta's offence, Rakoff repeated, was 'his egregious breach of trust'. Rajaratnam's gains were immaterial to the case, and Gupta would be guilty even if Rajaratnam had not made a cent.

'In the eye of the law,' Rakoff explained, 'Gupta's crime was to breach his fiduciary duty of confidentiality to Goldman Sachs; or to put it another way, Goldman Sachs, not the marketplace, was the victim of Gupta's crimes. Yet the Guidelines assess his punishment almost exclusively on the basis of how much money his accomplice gained by trading on the information. At best, this is a very rough surrogate for the harm to Goldman Sachs.' So Rakoff would ignore the Guidelines and rely, for sentencing, on the much higher law of Section 3553(a).

The first factor, then, to be considered was 'the nature and circumstances of the offence and the history and characteristics of the defendant'. This posed the fundamental problem of this sentencing, said Rakoff, 'for Mr Gupta's personal history and characteristics starkly contrast with the nature and circumstances of his crimes'. It was clear that Gupta had selflessly devoted a huge amount of time and effort to a very wide variety of socially beneficial activities, and this indicated his big heart and helping hand, which he extended without fanfare or self-promotion, to all with whom he came in contact. 'The USSG virtually ignore this measure of the man,' said Rakoff. '…[But] on this day of judgement, must not one judge the man as a whole?'

Yet Gupta was certainly guilty of crimes that, 'by any measure […] represented the very antithesis of the values he had previously embodied.

'So how does a court balance these polar extremes [when deciding on a sentence]?' asked Rakoff. By turning to the further mandates of Section 3553, Rakoff decided. The first was that the sentence should afford specific and general deterrence. 'As to specific deterrence,' said Rakoff, 'it seems obvious that, having suffered such a blow to his reputation, Mr Gupta is unlikely to repeat his transgressions, and no further punishment is needed to achieve this result. General deterrence, however, suggests a different conclusion. As this Court has repeatedly noted in other cases, insider trading is an easy crime to commit but a difficult crime to catch. Others similarly situated to the defendant must therefore be made to understand that when you get caught, you will go to jail. Defendant's proposals to have Mr Gupta undertake various innovative forms of community service would, in the Court's view, totally fail to send this message. Moreover, if the reports of Mr Gupta's charitable endeavours are at all accurate, he can be counted on to devote himself to community service when he finishes any prison term, regardless of any order of the Court.' Through this flawless interpretation of the statutes, Rakoff dismissed the notions of penitence in Rwanda.

'At the same time,' Rakoff admitted, 'no one really knows how much jail time is necessary to materially deter insider trading; but common sense suggests that most business executives fear even a modest prison term to a degree that more hardened types might not. Thus, a relatively modest prison term should be "sufficient, but not more than necessary", for this purpose.' In other words, if Gupta was sent to prison for a very short period, it would be enough to serve as a general deterrent.

But there was also the matter of 'just punishment'. 'Human beings, as social animals, are programmed to respect moral values,' said Rakoff. '...As people have come to understand that insider trading is not only a sophisticated form of cheating but also a fundamental breach of trust and confidence, they have increasingly internalized their revulsion for its commission. While no defendant should be made a martyr to public passion, meaningful punishment is still necessary to reaffirm society's deep-seated need to see justice triumphant. No sentence of probation, or anything close to it, could serve this purpose. After carefully weighing all these, and other, relevant factors, the Court concludes that the sentence that most fulfils all requirements of Section 3553 is two years in prison.'

This, then, was the sentence: 'Rajat K. Gupta is therefore sentenced to twenty-four months' imprisonment, concurrent on all counts, to be followed by one year of supervised release, on the terms stated from the bench and here incorporated by reference. The otherwise mandatory forfeiture has been waived by the Government, but Court imposes a fine in the sum of $5,000,000.'

It was a truly magnificent act of jurisprudence, and Rakoff had lived up to his reputation, upholding the spirit of the law, obeying every principle held sacred, and not for a moment losing sight of the true nature of the man who stood before him, awaiting judgement.

♦

Yet, the mystery refuses to go away, stubbornly declining to present itself as clear incontrovertible fact. And people who have known and worked with Gupta will never believe that he did what the US judiciary found him guilty of doing.

'Maybe this is all about wrong timing, about being at the wrong place at the wrong time,' said Ashok Syal, who had lived two rooms away from Gupta for five years at IIT Delhi. 'I don't believe anything else could have happened. I am simply unable to understand how else something like this could have come to pass.'

What about the desire to be more wealthy, what juror Ronnie Sesso described as 'need for greed'?

Rajendra Singh Pawar, founder-chairman of the NIIT Group, who worked closely with Gupta during the setting up of ISB and on other IIT-related issues, scoffed at the suggestion. 'All those people who say that he was unhappy being a millionaire and wanted to be a billionaire, they're all idiots,' he said.

'I know his family background,' said Syal. 'I have seen how his daughters were brought up, and Anita Mattoo would never pressure her husband to make more money. When she fell in love with Rajat, she had no idea about how high he would rise. She fell in love with a boy who had no parents, no ancestral wealth, nothing. She loved him for what he was, and that's the way I believe she has always loved him.'

Of course, there have been the expected jibes in the Indian media. The 'illegal' acts that Gupta supposedly committed, pointed out Indian commentators, are precisely what run Indian business and politics on an everyday basis. Writing on the news website firstpost.com after the jury verdict, columnist Anant Rangaswami noted: 'Many thousands of kilometres away, in India, many of us are bemused by the accusations and the conviction. A man goes to jail because he shared information with a friend? By that yardstick, half of India would be in jail.

'Knowing people in power and to benefit from the knowledge and contacts that they possess is the ladder to success that Indians have recognized centuries ago.

'It's an ethos and a culture—and it's deep-rooted... But that's what India is all about—having the contacts and taking advantage of the contacts to give one an edge. There's nothing wrong in that—everybody does it.

'That's what dragged Rajat Gupta down. He continued with his Indian trait, forgetting, tragically, that the trait is acceptable in India, the land of his origins, but not in America, the land he had adopted... Rajat Gupta has paid a price for being Indian.'

Speaking about the trial, Pawar referred to cultural differences. 'Americans are, at a level, simple transparent people,' he said. 'But the way they can flip their moral compass is not funny. In some ways their naïvety is frightening, at least to us who come from a much longer line of thought and experience.

'In Rajaratnam's case, you have evidence,' said Pawar. 'In Rajat's case, you don't have that. Plus he is fighting. They can't take a guy who's fighting because he has moral courage. This is so bloody unfair.'

What about all the circumstantial evidence? The swipe card, the phone calls, the trades...it all ties up logically, doesn't it? I asked Pawar.

Had I seen the film *Judgement at Nuremberg*? he asked.

I had.

Did I recall a certain scene between Judge Dan Heywood, played by Spencer Tracy, and Hans Rolfe, the defence counsel, played by Maximilian Schell?

I did.

In that scene, a private conversation between the two of them, Judge Heywood tells Rolfe: 'Herr Rolfe, I have admired your work in the court for many months. You are particularly brilliant in your use of logic... But to be logical is not to be right.'

It was strange, I thought, that while researching this book, I had now encountered the post-World War II trial of Nazi leaders at Nuremberg for the second time. As mentioned in Chapter

Eight, Viet Dinh, profiling US Attorney Preet Bharara for *Time* magazine, had mentioned that Bharara's hero was Robert H. Jackson, the chief prosecutor at the Nuremberg trial, a man who tempered 'zeal with human kindness, who [sought] truth and not victims, who [served] the law and not factional purposes and who [approached] his task with humility'.

It was even more interesting that while Preet Bharara, who idolized the prosecutor in the Nuremberg trial, had relied entirely on circumstantial logic to prove his case, in the scene Pawar was referring to, the judge (in this case, fictional) was emphasizing the possibility of logic—truth mismatches to the defence lawyer.

There was also the question that many in the US media had asked about Bharara's strategy: Was he going for the easy targets, the small fry, while the big fish whose reckless avarice had been instrumental in causing the collapse of the US markets were still sitting pretty in their corner offices and paying themselves jaw-dropping bonuses? Yes, Rajaratnam had committed extensive securities fraud, but he was a Wall Street player who in no way contributed to the economic catastrophe that hit the US in 2008 and then spread across many parts of the world.

To be fair, on the very first day of Rajat Gupta's trial, Judge Rakoff had explained to the jury very clearly that this trial had nothing at all to do with the 2008 Wall Street and housing market meltdown and the subsequent suffering that millions of Americans faced. But how deep had that message gone? The jurors were mostly working-class New Yorkers. Many of them may have been directly affected by the economic crisis. At the very least, many of them would certainly have had a close friend or relative who had seen his livelihood vanish or his loans foreclosed. One of Gupta's US-based friends, who spoke to me on the condition of anonymity (most of them, in fact, insisted on not being quoted by name), felt that the composition of the jury might also have had a bearing on the final judgement. 'They were all lower-middle class people,' he said. 'And given what the US economy is going through, the world of Rajat—his wealth, the circles he moves in—is light years away from their own reality. There could have been an unconscious bias. It's within the realms of possibility that a jury drawn from a different demographic might have reached a different verdict.'

And then there's the word denoting a certain type of bias that dares not speak its name. The three big players in the Galleon insider trading drama—the biggest in Wall Street history—are all of South Asian origin: Preet Bharara, Raj Rajaratnam and Rajat Gupta. Was it pure coincidence, or, as Bharara's detractors complained to me bitterly, was the prosecutor establishing his 'all-American' credentials beyond any doubt?

A few days after Gupta's conviction, the satirical blog India Update (shovonc.wordpress.com) carried an item headlined: 'Justice Department may prosecute white people on Wall Street.' The tongue-in-cheek news report read: 'Celebrated US attorney Preet Bharara confirmed that the subject of prosecuting white people on Wall Street was under active consideration. "It's not that we're targeting immigrants, or anything," he said. "It's just that security cameras tend to track them more, so it's easier to get footage."

'A Justice Department official, who chose to remain anonymous, admitted that demographics had played a role in the prosecution. "We wanted to favour sons-of-the-soil, like other countries," he said. "But most of them were killed in the nineteenth century. Instead, we're borrowing a well-known Inventory Management principle called LIFO, which means Last In First Out. It's very similar to puking. We want to use this principle to make Wall Street a whiter, cleaner place."

Gupta is appealing the verdict, and there is an outside chance that the New York jury's verdict will be overturned by the US Supreme Court. But will that ever repair Gupta's reputation? Even if he walks free one day, proved innocent, a cloud of calumny will always hang over his head. Those who believe that Gupta could never have helped Rajaratnam in his illicit schemes will continue to keep the faith, even as he serves time in prison. And those who believe he is guilty will never accept, either in their heads or their hearts, a 'not guilty' verdict that may come sometime in the future.

The orphan from Kolkata who reached heights no Indian had ever previously reached in the US corporate world will never outlive the curse that struck him at the end of a truly glorious career.

That curse, whether self-inflicted or the result of some venal cosmic injustice, will shadow him relentlessly, and even perhaps, entirely unfairly, define him in the decades to come, when his name is mentioned in business histories.

Why did this happen? How could this have happened?

Perhaps we should leave it to Judge Rakoff, clearly the most brilliant and irreproachable man in this whole story.

'So why did Mr Gupta do it?' he asked in his sentencing order. 'Since motive is not an element of the offences here in issue, it did not need to be proved at trial, and so one can only speculate. Having finished his spectacular career at McKinsey in 2007, Gupta, for all his charitable endeavours, may have felt frustrated in not finding new business worlds to conquer; and Rajaratnam, a clever cultivator of persons with information, repeatedly held out prospects of exciting new international business opportunities that Rajaratnam would help fund but that Gupta would lead. There is also in some of the information presented to the Court under seal an implicit suggestion that, after so many years of assuming the role of father to all, Gupta may have longed to escape the straitjacket of overwhelming responsibility, and had begun to loosen his self-restraint in ways that clouded his judgement. But whatever was operating in the recesses of his brain, there is no doubt that Gupta, though not immediately profiting from tipping Rajaratnam, viewed it as an avenue to future benefits, opportunities, and even excitement.'

Speaking to me on the phone from his Virginia home, Ashok Syal sounded distraught. 'What can one say now?' Even from across the oceans, one could hear the deep gloom and despair in his voice. 'This is something very sad. I hope something comes up in his favour. He's got so much wealth of knowledge and experience, he should be used for the benefit of society. And he was trying to give back so much to society, and to India. We all know that. And he would have been very successful at that.'

Yes, what can one say now?

1—DATE:	July 29, 2008	**GOVERNMENT EXHIBIT 534-T-R**
2		S2 09 Cr. 1184 (RJH)
3 TIME:	5:39 PM	
4		
5 WIRETAP:	OVER 917-907-2350	
6		
7 CALL FROM:	RAJAT GUPTA (203-977-6701)	
8		
9 CALL TO:	RAJ RAJARATNAM (917-907-2350)	
10		
11 OTHER PARTICIPANTS:	RENEE GOMES	
12		
13		
14 KEY:	Unintelligible:	UI
15	Inaudible:	IA
16	Phonetic Spelling:	PH
17	Voice Overlap:	//
18		

19
20 RAJ RAJARATNAM:	Hello?	
21		
22 RENEE GOMES:	Raj?	
23		
24 RAJ RAJARATNAM:	Yep.	
25		
26 RENEE GOMES:	Hi. It's Renee.	
27		
28 RAJ RAJARATNAM:	Hi Renee. How are you?	
29		
30 RENEE GOMES:	I'm good. How are you?	
31		
32 RAJ RAJARATNAM:	I'm good. Thanks.	
33		
34 RENEE GOMES:	Good. Good. I have Rajat. Are you available	
35	to talk to him now? Or...	
36		
37 RAJ RAJARATNAM:	Absolutely	
38		
39 RENEE GOMES:	O.K. One moment.	
40		
41 RAJ RAJARATNAM:	(Clears throat)	
42		
43 RAJAT GUPTA:	Hey, Raj. How is working from Connecticut?	

1		
2	RAJ RAJARATNAM:	It's good. I get more work done because
3		people don't... See I have open door, open
		(Clears throat) office policy, right?
4		
5	RAJAT GUPTA:	Right. Right. Right.
6		
7	RAJ RAJARATNAM:	Because you have to keep the culture so that
		people can come to
8		you anytime.
9		
10	RAJAT GUPTA:	Yeah. Yeah.
11		
12	RAJ RAJARATNAM:	But then, what happens you're not as productive
		as you are.
13		
14	RAJAT GUPTA:	Yeah.
15		
16	RAJ RAJARATNAM:	When you are... Um, I called you because I am
		meeting with Gary
17		Cohn on Thursday.
18		
19	RAJAT GUPTA:	Yeah.
20		
21	RAJ RAJARATNAM:	And there's a rumor, that Goldman might look
22		to buy a commercial bank.
23		
24	RAJAT GUPTA:	Uh-hum.
25		
26	RAJ RAJARATNAM:	You know? And you know this guy Bob Steele,
27		who was a senior guy at Goldman was under
		Secretary
28		
29	RAJAT GUPTA:	(UI) Yeah. At Wachovia.
30		
31	RAJ RAJARATNAM:	...at Paulson and went to Wachovia and they
		have a large demand,
32		I mean deposit base and all that.
33		
34	RAJAT GUPTA:	Yeah.
35		
36	RAJ RAJARATNAM:	Have you heard anything along that line?
37		
38	RAJAT GUPTA:	Yeah. This was a big discussion at the board
		meeting.
39		
40	RAJ RAJARATNAM:	Uh-hum.
41		
42	RAJAT GUPTA:	Uh, on whether we, uh...
43		

187

1	RAJ RAJARATNAM:	Buy a commercial bank?
2		
3	RAJAT GUPTA:	Buy a commercial bank. And, you know it
4.		was a uh, divided discussion in the board.
5		
6	RAJ RAJARATNAM:	Uh-hum.
7		
8	RAJAT GUPTA:	I think more people saying why, because in
		essence it's a low return business and while
9		yeah it may be interesting to develop a deposit
10		base which is a low cost source of funding.
11		
12	RAJ RAJARATNAM:	Right.
13		
14	RAJAT GUPTA:	Uh, you know, what we should probably
		explore more is, I mean, we aren't having
15		trouble funding ourselves but, you know we
16		should explore more global sources of funding.
17		And perhaps even you know uh, insurance or
18		other things which also are a low uh, cost, also.
19		
20	RAJ RAJARATNAM:	Return (UI).
21		
22	RAJAT GUPTA:	Now, having said all this...
23		
24	RAJ RAJARATNAM:	Right.
25		
26	RAJAT GUPTA:	...they are an opportunistic group, so...
27		
28	RAJ RAJARATNAM:	okay
29		
30	RAJAT GUPTA:	If Wachovia was a good
31		deal and they, you know, it's quite conceivable
32		they'd come and say let's go buy Wachovia.
33	RAJ RAJARATNAM:	Or even AIG, right?
34		
35	RAJAT GUPTA:	Or even AIG. Yeah.
36		
37	RAJ RAJARATNAM:	Uh-hum.
38		
39	RAJAT GUPTA:	A, AIG, it was definitely on, in, in, in, the
		discussion...
40		
41	RAJ RAJARATNAM:	Uh-hum.
42		
43	RAJAT GUPTA:	...mix. Um, and you know, their view was
		actually, which has

1		proven to be wrong, their view was very
2		bearish on the commercial banks, but uh
3		obviously, the commercial banks have had a
4		pop in the last.
5	RAJ RAJARATNAM:	Yes. That's maybe, just a dead cat bounce (UI).
6		
7	RAJAT GUPTA:	Yeah it could be that. I mean, because their view of credit losses
8		and all that is still more to come, credit cards,
9		retail. You know?
10	RAJ RAJARATNAM:	Right.
11		
12	RAJAT GUPTA:	But, but you now sometimes all that gets
13		factored into the market, as you know better
14		than I do and...
15	RAJ RAJARATNAM:	O.K.
16		
17	RAJAT GUPTA:	Uh, so, I would be extremely surprised if uh...
18		
19	RAJ RAJARATNAM:	There was anything active.
20		
21	RAJAT GUPTA:	Anything imminent. Yeah.
22		
23	RAJ RAJARATNAM:	Right. O.K. That was one that I wanted to just, you know, see whether there was any thoughts on that. But it gotta be a good
24		discussion point. I'm gonna start by saying
25		how do you see the future financial services
26		firms, the winners,
27		right?
28	RAJAT GUPTA:	Yeah. Yeah.
29		
30	RAJ RAJARATNAM:	You know, (Exhales) can they just fund for
31		short term? Commercial paper or do they need
32		deposits and insurance and things like that.
33		
34	RAJAT GUPTA:	Yeah.
35		
36	RAJ RAJARATNAM:	Because there are some values out there.
37		
38	RAJAT GUPTA:	Yeah.
39		
40	RAJ RAJARATNAM:	AIG and Wachovia and see what he, you know says.
41		
42	RAJAT GUPTA:	Yeah. Yeah.
43		

1	RAJ RAJARATNAM:	O.K. And then uh...
2		
3	RAJAT GUPTA:	Good.
4		
5	RAJ RAJARATNAM:	George, I'm gonna be out in the office on Thursday.
6		
7	RAJAT GUPTA:	O.K.
8		
9	RAJ RAJARATNAM:	So, I'm gonna get George to just uh, write the
10		balances, if you want.
11		
12	RAJAT GUPTA:	Well, what I did is I, you know, uh, as we had
13		agreed, I just did the calculations for the (UI).
14		
15	RAJ RAJARATNAM:	Yes. (UI) Right
16		
17	RAJAT GUPTA:	(UI) you know...
18		
19	RAJ RAJARATNAM:	Yeah. So George will just certify that and (UI),
20		send you uh...
21	RAJAT GUPTA:	Yeah.
22		
23	RAJ RAJARATNAM:	I mean, I, I'll you know, I'll do it on my
24		Galleon letterhead, (UI).
25	RAJAT GUPTA:	Yes, yes and, let, let, let, let him update it to
26		30th of June if you can, so, whatever it is. (UI).
27		
28	RAJ RAJARATNAM:	30th June, it will be slightly down.
29		
30	RAJAT GUPTA:	Slightly down is fine.
31		
32	RAJ RAJARATNAM:	You know because of the uh...
33		
34	RAJAT GUPTA:	Yeah. Cost of money. Yeah.
35		
36	RAJ RAJARATNAM:	Cost and all that so (UI)?
37		
38	RAJAT GUPTA:	Yeah. Yeah
39		
40	RAJ RAJARATNAM:	All right. Anything else? Anything interesting?
41		
42	RAJAT GUPTA:	No. No that's it. Otherwise you know uh, uh, I
		saw, (Sighs) you know, Anil, how, how is, I
43		mean, he seems, seems a little

1		unsettled yesterday. I don't know. (UI).
2		
3	RAJ RAJARATNAM:	He seemed unhappy.
4		
5	RAJAT GUPTA:	Yeah.
6		
7	RAJ RAJARATNAM:	Because he did come to me and asked me, do
8		you have deal with Rajat on Galleon
9		International.
10	RAJAT GUPTA:	Yeah
11		
12	RAJ RAJARATNAM:	And I just said, nothing concrete. I didn't
13		want to get into with him?
14		
15	RAJAT GUPTA:	Yeah. Yeah.
16		
17	RAJ RAJARATNAM:	I sort of dismissed it without getting him into it.
18		
19	RAJAT GUPTA:	Yeah.
20		
21	RAJ RAJARATNAM:	Because (Coughs) I'm getting a feeling that
22		he's trying to, just do a mini, you know, be a
		mini Rajat, right?
23		
24	RAJAT GUPTA:	Yes. Yes.
25		
26	RAJ RAJARATNAM:	Without bringing anything new to the party,
		right?
27		
28	RAJAT GUPTA:	Yeah. Yeah.
29		
30	RAJ RAJARATNAM:	Because then he was trying to talk about
31		whether he can participate somehow in
32		Galleon International and, you know at
		some point, you know I'm also running a
33		business for people who work hard and uh...
34		
35	RAJAT GUPTA:	Yes.
36		
37	RAJ RAJARATNAM:	You don't need to be compensated and you
38		know, you can't just keep on giving, right?
39		
40	RAJAT GUPTA:	Yeah. Yeah. Yeah.
41		
42	RAJ RAJARATNAM:	And I, you know, honestly, Rajat, I'm, giving
		him a million dollars a year for doing literally
43		nothing. Just because...

1		
2	RAJAT GUPTA:	I know, your being... I think your being very generous.
3		
4	RAJ RAJARATNAM:	Yeah, but you know I, sometimes...
5		
6	RAJAT GUPTA:	But he should sometimes say thank you for
7		that, you know?
8	RAJ RAJARATNAM:	Yeah but he's never ever, ever said, I mean,
9		look he is my friend so, take it with that spirit,
10		right?
11	RAJAT GUPTA:	Yeah. Yeah, I, I...
12		
13	RAJ RAJARATNAM:	But he just seemed uh, I don't know what, he
14		just seemed, I don't think he's, I mean that's
15		why I asked you, uh, I've never seen him
16		laugh and be really happy, you know?
17	RAJAT GUPTA:	Yeah, because.
18		
19	RAJ RAJARATNAM:	He is constantly, sche, not scheming is not the
20		right word, but constantly trying to figure out
21		what other people's angles are.
22	RAJAT GUPTA:	Right.
23		
24	RAJ RAJARATNAM:	And then he seems to know what everybody
25		else is worth, you know he leads with, "Oh,
26		Sunil Mittal is worth 20 billion dollars", you
27		know, when he starts thinking like that...
28	RAJAT GUPTA:	Yeah.
29		
30	RAJ RAJARATNAM:	You know, "and this guy he wants to make
		500 million dollars and...
31		
32		
33	RAJAT GUPTA:	Yeah.
34		
35	RAJ RAJARATNAM:	And (UI) wants to make 300 million dollars,
		and this guy"...
36		
37	RAJAT GUPTA:	Yeah. Yeah. Yeah.
38		
39	RAJ RAJARATNAM:	And you know he was tell me Vin Gupta
40		wants to make 100 million dollars on this deal
41		and you now if you start thinking like that.
42		
43	RAJAT GUPTA:	Yeah.

1	
2 RAJ RAJARATNAM:	It, you know, you build the business and the money will come,
3	you know?
4	
5 RAJAT GUPTA:	Yes. Yes. Yes.
6	
7 RAJ RAJARATNAM:	And...
8	
9 RAJAT GUPTA:	Add value and, and leave it to, you know I, I, I
10	look at how hard he was fighting for this two
11	percent and NSR equity, I mean it was just
12	kind of, you know.
13 RAJ RAJARATNAM:	You know without, without a leg to stand on. I
14	mean, you know, I think he (Coughs)
15	everybody was doing it (Coughs) because they
16	were magnanimous good people.
17 RAJAT GUPTA:	Look, his overall deal in NSR, as you was
18	agreeing, it is a very good, I mean, you know
19	he gets 400 thousand in cash, ten million in, in,
20	you know.
21 RAJ RAJARATNAM:	Carry.
22	
23 RAJAT GUPTA:	Carry.
24	
25 RAJ RAJARATNAM:	Uh-hum.
26	
27 RAJAT GUPTA:	And you know, six percent equity. I mean,
28	
29 RAJ RAJARATNAM:	Right. And I don't know, um, um, um, you know, I can argue that I did more for NSR than
30	he did.
31	
32 RAJAT GUPTA:	I, I, he, I... Absolutely right. Absolutely right. (UI).
33	
34 RAJ RAJARATNAM:	He, he, he coordinated the, he coordinated
35	those uh, telephone meetings, right?
36	
37 RAJAT GUPTA:	Yeah. Yeah. Yeah. Absolutely right.
38	
39 RAJ RAJARATNAM:	And that's about it, right?
40	
41 RAJAT GUPTA:	Yeah. Yeah. Yeah.
42	
43 RAJ RAJARATNAM:	I put in 50 million bucks, whatever...

1

2 RAJAT GUPTA: Yeah. Yeah.

3

4 RAJ RAJARATNAM: I went on the trips. Whatever, but...

5

6 RAJAT GUPTA: Yeah. Yeah. Yeah.

7

8 RAJ RAJARATNAM: And I, look, I'm happy with you know...

9

10 RAJAT GUPTA: You're happy. You're a different place. You

11 don't uh, uh...

12 RAJ RAJARATNAM: Yeah. I mean, I'm happy with it, but you

13 know there's a fairness,
right?

14

15 RAJAT GUPTA: Yeah.

16

17 RAJ RAJARATNAM: Now from, for the last three or four, I mean,

18 four or five years I've given him a million

19 bucks a year, right?

20 RAJAT GUPTA: Yeah. Yeah.

21

22 RAJ RAJARATNAM: After taxes, off shore cash.

23

24 RAJAT GUPTA: Yeah. Yeah.

25

26 RAJ RAJARATNAM: Right? And then he comes to me and he tells

27 me, "You know, moving to New York is going

28 to be expensive and I'm only moving to be

29 with NSR and you guys and, you know is

30 there anything more we can expect?" And you

31 know and it's like, I, I and I felt, between you

and I felt like he was putting a stake through

my...

32

33 RAJAT GUPTA: Yeah.

34

35 RAJ RAJARATNAM: ...you know stomach, because instead of

36 saying thank you for giving me 5 million

37 dollars after taxes.

38 RAJAT GUPTA: Yeah, other, other thing is I don't understand

39 why he doesn't ok you mention it once, and if

40 people want to do it, they will come. I mean,

41 like NSR thing, you mention it once, if people

42 want to do it, they will do it for you, otherwise,

you just say O.K. You know. Fine.

43

194

1 RAJ RAJARATNAM:	No (UI) if he comes and does a big deal and
2	he's instrumental in orchestrating a deal and
3	getting it done, right? People might say, hey
4	here is a bonus, you know?
5 RAJAT GUPTA:	Yeah.
6	
7 RAJ RAJARATNAM:	So, I don't know.
8	
9 RAJAT GUPTA:	Yeah.
10	
11 RAJ RAJARATNAM:	But anyway, I think it would be fun to do this uh, (UI).
12	
13 RAJAT GUPTA:	It'll be fun to this thing. I think (UI).
14	
15 RAJ RAJARATNAM:	But we'll uh, (Coughs) we'll, and keep your
16	eyes and ears open if you hear anything. Just
17	anything that you think may be interesting and
18	I will uh, I will track him down and see
	what's in the market and you know I'll bring
19	that angle to it you know?
20 RAJAT GUPTA:	Do, do you, do you have two more minutes?
21	
22 RAJ RAJARATNAM:	Yes. Of course.
23	
24 RAJAT GUPTA:	Uh, first I wanted to get your straight opinion
25	on whether uh, uh, I think, you think I should
26	do this KKR thing, and second I want to tell
27	you about what I learned kind of maybe the
28	deal he's gonna offer me.
29 RAJ RAJARATNAM:	Right
30	
31 RAJAT GUPTA:	Which I want to bounce off you, if you, first I
	mean...
32	
33 RAJ RAJARATNAM:	(UI).
34	
35 RAJAT GUPTA:	You know, do you, do you really feel in the
	gut that given everything it's a good thing to
36	do?
37	
38 RAJ RAJARATNAM:	I think so. I think if you do it in a way,
39	(Sniffles) see right now I think everybody
40	expects you to spend 100 percent of your time
41	other than charity on NSR, right? You know.
42 RAJAT GUPTA:	That should not, a full...
43	

1	RAJ RAJARATNAM:	Or 40 percent or 50 percent.
2		
3	RAJAT GUPTA:	(UI) 40.
4		
5	RAJ RAJARATNAM:	And I think you have to just kill that right away. Right?
6		
7	RAJAT GUPTA:	Yeah.
8		
9	RAJ RAJARATNAM:	And say that your value added is not to do
10		cash flows and not to, you know, (Clears
11		throat) that your value added is to bring
12		people together, deals together, at the right
13		time make the call, introduce people so on
14		and so forth. You know like the old merchant bankers use to do, you know?
15	RAJAT GUPTA:	And that's, that's, that's exactly what I've been doing.
16		
17	RAJ RAJARATNAM:	And that is, that is, yeah.
18		
19	RAJAT GUPTA:	Yeah.
20		
21	RAJ RAJARATNAM:	And that's what the, if anybody complains
22		that you're not spending one day or two days
23		or you promised that then they are not
24		understanding your value. Right?
25	RAJAT GUPTA:	No. No. Correct and I told Parag I said Parag,
26		if you can point to anything you would like
27		me to do for NSR that I'm not doing, please
28		say, do that, you know?
29	RAJ RAJARATNAM:	Yeah. So I think, I think you're instrumental
30		in uh, architecting this NSR in raising capital.
31		
32	RAJAT GUPTA:	Yeah.
33		
34	RAJ RAJARATNAM:	And in giving it huge credibility in India.
35		
36	RAJAT GUPTA:	Uh-hum.
37		
38	RAJ RAJARATNAM:	Huge credibility.
39		
40	RAJAT GUPTA:	Yeah
41		
42	RAJ RAJARATNAM:	In fact, giving part, and that is worth a lot, right?
43		

1 RAJAT GUPTA:	Yeah..Yeah.
2	
3 RAJ RAJARATNAM:	(Clears throat) But I think you should not be
4	boxed into NSR.
5 RAJAT GUPTA:	No. No. I'm not. I'm not. So...
6	
7 RAJ RAJARATNAM:	(UI).
8	
9 RAJAT GUPTA:	I think that the condition is, I, I have had that
10	discussion with Parag. I said, "Look, you
11	know, uh, firstly you know I don't buy any of
12	that and I'm gonna do what I'm good
13	at. I'm not gonna do other stuff.
14 RAJ RAJARATNAM:	Right.
15	
16 RAJAT GUPTA:	And that'll be of immense value.
17	
18 RAJ RAJARATNAM:	Yeah.
19	
20 RAJAT GUPTA:	And by the way, who are you to say anything because you said
21	you were gonna spend (Chuckles) 180 days in (UI) India."
22	
23 RAJ RAJARATNAM:	(UI).
24	
25 RAJAT GUPTA:	You've hardly done that
26	and are doing three other things. So Parag...
27	
28 RAJ RAJARATNAM:	Let's see, yeah.
29	
30 RAJAT GUPTA:	...you know, he automatically just shut up after
31	that. He never said anything else.
32	
33 RAJ RAJARATNAM:	So I think that you table that first, right?
34	
35 RAJAT GUPTA:	Yeah. That's done. That's that.
36	
37 RAJ RAJARATNAM:	The second thing I think is you create a
38	platform called whatever, right? (UI).
39	
40 RAJAT GUPTA:	In a way, it, it... In a way that's also there, I mean.
41	
42 RAJ RAJARATNAM:	Yeah.
43	

197

1	RAJAT GUPTA:	It's a portfolio of, of, I mean.
2		
3	RAJ RAJARATNAM:	A portfolio things that you enjoy doing and
		you want to do and that you, you can add
4		value at, right?
5		
6	RAJAT GUPTA:	Yeah.
7		
8	[11 min 45 sec]	
9	RAJ RAJARATNAM:	So Galleon International can be one....
10		
11	RAJAT GUPTA:	By the way, on that I want you to keep, us to
12		keep having the dialogue as to what...
13		
14	RAJ RAJARATNAM:	Yeah.
15		
16	RAJAT GUPTA:	...you know how I can be helpful in Galleon
17		International. By the way not Galleon
18		International, Galleon Group. I mean you've
19		given...
20	RAJ RAJARATNAM:	Galleon Group, right.
21		
22	RAJAT GUPTA:	...a position in Galleon International. That's
		good enough. I, I...
23		
24	RAJ RAJARATNAM:	Yeah, but you know what, I, I am now at the
25		point where I, in the last couple of years, I'm
26		building, right?
27	RAJAT GUPTA:	Yeah.
28		
29	RAJ RAJARATNAM:	Rather than just making returns, just and not
		building, right?
30		
31	RAJAT GUPTA:	Right. Right. (UI).
32		
33	RAJ RAJARATNAM:	So I'm putting the structure in place and all of
		that, right? So we will build this into a ten
34		billion dollar company, hopefully by the end
35		of 2009.
36		
37	RAJAT GUPTA:	Yes. Yes you will.
38		
39	RAJ RAJARATNAM:	You know?
40		
41	RAJAT GUPTA:	Yeah. Yeah.
42		
43	RAJ RAJARATNAM:	And so that's sort of the goal, right? 13

```
1
2  RAJAT GUPTA:          Yeah. Yeah. Yeah. Yeah.
3
4  RAJ RAJARATNAM:       And so I, my goal, what I told people was
5                        2010 we enter with 10 billion.
6
7  RAJAT GUPTA:          Right. Right. And there you know, I do want
8                        to, I, I, I, will now next week, I'll, I mean I've
9                        been having periodic meetings with these
10                       guys.
11 RAJ RAJARATNAM:       Right.
12
13 RAJAT GUPTA:          On the fund-raising side and I'll continue to
14                       do that and, you know, they pulled me in but
15                       I'm, you know, please keep telling them, they,
16                       they should pull me in wherever they think I
17                       can add value and, you know?
18 RAJ RAJARATNAM:       Yeah. And I think yeah...
19
20 RAJAT GUPTA:          And you should do the feel the same. Any
21                       meeting you want me you know come...
22
23 RAJ RAJARATNAM:       Right.
24
25 RAJAT GUPTA:          Not come...

26 [12 min 51 sec]
27
28 RAJ RAJARATNAM:       So, so that thing. So I think you know,
29                       having a portfolio of opportunities, right? To
30                       really leverage your, you know, experience, is
31                       the right way to do it, right?
32 RAJAT GUPTA:          Uh-hum.
33
34 RAJ RAJARATNAM:       And even this AT&T thing, right?
35
36 RAJAT GUPTA:          Yeah.
37
38 RAJ RAJARATNAM:       You can easily recruit the top notch guy a
                         Parag equivalent right?
39
40 RAJAT GUPTA:          Yes. Yes.
41
42 RAJ RAJARATNAM:       And give him 30 percent of the economic or
                         35% (UI).
43
```

1 RAJAT GUPTA:	Yes absolutely. Absolutely.
2	
3 RAJ RAJARATNAM:	And tell Parag look, this is my contact, right?
4	
5 RAJAT GUPTA:	Yeah.
6	
7 RAJ RAJARATNAM:	They are doing it because of that.
8	
9 RAJAT GUPTA:	Oh he knows that. He knows that and he acknowledges that. I mean this won't happen
10	without, you know?
11	
12 RAJ RAJARATNAM:	And then for me to execute this properly, right?
13	
14 RAJAT GUPTA:	Yeah.
15	
16 RAJ RAJARATNAM:	I will. I'm, I'm gonna recruit somebody. I
17	don't know who it is, but you know you
18	recruit somebody really good.
19 RAJAT GUPTA:	I already told that to him.
20	
21 RAJ RAJARATNAM:	O.K.
22	
23 RAJAT GUPTA:	That's' already...
24	
25 RAJ RAJARATNAM:	And that you, you know, might or might not use NSR's people on the ground because this
26	guy also might say look I don't think Vivek
27	(PH) is the right guy. I might need my
28	own guy, you know?
29 RAJAT GUPTA:	Vivek (PH) is not the right guy. Yeah.
30	
31 RAJ RAJARATNAM:	Right, for Telecom, right?
32	
33 RAJAT GUPTA:	Yeah.
34	
35 RAJ RAJARATNAM:	So he might create this way, right?
36	
37 RAJAT GUPTA:	(UI) yeah. Yeah. Yeah.
38	
39 RAJ RAJARATNAM:	He might craft it this way, right? (Sniffles)
40	
41 RAJAT GUPTA:	Yeah.
42	
43 RAJ RAJARATNAM:	And you say, you know, that, I mean just because Parag came to a

1		meeting or two AT&T doesn't mean that, you know?
2		
3	RAJAT GUPTA:	Well he didn't come in. It was a phone call. I
4		have done all the 4 meetings.
5		
6	RAJ RAJARATNAM:	Meetings, yeah. So I think you do that and you
7		get somebody that you enjoy working with.
8		
9	RAJAT GUPTA:	Yeah. Yeah.
10		
11	RAJ RAJARATNAM:	Like today (Cough) I got a call from a guy
12		called Varun Bery.
13	RAJAT GUPTA:	Oh I know Varun very well. A former McKinsey guy.
14		
15	RAJ RAJARATNAM:	(Cough) O.K. He called me and he said
16		there's this Singtel deal, right?
17		
18	RAJAT GUPTA:	Yeah.
19		
20	RAJ RAJARATNAM:	That we were looking at and whether I'd be
21		interested and I said look, I'm not doing
22		private equity but uh, talk to Parag, you
23		know? And he said I've been trying to get a
24		hold of Parag and you know, I could just send him an e-mail, right?
25	RAJAT GUPTA:	Yeah.
26		
27	RAJ RAJARATNAM:	He was only here for, and apparently he's
28		running like a 700 million dollar Asia fund or
29		something, you know?
30	RAJAT GUPTA:	Right. Correct. Correct
31		
32	RAJ RAJARATNAM:	Based on, based on India in, in, in India or?
33		
34	RAJAT GUPTA:	Telecom. It's a Telecom fund. I'm actually an
35		investor in that fund.
36		
37	RAJ RAJARATNAM:	O.K. He's running a Telecom fund, so maybe
38		then they're exiting this invest something,
39		right?
40	RAJAT GUPTA:	Yeah. O.K.
41		
42	RAJ RAJARATNAM:	But you know, they are people (Coughs) I, I, don't, I, remember meeting him because he
43		seemed very familiar with me and, "Hello

201

1		Raj. How are you?" And I just couldn't put a
2		face to a...
3	RAJAT GUPTA:	Yeah (Laughs).
4		
5	RAJ RAJARATNAM:	...name (Chuckles) so you know, I chatted like
		I knew him, right?
6		
7	RAJAT GUPTA:	Yeah. Yeah.
8		
9	RAJ RAJARATNAM:	But he is only here for two days.
10		
11	RAJAT GUPTA:	Yeah. Yeah.
12		
13	RAJ RAJARATNAM:	Today and tomorrow, but there are people like
14		that, that if you give em 25, 30 percent of the
		economics
15		
16	RAJAT GUPTA:	No. It'll be... Yeah. It'll be...
17		
18	[15 min 22 sec]	
19	RAJ RAJARATNAM:	See, you know, Rajat how I built a firm, was I
20		kept 50 percent of the profits.
21		
22	RAJAT GUPTA:	Yeah.
23		
24	RAJ RAJARATNAM:	For my, you know, talking to investors and to
25		uh, you know, building the thing and being
26		the resident shrink and all of that stuff, right?
27		
28	RAJAT GUPTA:	Yeah.
29		
30	RAJ RAJARATNAM:	And I gave 50 percent away.
31		
32	RAJAT GUPTA:	Yeah. Yeah (UI).
33		
34	RAJ RAJARATNAM:	And then, but I kept the equity, myself.
35		
36	RAJAT GUPTA:	Yeah.
37		
38	RAJ RAJARATNAM:	And then when the firm got to the point where
39		I needed to give equity, I gave equity.
40		
41	RAJAT GUPTA:	Yeah. Yeah. Yeah.
42		
43	RAJ RAJARATNAM:	You know? And so that model, and that's how
		I got reasonably

1		wealthy because in the early stages (Clears
2		throat) you know, you, you build and then your
3		capital grows for you, see.
4	RAJAT GUPTA:	No. No. No. That's fine. That's fine.
5		
6	RAJ RAJARATNAM:	I think the model of, you know, giving away
7		half to the team, is...
8	RAJAT GUPTA:	Right.
9		
10	RAJ RAJARATNAM:	...you know, if Shaukat raises money he is
11		gonna give half the incentive fee to his team.
12		
13	RAJAT GUPTA:	Uh-hum.
14		
15	RAJ RAJARATNAM:	You know?
16		
17	RAJAT GUPTA:	Uh-hum. Yeah
18		
19	RAJ RAJARATNAM:	And you do that. Right?
20		
21	RAJAT GUPTA:	Yeah.
22		
23	RAJ RAJARATNAM:	And don't give any e, equity right now.
24		
25	RAJAT GUPTA:	Yeah.
26		
27	RAJ RAJARATNAM:	Right? At some point if you think you need to
28		give equity, you give equity. You know?
29		
30	RAJAT GUPTA:	Uh-hum.
31	[16 min 19 sec]	
32		
33	RAJ RAJARATNAM:	Because I tell you what everybody forgets.
34		The first fund is the 34 oughest to raise.
35		
36	RAJAT GUPTA:	Uh-hum.
37		
38	RAJ RAJARATNAM:	The first Telecom fund is the toughest to raise.
39		
40	RAJAT GUPTA:	Uh-hum.
41		
42	RAJ RAJARATNAM:	To get the first anchor investor...
43		

1	RAJAT GUPTA:	Uh-hum.
2		
3	RAJ RAJARATNAM:	...is the toughest.
4		
5	RAJAT GUPTA:	Uh-hum.
6		
7	RAJ RAJARATNAM:	Once you get that and you get the first fund
8		going...
9	RAJAT GUPTA:	Uh-hum. Hm-hm.
10		
11	RAJ RAJARATNAM:	...then based on a few Wall Street stones you can raise...
12		
13	RAJAT GUPTA:	Yeah. Yeah.
14		
15	RAJ RAJARATNAM:	A lot of people won't even look at first time funds.
16		
17	RAJAT GUPTA:	Yeah. No. That's right. That's right. So, you
18		know going back to, I mean that is kind of the
19		set up that I have. I, I do agree that I've been
20		kind of you know, naturally on private
21		equity stuff, reaching out to NSR but I have
22		already told Parag that I wanted this Telecom
23		fund to be separate. So, um, you know, I have to, I have to, go and...
24	RAJ RAJARATNAM:	You just have to find one good guy who can
25		build it for you.
26	RAJAT GUPTA:	Yeah. Right.
27		
28	RAJ RAJARATNAM:	And once you get one good guy, you know,
29		whether it is Ramesh (PH) or whoever, right?
30		
31	RAJAT GUPTA:	Yeah.
32		
33	RAJ RAJARATNAM:	Who knows Telecom and who is willing to
34		work with you.
35	RAJAT GUPTA:	Yeah.
36		
37	RAJ RAJARATNAM:	Now you'll find that you know Anil will put
28		his hand up for some equity in that (Chuckles)
39		and (UI)...
40	RAJAT GUPTA:	I'm sure he... Yeah. Yeah.
41		
42	RAJ RAJARATNAM:	You know, and that I mean, (Clears throat) I
		mean I don't think he needs any, but, you
43		know, that's your call.

1	
2 RAJAT GUPTA:	Yeah, Yeah. I mean you know, uh, ah, that's, that's a minor point. I mean, I'm, I'm not... I mean, I'm even fine with it, but, um, but here is the KKR advice so...
3	
4	
5	
6 RAJ RAJARATNAM:	And the KKR I would do it in a heartbeat.
7	
8 * *	* *
9	
10	[END OF CALL]

------------------------------- x
UNITED STATES OF AMERICA

                 : <u>SEALED INDICTMENT</u>

    -v.-

                 : 11-Cr_____

RAJAT K. GUPTA,   : 11 CRIM 907

    Defendant.   :

                     :

------------------------------ x

COUNT ONE

(Conspiracy to Commit Securities Fraud)
The Grand Jury charges:

Relevant Entities and Individuals

1. At all times relevant to this Indictment, The Goldman Sachs Group, Inc. ("Goldman Sachs") was a global financial services firm with its headquarters in New York, New York. At all times relevant to this Indictment, Goldman Sachs was a public company whose stock traded on the New York Stock Exchange ("NYSE") under the ticker symbol "GS."

2. At all times relevant to this Indictment, RAJAT K. GUPTA, the defendant, served on the Board of Directors of Goldman Sachs (the "Goldman Sachs Board"). In his capacity as a member of the Goldman Sachs Board, GUPTA regularly received confidential information about Goldman Sachs's earnings, contemplated and actual corporate transactions, and other significant developments prior to Goldman Sachs's public announcement of such information.

3. At all times relevant to this Indictment, the Procter & Gamble Company ("P&G") was a global provider of branded consumer products with its headquarters in Cincinnati, Ohio. At all times relevant to this Indictment, P&G was a public company whose stock traded on the NYSE under the ticker symbol "PG."

4. At all times relevant to this Indictment, RAJAT K. GUPTA, the defendant, served on the Board of Directors of P&G (the "P&G Board"). In his capacity as a member of the P&G Board, GUPTA regularly received confidential information about P&G's earnings, contemplated and actual corporate transactions, and other significant developments prior to P&G's public announcement of such information.

5. At all times relevant to this Indictment, the Galleon Group ("Galleon") operated a family of hedge funds in New York, New York. Galleon Management, LP ("Galleon Management") managed a number of those hedge funds, including the Galleon Technology Offshore Fund, Ltd., and Galleon Diversified Fund, Ltd. (collectively, the "Galleon Tech Funds").

6. Raj Rajaratnam ("Rajaratnam") was the founder and head of Galleon. At all times relevant to this Indictment, Rajaratnam was the Managing Member of Galleon Management LLC, the general partner of Galleon Management. In addition, at all times relevant to this Indictment, Rajaratnam was a portfolio manager for the Galleon Tech Funds.

7. At all times relevant to this Indictment, Berkshire Hathaway Inc.

("Berkshire Hathaway") was a public holding company headquartered in Omaha, Nebraska, that owned a number of subsidiaries engaged in a variety of business activities, including the insurance business.

The Relationship Between GUPTA and Rajaratnam

8. At all times relevant to this Indictment, RAJAT K. GUPTA, the defendant, and Rajaratnam had numerous business dealings with each other. In addition, GUPTA and Rajaratnam maintained a personal relationship and friendship. Their business dealings included the following:

a. From in or about 2003 through in or about August 2005, GUPTA had money invested in at least two different Galleon offshore funds through an offshore entity that GUPTA had created. On or about March 31, 2005, the value of those investments was approximately $2,444,518.

b. In or about 2005, GUPTA and Rajaratnam, along with a third individual, formed an investment fund called Voyager Capital Partners ("Voyager"). At the time Voyager was formed, GUPTA invested $5 million and Rajaratnam invested $40 million. In or about early 2007, GUPTA invested an additional $5 million in Voyager, resulting in GUPTA having a 20% equity interest and Rajaratnam having an 80% equity interest. Certain of the asset in Voyager were invested in Galleon hedge funds, including funds managed by Rajaratnam.

c. In or about 2006, GUPTA and Rajaratnam, along with other individuals, became founding partners of a private equity fund focused on investments in emerging markets in Asia ("Private Equity Fund"). GUPTA made a commitment to invest approximately $22.5 million and Rajaratnam made a commitment to invest approximately $50 million. From inception through in or about March 2010, GUPTA served as the Chairman of the Private Equity Fund. From inception through in or about December 2008, Rajaratnam served as a limited partner of the Private Equity Fund and a member of the Private Equity Fund's investment committee.

d. In or about late 2007, Rajaratnam explored the possibility of launching a new Galleon fund that would invest in late-stage private equity in emerging markets in Asia. In connection with that contemplated fund, representatives of Galleon prepared marketing materials and contacted potential investors. GUPTA and Rajaratnam, among others, were to serve as members of the fund's investment committee.

Relevant Confidentiality Policies

9. At all times relevant to this Indictment, the directors who served on the Goldman Sachs Board, including RAJAT K. GUPTA, the defendant, had an obligation to maintain the confidentiality of information received in connection with their service as directors, and an obligation not to provide the information to others for the purpose of securities trading.

10. At all times relevant to this Indictment, the directors who served on the P&G Board, including RAJAT K. GUPTA, the defendant, had an obligation to maintain the

209

confidentiality of information received in connection with their service as directors, and an obligation not to provide the information to others for the purpose of securities trading.

The Insider Trading Scheme

11. From at least in or about 2008 through in or about January 2009, RAJAT K. GUPTA, the defendant, Raj Rajaratnam, and others known and unknown, participated in a scheme to defraud by disclosing material, nonpublic information relating to Goldman Sachs and P&G (the "Inside Information") and/or executing securities transactions on the basis of the Inside Information. GUPTA, Rajaratnam, and others known and unknown, effectuated the fraudulent scheme in the following ways:

a. GUPTA obtained the Inside Information in his capacity as a member of the Goldman Sachs Board and the P&G Board.

b. In violation of duties of trust and confidence that GUPTA owed to Goldman Sachs and P&G, and their respective shareholders, GUPTA disclosed the Inside Information to Rajaratnam, with the understanding that Rajaratnam would use the Inside Information to purchase and sell securities.

c. Rajaratnam, in turn, knowing that GUPTA had disclosed the Inside Information to him in violation of duties of trust and confidence, caused the execution of transactions in the securities of Goldman Sachs, P&G, and other companies on the basis of the Inside Information, and shared the Inside Information with other coconspirators at Galleon, thereby earning illegal profits (and illegally avoiding losses) of millions of dollars.

GUPTA'S Disclosure of Inside Information Concerning Berkshire Hathaway's $5 Billion Investment in Goldman Sachs

12. For example, on or about September 23, 2008, RAJAT K. GUPTA, the defendant, participated by telephone in a special meeting of the Goldman Sachs Board. During that meeting, the Goldman Sachs Board considered and approved a $5 billion investment from Berkshire Hathaway (at a time when the financial markets were experiencing significant distress in the wake of the bankruptcy filing of Lehman Brothers Holdings Inc. on or about September 15, 2008) . The public announcement of Berkshire Hathaway's investment in Goldman Sachs was announced following the 4:00 p.m. close of the NYSE on September 23, 2008. Prior to the public announcement, that information was confidential.

13. Approximately 16 seconds after RAJAT K. GUPTA, the defendant, disconnected his telephone from the special meeting of the Goldman Sachs Board on September 23, 2008, at approximately 3:54 p.m., GUPTA'S assistant called Rajaratnam at his office in New York, New York, and shortly thereafter, connected GUPTA to the call. During that call, GUPTA disclosed Inside Information to Rajaratnam concerning Berkshire Hathaway's investment in Goldman Sachs.

14. On September 23, 2008, at approximately 3:58 p.m., just two minutes before the close of the market, and prior to the

public announcement of Berkshire Hathaway's investment in Goldman Sachs, Rajaratnam caused the Galleon Tech Funds to order the purchase of approximately 350,000 shares of Goldman Sachs common stock, which was worth a total value of approximately $43 million. Of that amount, the Galleon Tech Funds purchased approximately 217,200 shares of Goldman Sachs common stock at approximately $124 per share, at a total cost of approximately $27 million.

15. Later on September 23, 2008, following the close of the NYSE, Goldman Sachs publicly announced the investment by Berkshire Hathaway. Goldman Sachs's stock opened the following morning, September 24, 2008, at $128.44 per share, reflecting an increase of more than $3.00 per share from the pre-announcement closing price of $125.05 per share.

16. On or about September 24, 2008, Rajaratnam caused the Galleon Tech Funds to liquidate its position in Goldman Sachs stock. The sale of the 217,200 Goldman Sachs shares that had been purchased at approximately 3:58 p.m. on September 23, 2008 generated for the Galleon Tech Funds an illegal profit of approximately $840,000.

17. On the morning of September 24, 2008, at approximately 7:05 a.m., Rajaratnam spoke by telephone with a trader at Galleon and, during that conversation, Rajaratnam told the trader that he had gotten a call at 3:58 p.m. the day before saying something good might happen to Goldman Sachs. Less than an hour later, at approximately 7:56

a.m., on September 24, 2008, Rajaratnam again spoke by telephone with the same trader and, during that conversation, Rajaratnam told the trader that he had gotten a call at 3:58 p.m. the day before saying something good was going to happen to Goldman Sachs.

GUPTA'S October 2008 Disclosure of Inside Information Concerning Goldman Sachs's Negative Interim Financial Results

18. As another example, on or about October 23, 2008, RAJAT K. GUPTA, the defendant, participated by telephone in a meeting of the Goldman Sachs Board in which senior executives of the company advised the members of the Goldman Sachs Board of significant developments and issues at the company. Goldman Sachs's confidential internal financial analyses showed that for the quarter ending November 28, 2008, the company had, at that point, lost nearly $2 per share. That information was particularly significant because in the firm's history as a public company, it had never before lost money in any quarter. Goldman Sachs did not publicly disclose those negative interim financial results, and that information was confidential.

19. Approximately 23 seconds after RAJAT K. GUPTA, the defendant, disconnected from the call with the Goldman Sachs Board on October 23, 2008, at approximately 4:49 p.m., GUPTA called Rajaratnam and spoke to Rajaratnam by telephone for approximately 13 minutes. During that call, GUPTA disclosed to Rajaratnam Inside Information concerning Goldman Sachs's negative interim earnings.

20. On the basis of the Inside Information provided by RAJAT K. GUPTA, the defendant, Rajaratnam caused the Galleon Tech Funds to execute transactions in Goldman Sachs securities that enabled the Galleon Tech Funds illegally to avoid a loss of several million dollars. Specifically, on the morning of October 24, 2008, shortly after the NYSE opened, beginning at approximately 9:31 a.m., Rajaratnam caused the Galleon Tech Funds to sell its entire long position in Goldman Sachs stock, which consisted of approximately 150,000 shares, at prices ranging from $97.74 to $102.17.

21. At approximately 12:08 p.m. on October 24, 2008, Rajaratnam spoke by telephone with a Galleon portfolio manager. During that conversation, Rajaratnam stated that he had heard the day before from someone on the Goldman Sachs Board that, among other things, Goldman Sachs was losing $2 per share, which was substantially worse than the prevailing market expectations at the time.

22. On or about December 16, 2008, Goldman Sachs publicly announced that for the quarter ended November 28, 2008, the company had lost approximately $2.12 billion, or $4.97 per share. By selling approximately 150,000 shares of Goldman Sachs common stock on October 24, 2008, the Galleon Tech Funds illegally avoided a loss of several million dollars.

GUPTA'S January 2009 Disclosure of Inside Information Concerning Procter & Gamble's Quarterly Financial Results

23. As another example, beginning

at approximately 9:00 a.m., on or about January 29, 2009, the day before P&G publicly announced its quarterly earnings, RAJAT K. GUPTA, the defendant, participated by telephone, from Switzerland, in a meeting of the Audit Committee of the P&G Board. During that call, the Audit Committee discussed the next day's earnings release, a draft of which had previously been circulated to the members of the Audit Committee, including GUPTA. That draft stated, among other things, that the company expected its organic sales (i.e., sales related to preexisting business segments) to grow 2-5% for the fiscal year, which compared negatively to the guidance that P&G had previously provided to the public.

24. At approximately 1:18 p.m., on or about January 29, 2009, RAJAT K. GUPTA, the defendant, called Rajaratnam from Switzerland and spoke to Rajaratnam for approximately eight minutes. During that call, GUPTA provided Inside Information to Rajaratnam concerning P&G's earnings release planned for the next day. That same afternoon, Rajaratnam told a portfolio manager at Galleon that he had heard from someone on the P&G Board certain information concerning P&G's organic sales growth. Thereafter, beginning at approximately 2:52 p.m., on or about January 29, 2009, on the basis of the Inside Information that GUPTA had provided to Rajaratnam, certain Galleon funds sold short approximately 180,000 shares of P&G common stock.

25. RAJAT K. GUPTA, the defendant, provided the Inside Information to Rajaratnam

215

because of GUPTA'S friendship and business relationships with Rajaratnam. GUPTA benefitted and hoped to benefit from his friendship and business relationships with Rajaratnam in various ways, some of which were financial.

The Conspiracy

26. From at least in or about 2008 up to and including in or about January 2009, in the Southern District of New York and elsewhere, RAJAT K. GUPTA, the defendant, Raj Rajaratnam, and others known and unknown, willfully and knowingly did combine, conspire, confederate and agree together and with each other to commit offenses against the United States, to wit, securities fraud, in violation of Title 15, United States Code, Sections 78j(b) and 78ff, and Title 17, Code of Federal Regulations, Section 240.10b-5.

Object of the Conspiracy Securities Fraud

27. It was a part and an object of the conspiracy that RAJAT K. GUPTA, the defendant, Raj Rajaratnam, and others known and unknown, willfully and knowingly, directly and indirectly, by the use of the means and instrumentalities of interstate commerce, and of the mails, and of facilities of national securities exchanges, would and did use and employ, in connection with the purchase and sale of securities, manipulative and deceptive devices and contrivances in violation of Title 17, Code of Federal Regulations, Section 240.10b-5 by: (a) employing devices, schemes and artifices to defraud; (b) making untrue

statements of material fact and omitting to
state material facts necessary in order to
make the statements made, in the light of the
circumstances under which they were made, not
misleading; and (c) engaging in acts, practices
and courses of business which operated and would
operate as a fraud and deceit upon any person,
all in violation of Title 15, United States
Code, Sections 78j(b) and 78ff, and Title 17,
Code of Federal Regulations, Section 240.10b-5.

Means and Methods of the Conspiracy

28. Among the means and methods by which
RAJAT K. GUPTA, the defendant, Raj Rajaratnam,
and their coconspirators would and did carry
out the conspiracy were the following:

a. GUPTA disclosed Inside Information
obtained from Goldman Sachs and P&G in violation
of (a) the fiduciary and other duties of trust
and confidence that GUPTA owed to those companies
and their shareholders, (b) the expectations
of confidentiality of the counterparties to
transactions with Goldman Sachs and P&G, and
(c) the policies of Goldman Sachs and P&G
regarding the use and safekeeping of confidential
and material, nonpublic information.

b. GUPTA, in breach of his duties
of confidentiality to Goldman Sachs and P&G,
and their respective shareholders, disclosed
Inside Information to Rajaratnam, with the
understanding that Rajaratnam would use the
Inside Information to purchase and sell
securities, and thereby receive illegal
profits and/or illegally avoid losses.

217

c. Rajaratnam, while in possession of Inside Information that Rajaratnam knew had been disclosed by GUPTA in breach of GUPTA'S duty to keep the information confidential, executed trades and caused others to execute trades based on the Inside Information and thereby received illegal profits and/or illegally avoided losses.

d. Rajaratnam shared the Inside Information provided by GUPTA with other coconspirators at Galleon.

Overt Acts

29. In furtherance of the conspiracy and to effect the illegal object thereof, RAJAT K. GUPTA, the defendant, Raj Rajaratnam, and their coconspirators committed the following overt acts, among others, in the Southern District of New York and elsewhere:

a. On or about June 3, 2008, Rajaratnam told a portfolio manager at Galleon that he had learned from someone on the P&G Board that P&G was selling its Folgers business to the J.M. Smucker Company.

b. On or about June 10, 2008, at approximately 5:41 p.m., GUPTA spoke by telephone with a senior executive officer of Goldman Sachs.

c. On or about June 10, 2008, at approximately 9:24 p.m, GUPTA called Rajaratnam.

d. On or about June 10, 2008, at approximately 9:31 p.m., GUPTA called and left a voice mail message for Rajaratnam.

e. On or about June 10, 2008, at

approximately 9:42 p.m., GUPTA spoke by telephone with Rajaratnam, who was in New York, New York.

 f. On or about June 11, 2008, at approximately 8:43 a.m., while in New York, New York, Rajaratnam called GUPTA.

 g. On or about June 11, 2008, beginning at approximately 9:35 a.m., Rajaratnam caused the Galleon Tech Funds to purchase approximately 5,500 Goldman Sachs call option contracts.

 h. On or about June 12, 2008, Rajaratnam caused the Galleon Tech Funds to purchase approximately 50,000 shares of Goldman Sachs common stock.

 i. On or about June 12, 2008, Rajaratnam caused the Galleon Tech Funds to purchase approximately 75,000 shares of Goldman Sachs common stock.

 j. On or about July 29, 2008, at approximately 5:39 p.m., GUPTA spoke by telephone with Rajaratnam and disclosed information that GUPTA had learned during a meeting of the Goldman Sachs Board.

 k. On or about September 23, 2008, from approximately 3:13 p.m. to 3:54 p.m. and 34 seconds, while in New York, New York, GUPTA participated by telephone in a meeting of the Goldman Sachs Board.

 l. On or about September 23, 2008, at approximately 3:54 p.m. and 50 seconds, at GUPTA'S direction, GUPTA's assistant called Rajaratnam at his office in New York, New York.

 m. On or about September 23, 2008, at

approximately 3:55 p.m., while in New York, New York, GUPTA spoke by telephone with Rajaratnam and disclosed Inside Information concerning Berkshire Hathaway's investment in Goldman Sachs.

n. On or about September 23, 2008, at approximately 3:58 p.m., while in New York, New York, Rajaratnam caused Galleon to purchase approximately 217,200 shares of Goldman Sachs common stock.

o. On or about September 23, 2008, at approximately 6:16 p.m., GUPTA called and left a voice mail message for Rajaratnam.

p. On or about September 24, 2008, at approximately 7:05 a.m., Rajaratnam spoke by telephone with a trader at Galleon who was in New York, New York ("Trader-A").

q. On or about September 24, 2008, at approximately 7:56 a.m., Rajaratnam spoke by telephone with Trader-A, who was in New York, New York.

r. On or about October 23, 2008, from approximately 4:16 p.m. to 4:49 p.m. and 47 seconds, GUPTA participated by telephone in a meeting of the Goldman Sachs Board.

s. On or about October 23, 2008, at approximately 4:50 p.m., GUPTA spoke by telephone with Rajaratnam, who was in New York, New York, and provided Inside Information concerning Goldman Sachs's negative interim earnings.

t. On or about October 24, 2008, beginning at approximately 9:31 a.m., Rajaratnam caused the Galleon Tech Funds to sell approximately 150,000 shares of Goldman Sachs common stock.

u. On or about October 24, 2008, at approximately 12:08 p.m., Rajaratnam spoke by telephone with a Galleon portfolio manager.

v. On or about January 29, 2009, at approximately 9:00 a.m., GUPTA, while in Switzerland, participated by telephone in a meeting of the Audit Committee of the P&G Board.

w. On or about January 29, 2009, at approximately 1:18 p.m., GUPTA, while in Switzerland, called Rajaratnam, who was in New York, New York.

x. On or about January 29, 2009, Rajaratnam told a. Galleon portfolio manager, who was in New York, New York, that he had received certain information concerning P&G's organic sales growth from a contact on the P&G Board.

y. On or about January 29, 2009, beginning at approximately 2:52 p.m., certain Galleon funds sold short approximately 180,000 shares of P&G common stock.

(Title 18, United States Code, Section 371.)

COUNTS TWO THROUGH SIX
(Securities Fraud)
The Grand Jury further charges:

30. The allegations contained in paragraphs 1 through 25 and 28 through 29 are repeated and realleged as if fully set forth herein.

31. On or about the dates set forth below, in the Southern District of New York and elsewhere, RAJAT K. GUPTA, the defendant, willfully and knowingly, directly

and indirectly, by the use of the means and instrumentalities of interstate commerce, the mails and the facilities of national securities exchanges, in connection with the purchase and sale of securities, did use and employ manipulative and deceptive devices and contrivances, in violation of Title 17, Code of Federal Regulation, Section 240.10b-5, by: (a) employing devices, schemes, and artifices to defraud; (b) making untrue statements of material facts and omitting to state material facts necessary in order to make the statements made, in the light of the circumstances under which they were made, not misleading; and (c) engaging in acts, practices, and courses of business which operated and would operate as a fraud and deceit upon any person, to wit, on the basis of Inside Information that GUPTA disclosed to Raj Rajaratnam in violation of GUPTA'S fiduciary and other duties of confidentiality, Rajaratnam executed and caused others to execute the securities transactions listed below:

COUNT	DATE	SECURITY	TRANSACTION
TWO	September 23, 2008 at approximately 3:58 p.m.	Goldman Sachs	Purchase of approximately 150,000 shares of common stock
THREE	September 23, 2008 at approximately 3:58 p.m.	Goldman Sachs	Purchase of approximately 67,200 shares of common stock
FOUR	October 24, 2008 at approximately 9:31 a.m.	Goldman Sachs	Sale of approximately 50,000 shares of common stock
FIVE	October 24, 2008 at approximately 10:09 a.m.	Goldman Sachs	Sale of approximately 50,000 shares of common stock

SIX	October 24, 2008 at approximately 10:37 a.m.	Goldman Sachs	Sale of approximately 50,000 shares of common stock

(Title 15, United States Code, Sections 78j (b) and 78ff ; Title 17, Code of Federal Regulations, Section 240.10b-5; and Title 18, United States Code, Section 2.)

FORFEITURE ALLEGATION

32. As a result of committing one or more of the foregoing securities fraud offenses alleged in Counts One through Six of this Indictment, RAJAT K. GUPTA, the defendant, shall forfeit to the United States pursuant to Title 18, United States Code, Section 981(a)(1)(C) and Title 28, United States Code Section 2461, all property, real and personal, that constitutes or is derived from proceeds traceable to the commission of the securities fraud offenses alleged in Counts One through Six, including but not limited to the following:

Money Judgment

a. At least a sum of money in United States currency which was derived from proceeds traceable to the commission of the securities fraud offenses alleged in Counts One through Six.

Substitute Assets Provision

33. If any of the above-described forfeitable property, as a result of any act or omission of the defendant:

a. cannot be located upon the exercise of due diligence;

223

b. has been transferred or sold to, or deposited with, a third party;

c. has been placed beyond the jurisdiction of the Court;

d. has been substantially diminished in value; or

e. has been commingled with other property which cannot be divided without difficulty;

it is the intent of the United States, pursuant to Title 21, United States Code, Section 853(p), to seek forfeiture of any other property of the defendant up to the value of the forfeitable property described above. (Title 15, United States Code, Sections 78j(b) and 78ff;

Title 18, United States Code, Section 981(a)(1)(C);

Title 28, United States Code, Section 2461(c); and Title 17, Code of Federal Regulations, Section 240.10b-5.)

Form No. USA-33S-274 (Ed. 9-25-58)

UNITED STATES DISTRICT COURT
SOUTHERN DISTRICT OF NEW YORK

UNITED STATES OF AMERICA
- **v.** -
RAJAT K. GUPTA,

Defendant.

INDICTMENT

11 Cr. ___
(Title 15, United States Code,
Sections 78j (b) and 78ff ;
Title 17, Code of Federal Regulations,
Section 240.10b-5; and Title 18, United
States Code, Sections 2 and 371.)

PREET BHARARA
United States Attorney.

UNITED STATES DISTRICT COURT
SOUTHERN DISTRICT OF NEW YORK
------------------------------ x
UNITED STATES OF AMERICA,   :
                             :
        -v-   :
                             :
                             : 11 Cr. 907 (JSR)
RAJAT K. GUPTA,   : <u>SENTENCING MEMORANDUM</u>
                             :   <u>AND ORDER</u>
        Defendant   :
--------------------------------------- x

JED S. RAKOFF, U.S.D.J.

The Court is called upon to impose
sentence on Rajat K. Gupta, who on June
15, 2012, was found guilty by a jury of
one count of conspiracy and three counts of
substantive securities fraud, in connection
with providing material non-public information
to Raj Rajaratnam. Federal law requires
a court to state, not only orally but in
writing, its reasons for imposing a sentence
"different from" a Guidelines sentence. 18
U.S.C. § 3553(c)(2). <u>See also United States
v. Rattoballi</u>, 452 F.3d 127, 128-29 (2d Cir.
2006). This will be a non-guidelines sentence,
and, accordingly, the Court will both read
this Sentencing Memorandum in open court and
docket it promptly thereafter.

Imposing a sentence on a fellow human
being is a formidable responsibility. It
requires a court to consider, with great care
and sensitivity, a large complex of facts and
factors. The notion that this complicated
analysis, and moral responsibility, can be
reduced to the mechanical adding-up of a small
set of numbers artificially assigned to a few

arbitrarily-selected variables wars with common sense Whereas apples and oranges may have but a few salient qualities, human beings in their interactions with society are too complicated to be treated like commodities, and the attempt to do so can only lead to bizarre results.

Nowhere is this more obvious than in this very case, where the Sentencing Guidelines assign just 2 points to Mr. Gupta for his abuse of a position of trust -- the very heart of his offense -- yet assign him no fewer than 18 points for the resultant but unpredictable monetary gains made by others, from which Mr. Gupta did not in any direct sense receive one penny.

It may be worth remembering that the Sentencing Guidelines were originally designed to moderate unwarranted disparities in federal sentencing by enacting a set of complicated rules that, it was hypothesized, would cause federal judges to impose for any given crime a sentence approximately equal to what empirical data showed was the average sentence previously imposed by federal judges for that crime. See generally Kimbrough v. United States, 552 U.S. 85, 96 (2007). From almost the outset, however, the Guidelines deviated from this goal. For example, even though a perceived racial disparity in sentencing was one of the evils the Guidelines were designed to combat, in actuality the Guidelines imposed in narcotics sentencing a huge racial disparity that dwarfed any prior such problem. Specifically, the Sentencing Commission, based on limited and faulty data, originally determined that an ounce of crack cocaine should be treated as the equivalent of 100 ounces of powder cocaine for sentencing purposes, even though the two substances were chemically almost identical and, as later studies showed, very similar in their effects. Since, however, 85 percent of crack cocaine offenders were black, while most of those who dealt in powder cocaine were Caucasian or Hispanic, the result of the 100-to-1 ratio was to force upon the courts a gross racial disparity in narcotics sentencing. See id. at 97-98. It was only in 2010 that the ratio was changed from 100-to-1 to 18-to-1; and even then as much on the basis of conjecture as evidence. See generally Dorsey v. United States, 132 S.Ct. 2321, 2326 (2012). For the Sentencing Commission had no more empirical basis for imposing the ratio of 18-to-1 than for earlier imposing the ratio of 100-to-1. In both cases, the numbers were plucked from thin air.

While this example is drawn from the area of narcotics, the fundamental point is equally applicable to the instant case. Here, as there, the numbers assigned by the Sentencing Commission to various sentencing factors appear to be more the product of speculation, whim, or abstract number-crunching than of any rigorous methodology -- thus maximizing the risk of injustice.

Another example of the deviation of the Guidelines from the original goals of the Sentencing Commission -- and one more directly relevant to the instant case -- is the huge increase in the recommended Guidelines sentences for securities fraud cases. The Guidelines' calculations for this offense are no longer tied to the mean of what federal judges had previously imposed for such crimes, but instead reflect an ever more draconian approach to white collar crime, unsupported by any empirical data. Take the hypothetical but typical case described by Professor Kate Stith of Yale Law School, involving a typical securities fraud defendant who pled guilty to inflating the financial figures of a public company, thereby causing at least 250 shareholders to collectively suffer a reduction of more than $12.5 million in the value of their shares. In 1987, such a defendant would have faced a Guidelines sentence of 30-37 months; but by 2003, the same defendant would have faced a Guidelines sentence of 151-188 months, a more than 500% increase. See Kate Stith, Federal Sentencing: The One-Way Ratchet, New York City Bar Association First Annual Conference on White Collar Crime (May 2012). Was such a crime really 500% worse in 2003 than it was in 1987? Had any of the factors that underlie rational sentencing so radically changed as to warrant such a huge increase?

In fairness, this vast increase in white collar sentencing was partly mandated by Congress, reacting in turn to public outcry over such massive frauds as Enron and WorldCom. But in implementing the Congressional mandate, the Sentencing Commission chose to focus largely on a single factor as the basis for enhanced punishment: the amount of monetary

loss or gain occasioned by the offense. By
making a Guidelines sentence turn, for all
practical purposes, on this single factor, the
Sentencing Commission effectively ignored the
statutory requirement that federal sentencing
take many factors into account, see 18 U.S.C.
§ 3553(a), and, by contrast, effectively
guaranteed that many such sentences would be
irrational on their face.

This Court has already had occasion to
comment on the unreasonableness of this approach
in United States v. Adelson, 441 F. Supp. 2d 506
(S.D.N.Y. 2006), and hereby adopts by reference
the observations made there. But there is
no better illustration of the irrationality of
this approach than the instant case: for of
the total of 30 Guidelines points calculated
by the Probation Department and endorsed by
the Government as reflecting the proper measure
of Mr. Gupta's crime and punishment, no fewer
than 20 -- or two-thirds of the total -- are
exclusively the product of Rajaratnam's and his
companies' monetary gain, in which Mr. Gupta
did not share in any direct sense.

It might be argued that the Guidelines
still work to minimize disparities. But if
the sentences so calculated are the product of
placing an overwhelming emphasis on a factor
that may be central to some frauds but largely
incidental to others, the effect is to create, in
the name of promoting uniformity, a sentencing
disparity of the most unreasonable kind.

The heart of Mr. Gupta's offenses here,
it bears repeating, is his egregious breach

230

of trust. Mr. Rajaratnam's gain, though a product of that breach, is not even part of the legal theory under which the Government here proceeded, which would have held Gupta guilty even if Rajaratnam had not made a cent. While insider trading may work a huge unfairness on innocent investors, Congress has never treated it as a fraud on investors, the Securities Exchange Commission has explicitly opposed any such legislation, and the Supreme Court has rejected any attempt to extend coverage of the securities fraud laws on such a theory. <u>See, e.g.</u>, <u>Chiarella v. United States</u>, 445 U.S. 222, 232-235 (1980). Prosecution of insider trading therefore proceeds, as in this case, on one or more theories of defrauding the institution (or its shareholders) that owned the information. <u>See, e.g.</u>, <u>Dirks v. SEC</u>, 463 U.S. 646, 660-64 (1983); <u>Carpenter v. U.S.</u>, 484 U.S. 19, 25-27 (1987). In the eye of the law, Gupta's crime was to breach his fiduciary duty of confidentiality to Goldman Sachs; or to put it another way, Goldman Sachs, not the marketplace, was the victim of Gupta's crimes as charged. Yet the Guidelines assess his punishment almost exclusively on the basis of how much money his accomplice gained by trading on the information. At best, this is a very rough surrogate for the harm to Goldman Sachs.

The Court is nonetheless mandated to calculate the defendant's Guidelines range, <u>see</u> 18 U.S.C. § 3553(a)(4)(A), even if, as the Court now holds, the non-guideline sentence that it intends to impose would not vary one whit if the Guidelines calculation was that proposed by the Government, that proposed by the defendant, or anywhere in between.

The parties agree that the base offense level for the offense of which Mr. Gupta stands convicted is 8 points, and that 2 points must be added for abuse of trust. To these 10 points must be added the number of points corresponding to the amount of monetary gain resulting from the offense. Such gain is defined in the official comment to the pertinent section of the Guidelines as "the total increase in value realized through trading in securities by the defendant and persons acting in concert with the defendant or to whom the defendant provided inside information." U.S.S.G. § 2B1.4 cmt. As Judge Holwell pointed out in connection with Mr. Rajaratnam's sentencing, this "phrase is not a model of clarity." United States v. Rajaratnam, No. 09 Cr. 1184 (RJH), 2012 WL 362031, at *14 (S.D.N.Y. Jan. 31, 2012). Nonetheless, it seems reasonably clear to this Court that the comment limits the calculation to gains made or losses avoided in trades that were based, in whole or in part, on the inside information.

In the instant case, however, it is also clear to the Court, both from the jury's split verdict and from the Court's own assessment of the evidence, that the trades in question were those made by Rajaratnam and his Galleon funds on September 23, 2008 and October 24, 2008, directly and immediately as the result of tips from Gupta.[1] In the former case, Gupta, late on the afternoon of September

232

23, tipped Rajaratnam about Warren Buffett's soon-to-be-announced infusion of $5 billion into Goldman Sachs, whereupon Rajaratnam caused various Galleon funds to purchase large quantities of Goldman stock just before the market closed. When the Buffett investment was announced the following morning, the stock surged, causing Galleon to realize an immediate gain of $1,231,630. In the latter case, Gupta, on October 23, tipped Rajaratnam that Goldman Sachs would soon report third quarter losses, whereas many analysts were predicting a profit. On the next day, Rajaratnam sold 150,000 shares of Goldman. Thereafter, as word began to seep out about Goldman's reduced prospects, the stock began to fall, and when the poor third quarter results were finally made public on December 16, 2008, it fell still further. Based on all the evidence, the Court concludes that it is more likely than not that Rajaratnam, in the absence of Gupta's tip, would not have caused Galleon to sell its valuable Goldman stock until the morning of December 17, 2008. The tip thus enabled Galleon to avoid losses of $3,800,565. Taken together, therefore, the September and October tip-based trades resulted in an illegal "gain" of $5,032,195.

---

[1] If the Court were assessing the evidence without the benefit of the jury's verdict, it might find that the Government had proved, at least by a preponderance of evidence, that some of additional Galleon trades were also, as the Government alleged, the product of Gupta's tips. But a decent respect for the jury's assessment of the evidence, albeit under a higher standard, properly informs this Court's assessment.

This figure, while large, is less than one-third of the $15,355,409 gain calculated by the Government and endorsed by the Pre-Sentence Report of the Probation Department. But in the arbitrary world of the Guidelines, this big difference makes little difference. Instead of adding 20 points to Gupta's Guidelines score, it adds 18 points, still overwhelming all other factors.

Although the defendant propounds a number of other theories for still further reducing the gain figure, see Sentencing Memorandum of Rajat K. Gupta at 55-67, the Court rejects these arguments, essentially for the reasons given by Judge Holwell in rejecting similar arguments at the time of the Rajaratnam sentencing, 2012 WL 362031, at *13-15, as well as the additional reasons set forth in the Government's two sentencing memoranda submitted in this case. Thus, the Court concludes that the total offense level is 28, the criminal history category is I, and the Guidelines range is 78 to 97 months' imprisonment.

But this Guidelines range does not rationally square with the facts of this case, not only for the reasons already stated but also because it does not take adequate account of the factors this Court is required by law to consider in imposing sentence. The Court therefore turns to the bedrock of all federal sentencing, section 3553(a) of Title 18, entitled "Factors to be considered in imposing a sentence." The very first factor is "the nature and circumstances of the offense and the

234

history and characteristics of the defendant" (emphasis supplied). Thus, at the very outset, there is presented the fundamental problem of this sentence, for Mr. Gupta's personal history and characteristics starkly contrast with the nature and circumstances of his crimes.

All the evidence before the Court -- not just the letters written on Mr. Gupta's behalf but also the objective facts of record -- establish beyond cavil that Mr. Gupta has selflessly devoted a huge amount of time and effort to a very wide variety of socially beneficial activities, such as the Global Fund to Fight AIDS, Tuberculosis and Malaria, the Public Health Foundation of India, the Indian School of Business, the Pratham Foundation (which provides quality education to underprivileged children in India), the Cornell Medical School, the Rockefeller Foundation, and many many more. As well summarized in his counsel's sentencing memorandum, such activities are but illustrations of Mr. Gupta's big heart and helping hand, which he extended without fanfare or self-promotion, to all with whom he came in contact.

While some have suggested that the large volume of poignant letters submitted on Mr. Gupta's behalf are simply the strategem of a rich, well-connected defendant endeavoring to derail the Court from focusing on his crimes, this is simply not the case, for the facts recited in most of the letters are well documented and, indeed, undisputed by the Government. The Court can say without exaggeration that

235

it has never encountered a defendant whose prior history suggests such an extraordinary devotion, not only to humanity writ large, but also to individual human beings in their times of need. The Guidelines virtually ignore this measure of the man, but here as elsewhere the Guidelines must take second place to section 3553(a), which requires a court to take account of a defendant's character in imposing sentence. And how could it be otherwise, for on this day of judgment, must not one judge the man as a whole? But when one looks at the nature and circumstances of the offense, the picture darkens considerably. In the Court's view, the evidence at trial established, to a virtual certainty, that Mr. Gupta, well knowing his fiduciary responsibilities to Goldman Sachs, brazenly disclosed material non-public information to Mr. Rajaratnam at the very time, September and October 2008, when our financial institutions were in immense distress and most in need of stability, repose, and trust. Consider, for example, his tip to Rajaratnam on September 23, 2008. With Goldman Sachs in turmoil but on the verge of being rescued from possible ruin by an infusion of $5 billion, Gupta, within minutes of hearing of the transaction, tipped Rajaratnam, so that the latter could trade on this information in the last few minutes before the market closed. This was the functional equivalent of stabbing Goldman in the back.

So why did Mr. Gupta do it? Since motive is not an element of the offenses here in issue, it did not need to be proved at trial, and so one can only speculate.   Having finished his spectacular career at McKinsey in 2007, Gupta, for all his charitable endeavors, may have felt frustrated in not finding new business worlds to conquer; and Rajaratnam, a clever cultivator of persons with information, repeatedly held out prospects of exciting new international business opportunities that Rajaratnam would help fund but that Gupta would lead.   There is also in some of the information presented to the Court under seal an implicit suggestion that, after so many years of assuming the role of father to all, Gupta may have longed to escape the straightjacket of overwhelming responsibility, and had begun to loosen his self-restraint in ways that clouded his judgment.   But whatever was operating in the recesses of his brain, there is no doubt that Gupta, though not immediately profiting from tipping Rajaratnam, viewed it as an avenue to future benefits, opportunities, and even excitement. Thus, by any measure, Gupta's criminal acts represented the very antithesis of the values he had previously embodied.

So how does a court balance these polar extremes?   In arguing for a non-guideline sentence in the Pre-Sentence Report, the experienced Senior U.S. Probation Officer Emily Frankelis had this to say: "We believe the defendant's commission of the instant offenses was aberrant behavior – not aberrant as defined by the U.S. Sentencing Guidelines, but rather as defined by Merriam-Webster: ' . . . atypical.'" The Court agrees, and finds that the aberrant nature of Mr. Gupta's conduct by

237

itself would warrant a non-guideline sentence, even aside from the other factors favoring leniency. But in order to find just the right sentence, the Court must also consider two further mandates of section 3553(a): first, "the need for the sentence imposed" to afford specific deterrence, general deterrence, "just punishment," and the like; and, second, the requirement that any sentence imposed be "sufficient, but not greater than necessary, to comply with [these] purposes."

As to specific deterrence, it seems obvious that, having suffered such a blow to his reputation, Mr. Gupta is unlikely to repeat his transgressions, and no further punishment is needed to achieve this result. General deterrence, however, suggests a different conclusion. As this Court has repeatedly noted in other cases, insider trading is an easy crime to commit but a difficult crime to catch. Others similarly situated to the defendant must therefore be made to understand that when you get caught, you will go to jail. Defendant's proposals to have Mr. Gupta undertake various innovative forms of community service would, in the Court's view, totally fail to send this message. Moreover, if the reports of Mr. Gupta's charitable endeavors are at all accurate, he can be counted on to devote himself to community service when he finishes any prison term, regardless of any order of the Court.

At the same time, no one really knows how much jail time is necessary to materially deter insider trading; but common sense suggests that most business executives fear even a modest prison term to a degree that more hardened types might not. Thus, a relatively modest prison term should be "sufficient, but not more than necessary," for this purpose.

There are, however, still other factors set forth in § 3553(a) that the Court must, and has, considered, of which perhaps the most difficult, but most important one, is the concept of "just punishment." While all the other factors under section 3553 partake to a lesser or greater degree of policy considerations, "just punishment" taps a deeper vein. Human beings, as social animals, are programmed to respect moral values. This is why people without shame or guilt are considered psychopaths, and also why violations of the moral order raise such deep passions in the human breast. As people have come to understand that insider trading is not only a sophisticated form of cheating but also a fundamental breach of trust and confidence, they have increasingly internalized their revulsion for its commission. While no defendant should be made a martyr to public passion, meaningful punishment is still necessary to reaffirm society's deep-seated need to see justice triumphant. No sentence of probation, or anything close to it, could serve this purpose.

After carefully weighing all these, and other, relevant factors, the Court concludes that the sentence that most fulfills all requirements of section 3553(a) is two years in prison. Rajat K. Gupta is therefore sentenced to 24 months' imprisonment, concurrent on all counts, to be followed by one year of supervised release, on the terms stated from the bench and here incorporated by reference. The otherwise mandatory forfeiture has been waived by the Government, but Court imposes a fine in the sum of $5,000,000. The Court will defer the determination of restitution for up to 90 days, as permitted by federal law. A formal Judgment embodying these terms and incorporating this Memorandum by reference will issue shortly. Meanwhile, Mr. Gupta is ordered to surrender to the designated prison by 2 p.m. on January 8, 2013.

SO ORDERED.

_____

JED S. RAKOFF, U.S.D.J.

Dated: New York, New York
          October 24, 2012

Acknowledgements

A palpable shockwave swept through the Indian—and international—corporate world after Rajat Gupta was convicted for securities fraud in June 2012. The effects of the judgement were greater among those who had known and worked with Gupta, and certainly among all IITians, for whom Gupta was a true icon.

One lazy evening towards the end of June, I was telling Pranab Dutta, my friend and partner in Aardvark Media, about my conversations with Gupta some years ago when I was researching my book *The IITians*. I recalled that of all the super-achiever IITians I had met during those months, Gupta had stood out: he was the only one who remained a mystery as a person to me. His always-alert intellect, cool rationality, total self-composure, and unfailing courtesy and humility indicated that he was either, quite simply, a perfect man (and all evidence, all that he said, pointed in that direction, and most of his acquaintances too think so), or he had built this perfect armour around himself that no one could penetrate. He had mystified me.

'There's a book there,' said Pranab. 'Write it.' And once he'd said it, the idea refused to let go.

I re-established my IIT contacts and tracked people down. Pradeep Gupta (PG), an old friend and loyal IIT Delhi alumnus, helped, introducing me to some of Rajat Gupta's IIT mates. Some agreed to speak on the condition of anonymity, but many refused to speak at all. This, to me, was rather surprising, since I knew that all of them greatly admired Rajat Gupta, and I had made it clear to everyone I contacted that I had no intention at all of doing some sort of hatchet job. I merely wanted to build as full a picture of the man as I could.

I am grateful to Tejinder Singh, US-based editor of *India America Today*, for passing on to me the leniency plea memo filed by Anil Kumar's defence lawyers.

Being in India, I had to rely mostly on reports in the international media to tell the story of the Rajaratnam and Gupta investigation and trials. For every stage of the investigation and every day of the trials that I have described, I have consulted multiple news reports, to create a detailed version, and to make sure that I did not miss anything important. Among the sources I used are *The New York Times*, *The Wall Street Journal*, *The Washington Post*, *The Financial Times*, *The Economist*, *The New Yorker*, *Time*, Bloomberg Markets, Bloomberg Businessweek, Thomson Reuters, *New York Post*, businessinsider.com, huffingtonpost.com and forbes.com. Wherever I have felt that I should use the voice of the writer because he or she was expressing a personal take on the events, I have acknowledged the source, and I have also done so in the case of exclusive interviews given by any of the actors in this drama. Where the statements quoted have been made to the media at large (for instance, by Gupta's lawyer Gary Naftalis), I have not mentioned any specific source.

Every effort has been made to recheck every fact—numbers, names, places, designations, dates. Where there has been a discrepancy between reports—usually to do with sums of money involved—I have taken the number mentioned in the court documents, and if that has not been possible, left it as an approximation—between $x and y million).

The one question that everyone who came to know that I was working on this book asked, was: 'What do you think? Is he guilty?' The only answer I have been able to come up with is that either way, it is a great and immeasurably humbling tragedy.